# Anabaptist Witness

*A Global Anabaptist and Mennonite Dialogue
on Key Issues Facing the Church in Mission*

VOLUME 7  /  ISSUE 2  /  OCT 2020

# Anabaptist Witness

*A Global Anabaptist and Mennonite Dialogue on Key Issues Facing the Church in Mission*

## Editor

Jamie Pitts, Anabaptist Mennonite Biblical Seminary

## Editorial Staff

**BOOK REVIEW EDITORS** Steve Heinrichs & Isaac S. Villegas
**MARKETING COORDINATORS** Carmen Andres
Matthew J. Krabill
**COPYEDITOR** Heidi King
**STUDENT ASSISTANT** Marcos Acosta
**WEB EDITOR** Laura Carr-Pries
**PRINT DESIGNER** Matt Veith Creative

## Editorial Committee

Sarah Augustine, Suriname Indigenous Health Fund and Dispute Resolution Center of Yakima and Kittitas Counties
Jessica Stoltzfus Buller, Peace Education Coordinator, Mennonite Central Committee U.S.
Steve Heinrichs, Mennonite Church Canada Indigenous-Settler Relations
Matthew J. Krabill, Fuller Theological Seminary, Pasadena, California, USA
Laura Carr-Pries, Mennonite Voluntary Service, Canada
Patricia Urueña, Iglesia cristiana menonita de (Bogotá) Columbia
Isaac S. Villegas, Pastor of Chapel Hill Mennonite Fellowship, North Carolina, USA

## About

*Anabaptist Witness* is published twice a year (April and October) and is indexed in the ATLA Religion Database® (ATLA RDB®), http://www.atla.com. It is a publication of Anabaptist Mennonite Biblical Seminary, Mennonite Church Canada, and Mennonite Mission Network. The views expressed in *Anabaptist Witness* are those of the contributing writers and do not necessarily reflect the opinions of the partnering organizations.

## Subscriptions, Additional Copies, and Change of Address

The annual subscription rate is $20 (US) plus shipping. Subscribers will receive an invoice to send with remittance to Anabaptist Mennonite Biblical Seminary. Single or additional copies of *Anabaptist Witness* are available for purchase through Amazon.com. Change of address or questions about purchasing the journal may be directed to the editor at the address below or by sending an email to subscriptions@anabaptistwitness.org.

## Editorial Correspondence

The editor makes a public call for submissions for each issue of the journal, soliciting contributions that facilitate meaningful exchange among peoples from around the world, across professions, and from a variety of genres (sermons, photo-essays, interviews, biographies, poems, academic papers, etc.). All submissions to *Anabaptist Witness* undergo a double-blind peer review process. For full details of the current call for submissions, visit www.anabaptistwitness.org. Questions or comments about the journal's print or online content may be directed to the editor:

Jamie Pitts
JPitts@AMBS.edu

## Copyright



ISSN 2374-2534 (print)
ISSN 2374-2542 (online)

---

Cover photo: JP Valery / Unsplash / CC 4.0

*Anabaptist Witness*
Anabaptist Mennonite Biblical Seminary
3003 Benham Avenue
Elkhart, IN 46517 USA

www.anabaptistwitness.org

# Anabaptist Witness

*A global Anabaptist and Mennonite dialogue
on key issues facing the church in mission*

VOLUME 7 / ISSUE 2 / OCT 2020

## Displacement: Indigenous Peoples, Land, and Mission

## PROCEEDINGS FROM THE AAR/SBL MENNONITE SCHOLARS AND FRIENDS SESSION: "MIGRATION, BORDERS, AND BELONGING"



## REVIEWS

# Editorial

Christian mission is often described in positive terms as a commitment to cross every boundary in order to share the gospel of Jesus Christ. This description perhaps has its origins in the Acts of the Apostles, which contains Jesus's call to witness to him "to the ends of the earth" (1:8, NRSV). The Acts narrative shows Paul, in particular, as a border-crossing witness; if Peter's response to Cornelius begins to overcome the Jewish-Gentile boundary (10–11), Paul's expansive ministry spreads the message of interethnic reconciliation throughout the Roman Empire. Beyond Acts, Christians have looked to the model of the wandering Israelites and even to the incarnation—in which Jesus is said to have crossed the barrier between divinity and humanity—to inspire and to justify an account of mission as inherently border-crossing.

There has been less reflection, to my knowledge, on the implications for mission of the limited geographical scope of Jesus's ministry, or even of Paul's ministry, confined as it was largely to the Eastern Mediterranean provinces of the Roman Empire. Paul, according to Acts, was even restricted by the Holy Spirit from ministering in the imperial provinces of Asia and Bithynia (16:6–8). What does it do to our conception of mission as border-crossing if we accept that the Spirit sometimes stops us from crossing borders? Is there anything to be learned from the tension between Jesus's command to go to the ends of the earth, and his Spirit's containment of missionary expansion?

Those questions are important to consider when we reflect on the history of mission, especially (but not only) on its past five hundred years, during which mission has become thoroughly entangled with colonialism. Would a theology of mission more attentive to the Spirit's no have prevented, or at least significantly modified, European Christians' journeys to the ends of the earth? As Christians are increasingly challenged to learn about the importance of personal boundaries—to heed, for example, women's no to abuse—it seems clear that we need a more nuanced conversation about mission and borders.

That conversation will need to take up as a central topic the theme of the present issue of *Anabaptist Witness*: the historic Christian contribution to the displacement of peoples and land. The legacy of boundary-crossing colonial mission includes massive displacement—of native peoples from their homelands in Africa and the Americas, and of the produce of many lands, such as sugar, tobacco, and opium, for imperial purposes. The coerced movement and violent destruction of bodies and goods entails further displacements of psyches and families, cultures and languages. Any theology of mission that commends

Jesus's call, that advises packing up and moving across borders, must reckon with the history of missional displacement.

This issue consists of two primary sections. The first section contains peer-reviewed articles submitted to address the issue theme. These articles are framed by two interviews conducted by white, settler Mennonites with indigenous leaders. In the first of these interviews, Katerina Friesen speaks with Maya scholar Manuel May about his work to engage Old Colony Mennonites whose farms are displacing Maya people in southern Mexico. Rebecca Janzen's article then addresses related conflicts over land stemming from the arrival of Old Colony Mennonites to northern Mexico in the early twentieth century.

While these articles give a glimpse into the history of Mennonite displacement of others, Luis Acosta's essay shows that Mennonites have sometimes helped displaced others recover their land. Acosta narrates his work with Mennonite Mission Network's team in the Argentine Chaco to support a Mocoví community in their efforts to buy back some of their land.

Peter Sensenig writes of Christians in Kenya who refer to Somali refugees—many of whom are Muslims—as "Samaritans," thereby highlighting the complex bonds of solidarity forged in the face of terrorism. For Sensenig, seeing Muslims as Samaritans has the potential to expand the Christian imagination of interreligious hospitality. Recognizing displaced others, moreover, as agents of peace, not just victims of violence, can reconfigure our sense of the possibilities of addressing legacies of displacement.

One important model for fostering the peacemaking activity of those displaced by violence is truth and reconciliation commissions (TRCs). Andrew Suderman draws on his careful study of South Africa's TRC to warn Canadians, at the end of their own TRC process, that genuine reconciliation requires sustained work many years after the commission meetings stop. While Christian churches have a theological mandate to be agents of reconciliation, they also have to face their own complicity in the mass displacement of First Nations peoples. Reconciliation requires justice.

The theological themes latent in the previous articles come to the fore in the next few pieces. Hyejung Jessie Yum seeks to "unsettle" Mennonite assumptions about our commitment to peace in light of Russian Mennonite participation in settler colonialism in Canada. The next two authors, Randolph Haluza-DeLay and Devon Miller, contend that core concepts in peace theology—they treat shalom and violence, respectively—have to be revised in light of the colonial legacy and indigenous perspectives. David Rensberger also focuses on land, arguing that a theology of the Earth as belonging to God challenges settler conceptions of land as property to be conquered and controlled. A related piece—an excerpt from a forthcoming book by Ched Myers and Elaine Enns on "decolonizing discipleship"—is available on our website (https://www.anabaptistwitness.org).

This section of articles concludes with the second interview of the issue, conducted by Anabaptist Witness book review editor Steve Heinrichs in conversation with Cayuga leader Adrian Jacobs. Jacobs urges Christians to join indigenous peoples in friendship within the community of creation.

The second section of articles contains the proceedings from the Mennonite Scholars and Friends session from the joint American Academy of Religion/Society of Biblical Literature Annual Meetings, held on November 22, 2019, in San Diego, California. The theme of the session was "Migration, Borders, and Belonging." Jennifer Graber's opening keynote address drew from her book *The Gods of Indian Country* to discuss how Mennonites' sense of themselves as having the gift of "family" to offer others has led to the disruption of those others' own family bonds. Joseph Wiebe's response to Graber highlighted her book's contributions to conversations around decoloniality and religion, and urged a form of scholarship attentive to the scholar's own positionality and relations to indigenous communities.

The next keynote presentation, by Felipe Hinojosa, shifted the focus to the US/Mexico border. Hinojosa developed material from his book *Latino Mennonites* to explore how white Mennonite missionaries imagined the borderlands—and how their imagination fed into a paternalistic form of mission. In her response to Hinojosa, Hyejung Jessie Yum praised his work for enabling a shift toward a postcolonial, hybrid conception of Mennonite identity. My thanks to the presenters and to the session organizer, Kyle Gingerich Hiebert, for permission to publish these papers, which make a significant contribution to our understanding of mission and displacement.

The book reviews that conclude the issue further address this central theme. In her review of a festschrift for missiologist Darrel Guder, Sarah Ann Bixler presses us to ask questions about common terms such as "missional" in light of their colonial "scaffolding." May this issue of *Anabaptist Witness* help nurture a practice and theology of mission that takes those questions seriously. May we become attentive to both Jesus's call and his Spirit's no.


Jamie Pitts, editor

# Land, Neoliberalism, and Mennonite/Maya Interconnections

An Interview of Manuel May by Katerina Friesen

**KATERINA:** Manuel, what are some of the things you most love about where you come from? How would you describe your community (including the land) for readers? How has the land shaped you?

**MANUEL:** Regarding the Maya landscape, I think what has shaped my life mission is a living connection with sacred places, the sacred sites, or what some call archaeological sites. Walking in the middle of the jungle and finding buildings that were built over one thousand years ago by our ancestors has a powerful revitalizing effect on my connection to ancestral lands and my cultural roots. I enjoy walking through these ancestral lands and finding the special sites, considered sacred by our forefathers—for example, hills, caves, natural wells, and the abundant archaeological sites. Visiting these sites gives me a lot of inner strength. When I'm there in the community, I really enjoy visiting these places that are abundant in the

*Manuel May is a Maya scholar working as a postdoctoral researcher at Ludwig-Maximilians-Universität München in the Department of Social and Cultural Anthropology. His specific areas of interest are the heritage and rights of Indigenous Peoples and the reintegration of cultural memory for the empowerment of Maya communities. He is part of Ka' Kuxtal Much Meyaj, a Maya organization focused on educational and economic initiatives to support the self-determination of their community (*https://www.kakuxtal.org/*).*

*Katerina Friesen is a pastor, educator, and prison-garden program facilitator who lives on Yokuts land in Fresno, California. She chairs the Arts and Education Committee of the Dismantling the Doctrine of Discovery Coalition (*https://www.dofdmenno.org*).*

*Katerina and Manuel first connected in 2018 when Manuel reached out to the Dismantling the Doctrine of Discovery Coalition about a dialogue his community hopes to initiate with the old colony Mennonites in Hopelchén, Campeche, Mexico.*

area. Sometimes we are not able to see them because of the colonial-based education we have received at school.

KATERINA: Are the sacred spaces known in the community, or did you have someone guide you or show you those spaces?

MANUEL: Most of these places are well known in the Maya region, especially by the elders in the community—the grandmothers and grandfathers. But not everyone knows about these sites, because of the cultural amnesia caused by colonial-based education. Especially the youth are more and more disconnected from the Maya territory. I also had to have some guidance, especially from the elders, to visit various sacred sites. They are keen to pass on this knowledge to us and to future generations, so I think I am lucky because I have them to teach me.

Back to your question about the Maya landscape . . . I love to walk under the forest, in the atmosphere darkened by the shade of the trees. Despite the intense heat and sunlight, it seems that we are immersed in another world, fresh with pure air and full of life. The contrast of this environment may be hard to imagine in such a warm tropical area, especially in the dry season when we have so much light and so much heat. But as soon as you enter the jungle, you enter a dark space, like a cave, created by the shadow of the trees. The birds and insects are singing; it's like entering into a different world. I love that. I enjoy the feeling that I am part of the whole, not as a superior being but, rather, equal to animals, plants, and insects.

I like to learn from the singing of birds, insects, etcetera. I enjoy seeing the hills on the horizon covered with jungle, the smell of morning dew, and the colors of the sky after a storm. To enjoy the trees of the jungle and learn their medicinal uses . . . Often, when I walk with my father and he teaches me which plant is useful for a particular sickness, I like to think that some wounds from colonization are healing. To me, recovering this knowledge and learning from the experience with him is a healing process in itself and helps me to walk the path of decolonization.

I really feel at peace in that environment, and I think one of the best memories I have is after a storm. When you walk through the jungle after a storm, you can identify a special sound in the birds' song. When they sing after the rain, it's like they're celebrating a party! I like being able to listen and learn from those differences. And I also enjoy watching the different colors of the sky. I remember when I was a child, I loved to see the sky changing colors: blue, purple, pink, orange, red, etcetera.

KATERINA: Beautiful. Thank you, Manuel. I hear your deep love and intimacy with the place. Last year, you shared an article with me about the impact of the Mennonite communities' industrial farming practices on Maya beekeepers. It really impacted my heart to read it. For me, it highlighted the ongoing land degradation and disrespect for Indigenous sovereignty happening under settler colonialism. It echoes the stories of my German Russian Mennonite ancestors' displacement of Indigenous Peoples, where I live in what's now the United States as a settler (https://www.national-geographic.com/environment/2019/04/unlikely-feud-beekeepers-menno-nites-simmers-mexico/). One of the quotes that impacted me was by the indigenous beekeeper Edi Alimi Sanchez about the Mennonite settler-colonists: "They're good people. It's just that they destroy nature."

How would you describe the Mennonite communities in Campeche? What do you see as the sources of their destruction of nature? What do you wish they might understand about Maya communities?

MANUEL: It is difficult to describe any community without falling into essentialism and prejudice. I'll do my best, but I apologize if I fall into generalizations. My impression of the Mennonite communities we are more connected with is that they maintain a very isolated way of life—more than others I've heard about. As a group or collective, they rarely make contact with the Maya communities in our area. They often hire Maya men to work as laborers in the fields. But, in general, there is almost no relationship with the Maya communities. That's sad on the one hand. But, on the other hand, some of them are getting involved in the environmental problems of the region and are open to begin discussions on these problems that affect us all at the same time.

I read some testimonies from Mennonites, and I was surprised to learn that in some communities there is no television, that the internet is forbidden in their communities, or that women are not allowed to talk to non-Mennonites. It seems that most men learn Spanish to communicate with people from other villages and to sell or buy products. I'm not sure to what extent this information is accurate; maybe some women speak Spanish too. But when I have visited a Mennonite community in the area, often stopping by to buy cheese, it is certainly difficult to talk to the women, for some reason. However, one of the things that surprised me the most is that at school they learn their own language—German, or *Plattdütsch,* I think. And it is surprising, because we do not enjoy that right—the right to study in our own language. In the Maya communities, Spanish is the official language, and that's what we learn at school.

KATERINA: Indigenous language is not taught in schools? You have to do your own language revitalization for your youth?

MANUEL: Yes.

KATERINA: Wow. I just want to emphasize that, because I think it's a really important contrast. And I think it may have been one of the original agreements with the Mexican government when they settled there—to be able to teach their kids the language.

MANUEL: Yes. In regard to the language, I think it's nice to have a diversity of languages spoken, and I also think it is important to criticize the lack of education in our own language in schools. Our stories are different. For example, we faced five centuries of colonization. But it would be wonderful if we could learn our language at school.

KATERINA: Yes, it seems like differing stories of privilege and oppression. The European descendants were able to preserve their language, but the language of the Indigenous descendants in your home place that was colonized is at risk because it is not officially recognized or given support.

MANUEL: Right! On the other hand, we are proud to say that language revitalization is on the agenda of some Indigenous organizations, such as *Ka' Kuxtal. Ka' Kuxtal* is an Indigenous organization formed by Maya elders and young people. And one of the points I'd like to emphasize is that the elders are able to speak and teach the language, which means it's possible to create a multicultural, intercultural society or community if desired.

Going back to the Mennonite communities. . . . I have the impression that their current way of relating to the land has been shaped by the neoliberal movement in recent decades. This would not be uncommon because agricultural policies are guided by neoliberal agendas promoted by the Mexican state. In fact, this gives us an idea of the ideological impact of neoliberalism on the peoples of the world, particularly in Indigenous contexts. From the 1990s onward, Mennonites began to arrive in Hopelchén, just as Mexico was entering into NAFTA with the United States and Canada. Hopelchén Mennonites began to produce grain (sorghum first, then genetically modified [GM] corn and soybeans) for international markets. At this time, the government began to give more support to the Mennonites for the purchase of agricultural machinery and to convert the jungle into large areas of cultivation. In need of land and fleeing the violence in the north of the country, Mennonites who settled in Hopelchén benefited from the neoliberal plan of the Mexican government in many ways.

In turn, the Maya communities have maintained a historical struggle against the marginalization and the dispossession of the territories by the Mexican State through colonial-based policies. The Maya were reluctant to accept any policy that would harm the territorial sovereignty of the communities. So, in my opinion, support for Mennonite communities had the political result of weakening resistance and creating division in Maya communities.

KATERINA: So that happened in the 90s? I didn't realize it was that recent. Around the land title issues, was the land communally owned by the Maya before? How did the government transfer the land from the Maya to the Mennonites?

MANUEL: It is a long process that was reinforced by NAFTA-aligned policies and concrete changes in the law. After the Revolution, Indigenous communities obtained land to cultivate.[1] As a result, *ejidos* were created based on communal land ownership. But the ejido lands could be privatized if the assemblies so decided. That is why the 1992 constitutional reforms in Mexico promoted the subdivision of ejido lands as a necessary measure to be privatized after a careful legal procedure. This would allow land to be purchased, and, on the other hand, the government could use the expropriation of land to allocate it to Mennonites. Expropriation is a legal remedy based on the imposition of state dominion over the sovereignty of Maya peoples, very much in line with the Doctrine of Discovery.

With NAFTA, privatization was promoted. So, assemblies could sell off parts of the land. But, of course, the assembly members were also connected to the political parties, and through co-optation and corruption, certain leaders could be convinced to sell the land. It is also the case that

---

1 Following the Mexican Revolution, the Mexican government created a system of land reform for Indigenous and peasant communities based on the *ejido* system of Indigenous communal land tenure. The North American Free Trade Agreement (NAFTA) in 1991 effectively ended the *ejido* system.

individuals can sell their plots. For example, my father could obtain a plot of land to cultivate, and after some years of possession, he could ask for a change of use to sell it to private investors. Thus, the legal framework facilitates the dismantling of communal land tenure.

KATERINA: It sounds very intentional. It was created to dispossess or dismantle that communal system, like you said.

MANUEL: Right. But fortunately not all of the ejidos have been dismantled, and, in Hopelchén, some communities still keep land in common use and also develop different programs to protect it. In this sense, the Indigenous organization *Ka' Kuxtal* collaborates and supports several programs to protect and defend the territory in the region. The problem with the state's neoliberal policies is that they ignore the resistance of Maya communities to the practice of such a massive crop due to cultural and religious reasons. Cultivation in the Indigenous tradition is often carried out with great respect for Mother Earth. For example, before planting, ceremonies are held to ask permission from the spiritual protectors of the land and nature (*Yúumtsilo'ob*). So the very idea of clearing the forest to produce industrial and genetically modified corn goes against some basic principles of the relationship between the Mayas and the land.

But such respect is not easy to understand for people who come from other regions and have no spiritual connection to the earth. So, in my opinion, this was an advantage for the state that allowed it to channel Mennonite communities into industrial exploitation of the land.

KATERINA: Was it an advantage because the Mennonites were disconnected from the land, so they could be used almost as a tool to cultivate in an industrial way and take land in a way that the government wanted?

MANUEL: Yes, definitely. That was an advantage, and, besides, these communities were migrants trying to escape violence, which makes it easier for them to be instrumentalized and made dependent on the system.

KATERINA: It's a whole other conversation, but there are parallels between them [the Mennonites] escaping violence in Russia to come to Mexico,

Canada, the United States, or Paraguay. And that violence, maybe sometimes trauma, can blind us to the violence that we create.[2]

MANUEL: Yes, I think you're right. I hadn't seen it that way. . . . On the other hand, the government promotes certain violence by creating communities dependent on state money. All of a sudden, we have marginalized communities that seemingly become rich communities because of the resources that the state provides to buy machinery and new technologies for industrial cultivation.

KATERINA: So they started out marginalized and then became wealthy, partly because of the governments and the grants along the way for machinery and the land transactions.

MANUEL: Yes, I am certainly generalizing after talking to some people and reading a little more about the economic changes in Mexico in our region, and, of course, I also heard that there are problems mainly because the money granted is not free but works as a loan. Eventually, if there is a storm or a hurricane and crops are lost, everything is lost—even machinery, because it is bought with bank loans. This problem affects both Maya and Mennonites.

KATERINA: And would some people from the Maya communities—because of colonization—were they farming in similar ways? Had some people drifted away from the more, like you said, traditional practices of small cultivation and doing so in a more sacred way?

MANUEL: Yes. And I think it's all connected. For example, when people have lost their crops due to some natural phenomenon and need money, they can get loans and resources from the state, but sometimes these supports are provided for the cultivation of modified corn and soybeans. In several communities, the elders are reluctant to plant soybeans because some of the production is for self-consumption, so it is better to plant corn. But, in any case, genetically modified corn is sold, while native corn is preserved for consumption.

---

2 For more on intergenerational Russian Mennonite trauma as a barrier to Indigenous solidarity, see Elaine Enns, "Trauma and Memory: Challenges to Settler Solidarity," *Consensus* 37, no. 1 (2016), article 5; and "Facing History with Courage: Towards 'Restorative Solidarity' with Our Indigenous Neighbors," *Canadian Mennonite* 10, no. 5 (March 2, 2015): 4–9.

On the other hand, we have seen in the past decade that Mennonite communities began to create wealth, and you can see some young people with new trucks, nice and luxurious cars, and other machines. So imagine the young Maya looking at that! It's easy to be convinced to plant soybeans, for example, or modified corn. This creates another problem: the division within the Maya communities because some people want to switch to industrial cultivation. Of course, in the short term it seems to be better, or more profitable, but the elders—those who have more experience and have gone through several crises—are reluctant. They say that this improvement is temporary; it won't last forever.

In that sense, I think Mennonite communities have also begun to reflect. Because these problems affect us all in general. Regarding wealth, it is true that farmers get more money today because of the industrial way of farming. But it's not that much, to be honest, because nice cars, luxury cars, and machines are mostly bought on credit. When they cannot pay, they lose these goods, and, at the end of the day, people—whether they are Maya or Mennonite—are producing to benefit others.

I would also like to point out that many politicians are also businessmen in Mexico. Not only do they deal with changes in the law to allow massive industrial cultivation of GMOs but they also benefit directly from owning or partnering with companies that export soybeans, maize, or animals that feed on these grains to supply the world market. For example, the pigs and chickens that are sent to Asia, basically to China and other countries, are produced in the Yucatán Peninsula. Pigs and chickens feed on soybean products and modified maize. So, basically, the people who are getting really rich are not the Mennonites or the Maya who grow GMOs. In my opinion, they are one of the last links in the chain to benefit from the neoliberal system. And above them are the businessmen who make the most profit by feeding the global market.

KATERINA: What do you wish the Mennonites understood about the Maya community?

MANUEL: As I was thinking about that question, I was also doing a little self-reflection. Now there are Maya who are more in favor of industrial agrobusiness because they have seen the economic "success" of the Mennonite community. So, I would like *all of us* to go back to the ancestral teachings and to the forms of respect and gratitude toward Mother Earth, Mother Nature. This is not to romanticize or idealize, because I would say that much of this knowledge has been lost due to colonization or has been transformed. But we can still identify ideas, especially in the words of grandmothers and grandfathers—basic ideas or principles about how to relate to Mother Earth. So, I wish that together with the Mennonite communities and the Maya younger generation, we can *listen* and learn from the grandmothers and grandfathers.

KATERINA: I think that opens up the next question, which is about your desire to start a dialogue with Mennonite settlers—around Maya teachings and spirituality, Doctrine of Discovery, and your common interests—that you've described as neighbors, as links in this chain together. Maybe creating a different chain! What would be some of your hopes for this dialogue, and what might a repaired relationship look like if you can imagine it for your and our communities (linking myself to those communities as well)?

MANUEL: Honestly, when we talked last time, I had clearer ideas about how to respond. But when I was thinking about the nuances, I realized that there are complexities to think about. Thank you for giving me the opportunity to go deeper. In terms of the way our elders related to nature and the way we do it now and the way Mennonite communities do it in a more industrial way, I think we should start rethinking our relationships as a community, not just restricted to Indigenous people but also including Mennonites. As I said, the effects of industrialized crops are more evident now. We are getting sicker because of the use of chemicals like glyphosate, which is used to kill other plants for the benefit of GM crops. Now, it is more evident that after a few years with this type of farming, nature is destroyed in a dramatic way.

A few weeks ago, during tropical storm Cristobal, many Maya villages were flooded due to the way the terrain has been modified. The natural water courses that filled the natural wells were modified and blocked in the process of industrial cultivation. This resulted in flooding of neighboring communities and crops. It is clear that this way of relating to nature is harmful to all of us, and I think it is time for us to reflect deeply on how to treat nature more respectfully and with gratitude.

With respect to young Maya, I would say that it is urgent to discuss the historical roots that place us in the situation of oppression and injustice that we live in, and to reflect on the colonial process and the ideologies that support it, such as, for example, the Doctrine of Discovery. This is a necessary topic of discussion because many Protestant churches still perpetuate these ideologies.

KATERINA: In what ways do you see them perpetuating these ideologies?

MANUEL: For example, ancestral ceremonies for the cultivation of maize that, in fact, transmit values based on respect and gratitude toward nature are being demonized by the contemporary Protestant movement. I honestly don't know the position of the Mennonite church, but the Protestant churches in Maya communities qualify the ceremonies as acts of witchcraft, along with perpetuating the idea that land can be owned, dominated, and colonized. So, we need to examine the roots of these colonial ideologies and at the same time reclaim the ancestral Indigenous forms of respect and gratitude to Mother Earth.

KATERINA: Thank you for that. This seems like a big part of the work, as we've talked about in previous conversations, for Christians to undo the relationship between their spirituality and capitalism, and rediscover some of the roots in the Bible and in their own tradition that have a different relationship. Or, different stories for them to connect to the land rather than dominate the land.

MANUEL: Yes, in that sense, we haven't had that discussion yet [within the Maya community]. I was happy to know that there are Mennonite communities like the one you belong to that are developing this conversation in alliance and solidarity with Indigenous people in the United States. I was excited to share this with my community in Hopelchén, and they were also excited. To be honest, we were inspired by this initiative [the Dismantling the Doctrine of Discovery Coalition].

I think it is important that both Maya and Mennonites, who share the fruits of Mother Earth, have a conversation about the historical conditions and ideologies that have led us to this moment and to this particular situation of oppression, dependency, and injustice, where both Maya and Mennonites are immersed.

It would be important to discuss the colonial ideologies and strategies of demonization that were used by the colonizers to dominate Indigenous Peoples and that continue to be used by the different economic and political powers to maintain the oppression of entire peoples, whether Indigenous or non-Indigenous.

As we know, the Doctrine of Discovery has been discussed in United Nations forums, and various Indigenous Peoples around the world advocate its dismantling and the scrutiny of national laws that are influenced by such invalid principles—"racist, scientifically false, legally invalid, morally condemnable and socially unjust" (UNDRIP). We have also seen a beacon of hope in the conversations Mennonites are having with Indigenous Peoples in the United States and with society at large (for example, the coalition of which you are a part). Yet, these conversations do not exist between the Maya and Mennonites in Hopelchén and throughout the peninsula. For example, there are similar issues in Quintana Roo with the Maya and Mennonite communities as well.

The questions we'd like to start the conversation with are: How does the Doctrine of Discovery affect the formation of Mexico as a country? How does it perpetuate racist, scientifically false, legally invalid, morally condemnable, and socially unjust ideologies in the policies of the State?

Perhaps in the past I had doubts. But now, I think it is possible to start a dialogue with the Mennonite communities of Hopelchén, and we could start with the communities that are most willing to do so. I remember you once mentioned that there are people who interpret the teachings of Jesus from a capitalist current of thought but that there are other ways of understanding the teachings of the Bible, right? I agree with you, and, in that sense, I am convinced that Maya communities can contribute from Indigenous thought.

I wanted to emphasize that our ancestors and elders, during the colonization process, knew how to develop a profound theological and hermeneutical reflection on the teachings of the Bible. To give an example, in the ceremonies of the rain, we often see Jesus there, in the center of the altar. And, while taking part in the ceremony, while listening to the sacred messages, I realized that our elders—even in the most dramatic time of the colonial period—managed to capture the messages of God and the sacredness of God from Christianity. They reinterpreted and integrated these messages into Indigenous ceremonies such as the rain ceremony and had no problem doing so. Whereas, for the Christian colonizers of that time, using any Indigenous symbol was an offense and a reason for punishment. In that sense, I think our ancestors also gave that way of interpreting the teachings of Jesus as a legacy and I think that would be a good topic of conversation with Mennonite communities and Maya youth. Some Protestant churches could also learn from that experience.

I believe that when we deepen theological reflection and go beyond material symbolism, ideological barriers are removed, and that facilitates conversations. I think this benefits all of us in the region.

KATERINA: My final question is something that I'm open to you answering however you'd like, because I'm aware of the ways that white people or those of European descent have sometimes tried to appropriate Indigenous spirituality for themselves rather than being respectful. What do you think that Christians can learn, especially those from European descent, from Maya traditional practices?

MANUEL: I don't know if I'm the right person to answer that, but I can share what I've learned from our elders. When I was a teenager, I started to question some ideas, particularly because I belong to a family that is Protestant. But after being a child who often went to the Protestant church, I began to explore our ancestral spirituality. In the process, I learned that there is much damage in the colonial process that is perpetuated at school and the Protestant churches. I learned about human centrism [from the Protestant school and churches]. But the very idea that humans can control and dominate Mother Earth is very contradictory and goes against Maya spirituality. Moreover, in this anthropocentrism, the male role dominates, and this does not go unnoticed by Maya grandmothers and grandfathers. For example, I remember that in a ceremony in Guatemala, I was assisting a *ChuchAlcal-MamAlcal* couple—a Maya grandmother and grandfather—while in the distance we were listening to the service of the Protestant church. And through the speakers, the pastor often repeated, "God our Father. . ." on several occasions, until the grandmother said, "This pastor often forgets our Mother. God is both Mother and Father."

KATERINA: I agree with her!

MANUEL: Me too! And these messages are intrinsic to the ceremonies. For example, when you offer food or drinks, you offer for both mother and father. The Father is in Heaven, the Mother is Earth. Mother/Father is all of nature together. Due to the colonial education we receive, we often do not listen properly, but often our elders express profound messages clearly. We just have to learn how to listen better.

And we must also question the anthropocentric gaze. For example, when we attend ceremonies requesting permission from nature, from Mother Earth, to collect medicinal plants, a message of humility is transmitted to us. We are not superior to that little plant. We cannot assume ourselves as superior when we receive health and nutrition from plants. The same works for animals, from whom we also learn about medicine. As we see, the messages make it clear that we are not above the work of the Creators and Shapers, Mother-Father. And I wish this would be discussed in our communities, and that Protestant churches in the Maya region would join in the conversation.

KATERINA: Is there anything else you'd like to share that you didn't get a chance to share as we've talked today?

MANUEL: I would like to extend an invitation to all interested parties to join this conversation. The way we are treating Mother Earth affects all of humanity in the short term. The thirst for the accumulation of wealth is leading us to an environmental catastrophe, and Indigenous territories are the target of the capitalist system right now, precisely because they contain the last reserves of biodiversity on the planet. However, the accumulation of material wealth impoverishes the spirit. And I don't think Jesus was in favor of that.

KATERINA: I couldn't agree more. Yes. There's a verse in the book of Romans that talks about how all Creation is groaning for the liberation of humans. I think of that now—Mother Earth groaning. We can hear her groans. Thank you for bringing this full circle—that this conversation is not only healing for us humans but also for Earth. Thank you for your time today.

MANUEL: Thank you, Katerina, and thanks to the Mennonite Coalition for starting this conversation. We look forward to continuing to walk together. *Jáach Nib óolal!* (Many thanks!)

# Land Conflict in Mexico between Mennonite Colonies and Their Neighbors

Rebecca Janzen

Mennonites from Canada migrated to Mexico to pursue religious freedom by living in communities of villages called colonies.[1] Mexico welcomed them, as it believed the Mennonites would improve the economy of an unstable region. In the midst of this mutually convenient agreement with the federal government, however, Mennonites have experienced altercations with their neighbors over land use. This article situates Mennonites' land-related conflict within various changes in Mexican policy toward land and Indigenous people. It proposes that the Mennonites in Mexico, much like Mennonites in Canada, were able to continue their way of life "as a peaceful agricultural people" because Mexico's political and social structure favored them.[2] It shows that, in

---

*Rebecca Janzen is Assistant Professor of Spanish and Comparative Literature at the University of South Carolina, and is the author of* The National Body in Mexican Literature: Collective Challenges to Biopolitical Control *(New York: Palgrave Macmillan, 2015) and* Liminal Sovereignty: Mennonites and Mormons in Mexican Culture *(Albany, NY: State University of New York, 2018).*

Portions of this article were reprinted by permission from *Liminal Sovereignty: Mennonites and Mormons in Mexican Culture* by Rebecca Janzen, the State University of New York Press, © 2018, State University of New York, All Rights Reserved. Other portions come from "Whose Land? Conflict between Colonies and Ejidos in the Mexican State of Chihuahua," *Preservings*, no. 37 (2017): 45–50.

1 This article refers to Mennonites in Mexico who speak Low German and are descendants of Canadians who emigrated to Mexico between the 1920s and the 1940s, with the largest groups emigrating to Chihuahua and Durango between 1922 and 1926. The majority belonged to the Old Colony Mennonite Church, and a smaller number belonged to the Sommerfelder Mennonite Church. Royden Loewen's *Village among Nations: "Canadian" Mennonites in a Transnational World, 1916–2006* (Toronto: University of Toronto Press, 2013) provides a comprehensive overview of their history.

2 This terminology comes from Joseph R. Wiebe, "On the Mennonite-Métis Borderlands: Environment, Colonialism, and Settlement in Manitoba," *Journal of Mennonite Studies* 35 (2017): 112.

many cases, Mennonite settlement in Mexico adversely affected the surrounding population—either Indigenous or *mestizo* (mixed race)—contributing to their displacement and changing the people's ways of life.[3]

This article examines a few of many examples of Mennonite migration contributing to a country's existing colonization project—that is, to a government seeking to create loyal subjects throughout its territory and to marginalize or displace existing populations in order to contribute to that country's economic growth or capitalist expansion.

Mennonites arrived in Mexico in 1922, shortly after the government had reasserted control over Mexican territory following the Mexican Revolution.[4] This is significant to our discussion here because the revolution was fought, in large part, over land use. Mexican people in rural areas wanted to end the hacienda (large rural estate) system. In this system, landlords held most of the power in Mexico's rural areas because they owned most of the land. Peasants lived in a situation similar to debt peonage, of constant indebtedness and poverty. For this reason, leaders during and after the revolution made provisions for a more just land-use system.

In 1915, the federal government, under president-elect Venustiano Carranza, had passed a law that rendered any occupation of communal land illegal, even by soldiers.[5] When Carranza became president in 1917, his government passed a new constitution that continued this commitment to the question of land use and established the conditions for a land redistribution program. Article 27 stated: "La propiedad de las tierras y aguas comprendidas dentro de los límites del territorio nacional, corresponde originariamente a la Nación." (Land

---

3 In their early years of settlement in Mexico, Mennonites considered their neighbors to be of a uniform background and did not distinguish between Indigenous or *mestizo*. Andrea Dyck, "'And in Mexico We Found What We Had Lost in Canada': Mennonite Immigrant Perceptions of Mexican Neighbours in a Canadian Newspaper, 1922–1967" (master's thesis, University of Winnipeg, 2007), 1n2.

4 This article joins the position of historians who claim that the Mexican Revolution ended in 1920 following a decade of violent conflict. Other relevant dates include 1917, when the Constitution was passed, and the 1926–1929 Cristero War, an armed conflict between conservative Catholics and the Mexican government. Lázaro Cárdenas, who was president from 1934 to 1940, brought stability to the country under the Mexican Revolutionary Party (PRM). Manuel Ávila Camacho, president from 1940 to 1946, created the Institutional Revolutionary Party (PRI). His presidency began the PRI's single-party control, which lasted until 2000. Paul Gillingham and Benjamin T. Smith's edited collection, *Dictablanda: Politics, Work, and Culture in Mexico, 1938–1968* (Durham: Duke University Press, 2014), offers more information about the way the PRI maintained power in twentieth-century Mexico.

5 Gerardo N. González Navarro, *Derecho Agrario*, 2nd ed. (Oxford: Oxford University Press, 2015), 56.

and water found within national borders originally belongs to the Nation.)[6] This highlighted the nation's inalienable dominion and implied that landowners, regardless of their background, were to be subordinate to the government. Mexican people hoped this would mean they could own the land they had already been farming.

## Mexico Grants Mennonites Exceptions

As people in Mexico were experiencing a revolution, a much smaller group of people—Mennonites in Canada—were dealing with the aftermath of World War I (1914–1918). They were worried when men were drafted for military service, and some opposed the options for alternative service. Moreover, anti-German sentiment was on the rise, putting pressure on these Mennonites to educate their children in public schools in English rather than private religious schools in German. Many Mennonites found these changes to be an unreasonable attack on their lifestyle.

A group of Mennonite leaders representing those who did not want to integrate with their surrounding communities began to look for a new place to live. These leaders were pleased with the reception they received in Mexico. They were able to negotiate a special immigration agreement with Mexican president Álvaro Obregón (1920–1924) that accommodated their needs by granting them exception to multiple Mexican laws. The agreement stated:

1. You [the Mennonites] will not be forced to accept military service.
2. In no case will you be compelled to swear oaths.
3. You will be completely free to exercise your religious principles and to observe the regulations of your church, without being in any manner molested or restricted in any way.
4. You are fully authorized to establish your own schools, with your own teachers, without any hindrance from the government. Concerning this point, our laws are exceedingly liberal.
5. You may dispose of your property in any way you desire. The government will raise no objections to the establishment among the members of your sect of any economic system which they may voluntarily want to adopt.[7]

---

6 All translations are the author's unless otherwise noted. "Constitución de los Estados Unidos Mexicanos," *Diario Oficial de la Federación*, February 1, 1917, 2.

7 Calvin Wall Redekop, *The Old Colony Mennonites: Dilemmas of Ethnic Minority Life* (Baltimore: Johns Hopkins University Press, 1969), 251. The exceptions were an agreement, not a contract for colonization or immigration, and so depended on individual Mexican leaders for their enforcement. For more information on some challenges associated with having an agreement, see Martina E. Will, "The Mennonite Colonization of Chihuahua: Reflections of Competing Visions," *The Americas* 53, no. 3 (1997): 357n5.

These stipulations allowed the Mennonites to continue educating their children in their own schools and to avoid mandatory military service, both of which were important to them.

The agreement was signed by a president who was trying to reestablish stability and authority immediately following the somewhat dubious resolution of armed conflict by a government that had just passed a constitution guaranteeing free public education and land for all. The Mexican president was willing to sign such a generous agreement in part because he needed to populate the politically unstable region with loyal subjects who would contribute to its economy through agricultural production. The government wanted to use the Mennonite example to show that Mexico was a place where foreigners and their investments were safe.[8]

Chihuahua, one of two states where Mennonites entered into land-lease agreements, borders the United States, making it vulnerable to American interests. By 1920, when the Mennonite leaders were engaging in negotiations with the Mexican president, revolutionary fighting and an influenza epidemic had decimated the area's population, making it especially vulnerable. The state's agricultural production had fallen by three-fourths and the number of cattle by 90 percent.[9] The government wanted to rebuild Chihuahua's economy as a way to reduce the chances of future US incursions.[10]

The way President Obregón concluded the agreement confirms this impression: "It is the most ardent desire of this government to provide favorable conditions to colonists such as Mennonites who love order, lead moral lives, and are industrious. Therefore, we would deem it a pleasure if this answer would satisfy you. The aforementioned privileges being guaranteed by our laws, we hope that you will take advantage of them positively and permanently."[11] These Mennonite immigrants, in his view, would bring order to Mexico because of their Canadian ways and, because of the exceptions granted to them, would be able to contribute to the economy with their farms, ensuring that post-Revolutionary Mexico would prosper.

The Mennonites were satisfied with this agreement and acquired land in the states of Chihuahua and Durango. There, they established colonies, or groups of villages, that to this day remain crucial to their way of life—living separately from other parts of society and closely connected with one another.

---

8 Will, "Mennonite Colonization," 363–67.

9 Jason H. Dormady "Mennonite Colonization in Mexico and the Pendulum of Modernization, 1920–2013," *Mennonite Quarterly Review* 88, no. 2 (2014): 172.

10 Will, "Mennonite Colonization," 366.

11 Redekop, *The Old Colony Mennonites*, 251.

## Conflict in the 1920s and 1930s

The Mennonites' early years in Mexico included overt conflict that arose because the land they purchased had already been claimed by other people. In 1921, Mennonites from Canada acquired 225,000 acres (91,054 hectares) in two large blocks of land in Chihuahua, primarily from the Bustillos Hacienda, which belonged to Carlos Zuloaga's heirs, and a smaller tract from David S. Russek's hacienda. In Durango, they purchased 35,000 acres (14,164 hectares). These land transactions were finalized as century-long lease agreements with the government since, at that time, foreigners could not purchase land in Mexico.[12] But in Chihuahua, the Zuloagas had not been honest. Daniel Nugent observes that Mennonites paid ten times the going rate for land in Chihuahua, which pleased the Zuloagas.[13] H. Leonard Sawatzky adds that the seller was aware that groups of people, who had likely worked on the Bustillos hacienda prior to the Revolution, were living on land the Mennonites had just purchased.[14]

In 1920, before the Mennonites had migrated, eight different *agrarista* settlements—a term Mennonites used for people they perceived as squatters—surrounded what would become the Manitoba and Swift Current Mennonite colonies in Chihuahua.[15] The agrarista settlements were still there when the Mennonites arrived a year later. By that time, counting on the revolutionary promises, the settlements had filed to have the land granted to themselves.[16] In September 1921, Chihuahua's governor, Ignacio Enriquez, awarded provisional possession of 7,323 hectares of Zuloagas's land to those who had made the petition. The provision became permanent in 1923 when the governor ordered that 7,344 hectares of land be expropriated, including 5,000 hectares of land that the Mennonites had bought but not yet occupied.[17]

---

12 Harry Leonard Sawatzky, *They Sought a Country: Mennonite Colonization in Mexico* (Berkeley: University of California Press, 1971), 67.

13 Daniel Nugent, *Spent Cartridges of Revolution: An Anthropological History of Namiquipa, Chihuahua* (Chicago: University of Chicago Press, 1993), 89. Ana María Alonso details the understanding of the relationship between honor, personal relationships, and the accumulation of wealth in Northwestern Mexico in late nineteenth and early twentieth century (*Thread of Blood: Colonialism, Revolution, and Gender on Mexico's Northern Frontier* [Tucson: University of Arizona Press, 1995], 181–85). For them, land was also a means to preserving a way of life. This would continue in the period beyond Alonso's study.

14 Sawatzky, *They Sought a Country*, 45.

15 Walter Schmiedehaus, *Ein feste Burg ist unser Gott: Der Wanderweg eines christlichen Siedlervolkes* (Cuauhtémoc, Mexico: G. J. Rempel, 1948), 93–94; Sawatzky, *They Sought a Country*, 45.

16 Will, "Mennonite Colonization," 360.

17 Will, 360–61.

The Mennonites knew little about campesinos and their long struggle for land or about the new legal provisions to make land available for the people.[18] And the campesinos were undoubtedly perplexed that the land promised to them appeared to have changed hands. Over the course of these early years of settlement, "angry confrontations" took place between the Zuloagas, Mexican peasants, and Mennonites. For example, once the Mennonites had established their communities, free-ranging cattle repeatedly destroyed their crops. Building stronger fences did not resolve the issue; the fences were cut time and again.[19]

In 1924, the government redistributed more land from the Zuloagas' hacienda to the Mennonites and ordered the Zuloaga family to build a dam and reservoir so that the people living on newly redistributed land would have access to water.[20] The government also met the Mennonites' expectations as it sent troops to protect them.[21]

The tract of land acquired by the Mennonites in the state of Durango also came with issues; at the same time that Mennonites were purchasing what would become the Nuevo Ideal Colony, nearby peasants were petitioning for ownership of it.[22] Tensions remained even after the Mennonites settled there. At one point in the 1930s, the situation became so tense that Durango's governor ordered the Mennonites to close their schools. In other words, he forced them to comply with Mexican law—even though the Mennonites thought they had been exempted from it. In 1936, very concerned Mennonite leaders sent representatives to Mexico City to meet with then-president President Lázaro Cárdenas (1934–1940). The president was sympathetic to them and requested that the governor order people off the land that the Mennonites had purchased and also allow the schools to be reopened.[23]

In these cases, even though the Mexican federal government was ostensibly in favor of ejidos that recognized peasant land claims, it was particularly willing to accommodate the Mennonites. Events in Durango and Chihuahua show that because the government valued the Mennonites' economic contributions, it would use force to remove obstacles for them, even when those obstacles were other people.

---

18 Gerhard Rempel and Franz Rempel, *75 Jahre: Mennoniten in Mexico* (Cuauhtémoc, Mexico: Comité Pro Archivo Histórico; Museo Menonita, 1998), 299.

19 Sawatzky, *They Sought a Country*, 68–69.

20 Will, "Mennonite Colonization," 361.

21 Will, 368.

22 Dormady, "Mennonite Colonization" 181; Sawatzky, *They Sought a Country*, 194.

23 Dormady, "Mennonite Colonization," 182–83.

## Mexican Government Policies

These conflicts overlapped with the beginning of a land redistribution program. In Mexico, this program was formalized through the *ejido* system,[24] in which groups of people could claim land based on historical occupancy patterns for Indigenous groups, provided they were recognized in writing.[25] Groups of peasants could also petition for land for farming or ranching simply because they did not own any land.[26]

The Mexican government's federal *Secretaría de la Reforma Agraria* (Secretariat of Agrarian Reform) (SRA) organized land redistribution.[27] It worked with similar bodies on the state level.[28] A five-member decision-making body, the *Cuerpo Consultivo Agrario* (Agrarian Consultation Body) (CCA), would make final all decisions related to land redistribution.

In addition to creating these decision-making bodies, the government enacted the agrarian code, a series of rules for land redistribution. This code explained under which circumstances land from large landowners could be eligible for redistribution: the process would begin with a group of people coming together to file a petition asserting that they were farmers with no land and needed land to support themselves and their families. As *ejidatarios* (people liv-

---

24 Some scholars have incorrectly stated that this system was a return to pre-contact landholding. These include Samuel Baggett's "Article 27 of the Mexican Constitution: The Agrarian Question," *Texas Law Review* 5, no. 1 (1926): 1–9. In reality, the *ejido* system is similar to colonial-period landholding patterns common in Mexico from the sixteenth through the nineteenth centuries (González Navarro, *Derecho Agrario*, 29).

25 For more information about the role of Indigenous people in Mexico, see, for example, Miguel Bartolomé, "Etnicidad, historicidad y complejidad: Del colonialismo al indigenismo y al Estado pluricultural en México," *Cuicuilco: Revista de Ciencias Antropológicas* 24, no. 9 (2017): 40.

26 The Mexican situation is different from situations in Canada, the United States, or other countries as the relationships between the state and Indigenous people are not defined by treaties. For a comparative example, see Alonso's chronicle of serrano communities who settled in Northwestern Mexico on land they were given after fighting wars against Apache Indigenous people (*Thread of Blood*, 7–10).

27 This institution grew out of the Secretariat for Education's Department of Indigenous and Cultural Affairs, established in 1921. In 2003 it was renamed the National Commission for the Development of Indigenous Peoples and in 2018 the National Institute of Indigenous People. For more information, see Gonzalo Aguirre Beltrán, *El pensar y el quehacer antropológico en México* (Puebla, Mexico: Benemérita Universidad Autónoma de Puebla, 1994), 144–45; and Carlos Zolla and Emiliano Zolla Márquez, *Los pueblos indígenas de México: 100 preguntas*, 2nd ed. (Mexico City: UNAM, 2010), 304–11.

28 Manuel Fabila, *Cinco siglos de la legislación agraria en México (1493–1940)* (Mexico City: Procuraduría Agraria, 2005), 482.

ing on an ejido), they would have the right only to use the land, not to own it, and would be part of a collective run by an ejido leader. They were to apply just for land that could be cultivated—that is, that had sufficient access to water. The landowner also had to own more than fifty hectares.[29]

The agrarian code was later modified to apply only to people who owned more than one hundred and fifty hectares of land—if the land required irrigation—or three hundred hectares if it did not.[30] Landowners could also get out of the land redistribution program if they successfully petitioned for certificates of ineligibility for land reform.

As Cárdenas's government applied this code, seventeen million hectares (forty-two million acres) were distributed among eight hundred thousand people, and agricultural productivity increased throughout Mexico.[31] Thousands of people were now ejidatarios, with rights to cultivate land the ejidos understood to be theirs for the first time.

Although these were positive changes for Mexican peasants, the federal government irregularly implemented the agrarian code, and already wealthy landowners continued to own the best land and hold the most power in rural Mexico. Susan Walsh Sanderson's *Land Reform in Mexico: 1910–1980* explains that while land reform was a politically viable and popular decision, it was never done well.[32] Moreover, people who petitioned for *ejidos* in areas that had been active in the revolution could expect better land.[33] In addition to all of this, the bureaucrats in the SRA and the CCA, as well as ejido leaders, were notoriously corrupt.[34] Overall, from the 1920s to the 1990s, the government sporadically redistributed land, and when it did so, the land was of varying quality.[35]

---

29 Fabila, 482, 488, 491.

30 Fabila, 547.

31 Gerardo Otero, "Agrarian Reform in Mexico: Capitalism and the State," *Searching for Agrarian Reform in Latin America*, ed. William C. Thiesenhusen (Boston: Unwin Hyman, 1989), 284.

32 Susan R. Walsh Sanderson, *Land Reform in Mexico: 1910–1980* (Orlando: Academic, 1984), 2.

33 Sanderson, 47.

34 James J. Kelly, "Article 27 and Mexican Land Reform: The Legacy of Zapata's Dream," *Columbia Human Rights Law Review* 25 (1994): 554.

35 The ejido system officially ended when Mexico entered NAFTA in 1994. However, groups with active petitions could continue with the ejido process, and existing ejidos would continue to have a relationship with the Mexican state through bureaucratic channels. For more information, see González Navarro's *Derecho agrario*.

## Conflicts in the 1960s and 1970s

From the 1940s to the 1960s, Mexico experienced rapid urbanization and industrialization. Comparable development occurred in rural areas, in part due to the Green Revolution.[36] Mennonites, for their part, were able to deal with their many challenges in Mexico—such as droughts and religious divisions—without the added stress of what they perceived as interference from the government, or from conflict over land ownership.[37] But then, in the 1960s and 1970s, conflicts resurfaced as, in the 1920s, landowners sold Mennonites land that was already involved in the land reform process. Simmering conflicts came to a head as Mennonites expanded their land ownership in Mexico in the midst of widespread unrest in the Mexican population and a president committed to ejidos. In many cases, while having an ideological position in favor of the ejidatarios, the federal government resolved the ensuing land conflicts in the Mennonites' favor because it valued their economic contributions. In some cases, it again forcefully removed people from the Mennonites' property.

Mennonites had not needed to expand their land holdings until this time period primarily because of out-migration, even though their community had a high birth rate. Indeed, most conservative Old Colony people preferred to migrate to other countries rather than to assimilate, and some migrated to Canada seeking work when their crops did not perform well. Moreover, the Mennonites had purchased more land than was necessary for their initial population. Thus, it was not until the 1960s that the residents of the Nuevo Ideal colony in Durango and the increasingly connected Mennonite colonies in Chihuahua had grown enough that their residents needed more farm land.[38]

---

36 This initiative supported health, education, and rural development in Mexico. The Rockefeller initiative partially funded this project and ensured Mexican farmers would produce profitable crops with high yields (Nick Cullather, *The Hungry World: America's Cold War Battle against Poverty in Asia* (Cambridge: Harvard University Press, 2013), 57. Technologies of the Green Revolution expanded the amount of land cultivated in Mexico in low-tech, but not necessarily low-impact, ways (Christopher R. Boyer, *A Land between Waters: Environmental Histories of Modern Mexico* [Tucson: University of Arizona Press, 2014], 5). Indeed, many of Mexico's environmental issues can be traced to these developments. Flavia Echánove Huacuja details this process with regard to corn production and includes examples of Mennonite farmers ("Políticas públicas y maíz en México: El esquema de agricultura por contrato," *Anales de geografía* 29, no. 2 [2009]: 65–82).

37 Luis Aboites Aguilar's *El norte mexicano sin algodones, 1970–2010: Estancamiento, inconformidad y el violento adiós al optimismo* (Mexico City: El Colegio de México, 2018) provides more information about this time period.

38 Mennonite farmers had already vastly increased oat production and apple orchard production in Mexico and aligned with Mexican government goals (spurred on by the Rockefeller Foundation and the Green Revolution) to increase dairy production and

At the same time, Mexican peasants were also needing land for their own growing numbers and, as a result, were engaging in the ejido process and land occupation. Once the Mennonites realized this, they worked with local and federal officials to ensure that they would be the group retaining the maximum amount of land. The Mexican officials, for their part, were interested in the Mennonites' economic contributions and the possibility of creating positive relationships with them to ensure economic progress and a population of loyal taxpayers. Throughout the 1960s, massive unrest was brewing in Mexico. One catalyst for channeling this unrest into action was a railway worker strike in 1958, after which students and workers organized protests against widespread injustice.[39] Rural people began to organize outside of official channels, creating, for instance, a national union for peasants, which existed in a close relationship to the federal government. To avoid this close relationship, peasants organized through the *Central Campesina Independiente* (CCI), an independent group. This organizing was met with massive state repression, most notably expressed in the 1968 Tlatelolco massacre in downtown Mexico City.

*President Luis Echeverría, who came to power in 1970, needed to appease the population to avoid further protest.*[40] He was especially interested in doing so because as Secretary of the Interior he had orchestrated the Tlatelolco massacre—the first state violence meted out in an obvious way in an urban area against people from the working, middle, and upper classes. His administration committed itself to policies that would appear to bring about the revolutionary promises of land in rural areas, especially for Indigenous people.[41] Peasants

---

consumption (Dormady "Mennonite Colonization," 177). Luis Carlos Bravo Peña et al., include examples of the effects of Mennonite farming practices ("Cultura y apropiación del espacio: Diferencias en los paisajes culturas de menonitas y mestizos de Chihuahua, Mexico," *Journal of Latin American Geography* 14, no. 2 [2015]: 90–96). Carolina Vargas Godínez and Martha García Ortega focus on Mennonites and deforestation in Southern Mexico (in "Vulnerabilidad y sistemas agrícolas: Una experiencia menonita en el sur de México," *Sociedad y Ambiente* 6, no. 16 [2018]: 137–56). Evelyn Alarcón Quezada offers a case study about Mennonite agricultural practices in that state (in "Análisis del sistema agrario menonita, un enfoque desde la geografía sistémica, caso colonia la Honda, municipio de Miguel Auza, estado de Zacatecas" [Lic. Thesis, Universidad Autónoma del Estado de México, 2014]).

39 For more information on this period, see, for example, Jaime Pensado, *Rebel Mexico: Student Unrest and Authoritarian Political Culture during the Long Sixties* (Stanford: Stanford University Press, 2013).

40 Gabriela Soto Laveaga, *Jungle Laboratories: Mexican Peasants, National Projects, and the Making of the Pill* (Durham, NC: Duke University Press), 116.

41 "El pensamiento indigenista del Presidente Echeverría," *Acción indigenista* 264 (June 1975): 1.

rightly understood this as an opportunity to continue to apply for new ejidos or to expand existing ones.

## Conflict in Chihuahua

The factors that contributed to Tlatelolco were also in play in the state of Chihuahua in the 1960s. This period of widespread unrest, which had led to a massacre in Mexico City in 1968, also led to peasants in Northwestern Mexico to apply for new or expanded ejidos. These included ejidatarios near what are now the Santa Rita, Santa Clara, and Ojo de la Yegua Mennonite colonies.

Mennonites first settled in this area—to the north of the larger Manitoba and Swift Current colonies—in 1922. A group of Sommerfelder Mennonites had bought most of the land in this area from Russek's hacienda.[42] They faced difficult initial years of settlement without water for wells, a problem compounded by stony soil that made it difficult to grow crops.[43] In 1946, the Ojo de la Yegua and Santa Rita colonies were established, bridging the distance between the Santa Clara colonies and the larger Mennonite settlements just south of them.[44] These colonies began to prosper in the 1960s and 1970s because the Mennonites had developed better well-drilling technology and improved irrigation systems.[45]

The neighboring La Paz and Namiquipa *ejidos* were attuned to the expanding Mennonite settlement and agricultural technology. The Namiquipa ejido had grown so much that in 1962, it petitioned to create a new ejido, Nuevo Namiquipa.[46] When the government approved this expansion in 1965, it did not affect any of the Mennonite colonies, but when the La Paz ejido followed suit

---

42 Sawatzky, *They Sought a Country*, 51.

43 Sawatzky, 71.

44 Cornelius Krahn and Helen Ens, "Nord Colony, Mexico," *Global Anabaptist Mennonite Encyclopedia Online*, 1989, rev. November 20, 2016, http://gameo.org/index. php?title=Nord_Colony,_Mexico&oldid=141245.

45 Mennonites were associated with prosperity while other farmers were not. See an analysis of newspaper articles from this time period in Royden Loewen and Ben Nobbs-Thiessen, "The Steel Wheel: From Progress to Protest and Back Again in Canada, Mexico, and Bolivia," *Agricultural History* 92, no. 2 (2018): 179–80. For a comparative example, see also Ben Nobbs-Thiessen's analysis of Bolivian Mennonites' agricultural production, titled *Landscape of Migration: Mobility and Environmental Change on Bolivia's Tropical Frontier, 1952 to the Present* (Chapel Hill, NC: University of North Carolina press, 2020), 13.

46 "Solicitud de vecinos radicados en el poblado de Namiquipa, Municipio del mismo nombre, Estado de Chihuahua, para la creación de un centro de población agrícola que se denominará Nuevo Namiquipa," *Diario Oficial de la Federación*, August 1, 1962, 16.

in 1968 and petitioned to create the La Nueva Paz ejido, it was a different story. Part of the new ejido's land was redistributed from several Mennonite farmers in 1970.47 The same thing happened when the Nuevo Namiquipa ejido applied to expand in 1968—some Mennonite farmers' land was redistributed in 1970.48 In 1983, farmers in the same colony then "donated" land to quickly resolve the Nuevo Namiquipa ejido's second expansion.49

This transition depended on soft power and diplomatic compromise. Following a similar approach, some farmers, like Heinrich Klassen and Jacobo Wiebe Froesse, whose land had already been redistributed, applied for certificates to secure their remaining land against what they perceived could be further property loss.50 They were particularly fearful of losing access to their water source, the Santa Clara river.51 Another farmer, a Mr. Peters, made himself less

---

47 The farmers [corrected spellings] included Heinrich [Voth Sawatzky], Tobías [Dueck], Ernesto [Loewen], Jacob [Wiebe], Jacob Voth, Heinrich Friessen, Heinrich Hildebrand, Bernard [Stoesz], Katarina Voth de Friessen and Heinrich Klassen. "Resolución sobre la creación de un nuevo centro de población agrícola que se denominará La Nueva Paz, en Riva Palacio, Chih.," *Diario Oficial de la Federación*, September 12, 1970, 15.

48 "Resolución sobre ampliación de ejido al poblado Nuevo Namiquipa, Municipio de Namiquipa, Chih.," *Diario Oficial de la Federación*, December 5, 1968, 14–16, states that Johan Redekop, Ernst Fehr Boehlig, Johan Wiebe Peters, David Dyck Peters, David Martens, Jakob [Teichroeb Sawatzky], Jakob Friesen Friesen, and Benjamín Froese Dyck donated land.

49 "Resolución sobre segunda ampliación de ejido solicitada por vecinos del poblado denominado Nuevo Namiquipa, ubicado en el Municipio de Namiquipa, Chih. (Reg-316)," *Diario Oficial de la Federación*, August 24, 1983, 1st section, 16–18.

50 "Acuerdo sobre inafectabilidad agrícola, relativo al predio rústico denominado Lote 12 del predio La Campana, ubicado en el Municipio de Riva Palacio, Chih.," *Diario Oficial de la Nación*, January 2, 1984, 15–16;"Acuerdo sobre inafectabilidad agrícola, relativo al predio rústico denominado Lote 7 del predio La Campana, ubicado en el Municipio de Riva Palacio, Chih.," *Diario Oficial de la Nación*, January 2, 1984, 14–15.

51 Other farmers [corrected spellings] include Johan Heide Bueckert, Franz Enns Krahn, Jacob Klassen [Fehr], Heinrich [Enns] Reimer, Jacob W. Penner [Wolfe] and Abraham Dick Friessen" ("Acuerdo sobre inafectabilidad agrícola, relativo al predio rústico denominado Lote 14 de Santa Rita, ubicado en el Municipio de Riva Palacio, Chih.," *Diario Oficial de la Federación*, December 21, 1983, 25–26; "Acuerdo sobre inafectabilidad agrícola, relativo a los predios rústicos denominados Lote 12 y 13 La Campana, ubicado en el Municipio de Riva Palacio, Chih.," *Diario Oficial de la Federación*, December 30, 1983, 55–56; "Acuerdo sobre inafectabilidad agrícola, relativo al predio rústico denominado Lote 1 de La Campana, ubicado en el Municipio de Riva Palacio, Chih.," *Diario Oficial de la Federación*, December 30, 1983, 31; "Acuerdo sobre inafectabilidad agrícola, relativo al predio rústico denominado Lote 17 de Santa Rita, ubicado en el Municipio de Riva Palacio, Chih.," *Diario Oficial de la Federación*, January 2, 1984, 17–18; "Acuerdo sobre inafectabilidad agrícola, relativo al predio rústico denominado Lote 25 de Santa

vulnerable by deeding to his daughters—Justina Peters Boldt de Friessen and Sara Peters Boldt de Friessen—land that could have been eligible for redistribution. He received a certificate of ineligibility for the rest of his property.52 These Mennonite farmers came up with creative ways to avoid negative consequences of land redistribution in their own communities.

## Conflict in Zacatecas

Mennonites also experienced conflict with their neighbors in the state of Zacatecas. The La Batea and La Honda colonies were started there in the 1960s by people from Durango who needed more land. In these cases, the government acted in favor of the Mennonites, in part because the peasants were organizing outside of government-approved channels.

The situation began in a similar way as the land purchases in the 1920s. A Mennonite leader from Durango, Isaac Bueckert, traveled to the state of Zacatecas to inquire about land owned by a man called Ángel Mier. After Bueckert came to a favorable understanding with the owner, he told Mier he would inquire with the SRA about any ejido claims on the land. Mier, however, did not want him to do that, so Bueckert backed away from the venture.[53] Rightly so, as Mier is said to have thought a group of people might petition the SRA to create an ejido there.[54] Sometime later, Diedrich Braun, another Mennonite from Durango, took up the matter with Mier and proceeded to make the purchase in spite of potential issues. In 1961, a group of Mennonites from Nuevo Ideal, Durango, moved to land on Mier's property. In 1962, they finalized their purchase of three thousand hectares of land, now called the La Batea Colony.[55]

Neighboring Mexican peasants on the Niño Artillero ejido protested La Batea's establishment For instance, they destroyed the water pipes that the Mennonites had installed for their cattle. In response, soldiers were brought in

---

Rita, ubicado en el Municipio de Riva Palacio, Chih.," *Diario Oficial de la Federación*, January 2, 1984, 18; "Acuerdo sobre inafectabilidad agrícola, relativo al predio rústico denominado Lote 42 de Santa Rita, ubicado en el Municipio de Riva Palacio, Chih.," *Diario Oficial de la Federación*, January 2, 1984, 19.

52 "Acuerdo sobre inafectabilidad agrícola, relativo al predio rústico denominado Lote 106 Fracción A del predio La Campana, ubicado en el Municipio de Riva Palacio, Chih.," *Diario Oficial de la Federación*, March 26, 1984, 12–13; "Acuerdo sobre inafectabilidad agrícola, relativo al predio rústico denominado Lote 106 Fracción B del predio La Campana, ubicado en el Municipio de Riva Palacio, Chih.," *Diario Oficial de la Nación*, January 2, 1984, 19–20.

53 Peter T. Bergen, *La Batea: 55 Jahre* (La Honda, Mexico, 2017), 3, 5, 6.

54 Sawatzky, *They Sought a Country*, 182n36.

55 Bergen, *La Batea*, 73; Sawatzky, *They Sought a Country*, 180.

to force the peasants to leave.[56] The situation worsened after Mennonites purchased land for a fourth village in 1963. In 1973, the neighboring ejido for that village, Niño Artillo, petitioned the federal SRA to include that land, which was near a water source. This was a wise move on the part of the ejido, given that the newly installed federal government appeared to be committed to rural development and land redistribution.

In line with protest movements of the previous decade, the ejidatarios also began to occupy that land. According to Peter T. Bergen, who has written the history of the La Batea colony:

> Dann im Jahre 1973 kamen mehr Agraristen und siedelten in der Gegend an wo Niño Artillero heute ist. Am ersten waren sie auf der Arenas Fence. Da bauten sie Kleine Häuser aus Pappe. Zum Schauder der Mennoniten fingen diese Mexikaner an, die Felder der Mennoniten zu bearbeiten.

> [Then in 1973 more *ejidatarios* came and settled where Nino Artillero is today. At first, they were on the Arenas Fence. There they built small houses made of cardboard. To the horror of the Mennonites, the Mexicans then started to work on their fields.][57]

The ejidatarios acted in this way because they believed the land was theirs and that these actions would help their claim.

Also believing the land was rightfully theirs, the Mennonites appealed to the authorities. The community's religious and secular leaders employed notaries and worked with local officials to advocate for themselves. In 1971, colony leader Isaak Dyck Thiessen, via the notary, Rodolfo Soriano Duarte, submitted documents to the SRA to encourage the CCA to deny the ejido's request. He pointed out that each Mennonite family possessed a modest amount of land not exceeding the amount allowed by the land reform program.[58]

During this period, peasants attacked Mennonite crops and animals and threatened Mennonite people. Mennonite leader Jakob. K. Giesbrecht worked with local *presidente municipal* (similar to a mayor) Toño (Antonio) Herrera Bocardo to resolve these issues.[59] Isaak Dyck, who had already submitted documents to the SRA, increased his efforts on a federal level. He sent a telegram to officials in the Department of Agrarian Affairs in Mexico City explaining their situation in such abrupt terms that uses neither articles nor prepositions:

---

56 Sawatzky, *They Sought a Country*, 196.

57 Bergen, *La Batea*, 4.

58 Rodolfo Soriano Duarte, Report titled "Relación de las propiedades rústicas ubicadas en el predio denominado 'La Batea' de este municipio, que aparecen inscritas a nombre de los menonitas que a continuación se detalle," January 26, 1971, Ejido Niño Artillero Collection, Archivo General Agrario, Mexico City.

59 Bergen, *La Batea*, 4.

> Estamos quieta pacífica posesión terrenos forma colonias menonitas que
> representó a título dueños según documentos . . . negligencia absoluta auto-
> ridades estatales . . . tuvieron pleno conocimiento hechos situación tornase
> angustiosa . . . ataques a familias, cosechas y semovientes amenazas de muerte.
> . . . invasores dicen recibir ordenes central campesina independiente . . .
> [Somos] pequeños propietarios ofendidos inmensa mayoría nacidos territorio
> nacional.
>
> (We are peaceful own land form Mennonite colonies documents show that
> we are owners . . . state authorities have completely neglected us . . . they had
> full knowledge facts situation became awful . . . attacks on families, harvests,
> livestock and death threats . . . invaders claim to receive orders from the Inde-
> pendent Campesino Organization . . . [we are] small landowners offended the
> majority are born in national territory.)[60]

The telegram indicated that the Mennonites were peaceful *Mexican* victims who legally owned modest amounts of land and that if they were allowed to farm their land in peace, they would continue contributing to Mexico's econo-my. It added a veiled threat that the invaders were taking orders from the CCI, a peasant organization unaffiliated with the governing political party, the PRI. The Mennonites, the telegram concluded, were born in Mexico, implying that they would never do such a thing.

The government resolved the ejido's position in two ways: (1) According to Bergen, "Dieses Land haben die Mennoniten hier schließlich ganz verloren. Den Agraristen war diesen Land schon versprochen bevor die Mennoniten her-zogen." (In the end, the Mennonites lost this land. The ejidatarios had been promised this land before the Mennonites moved there)."[61] This would have been a small portion of land in the colony. (2) The government granted the remainder of the landowners in that colony exemption from future land claims; the certificates explained that while the Mennonites had come from elsewhere, their "descendientes son mexicanos por nacimiento que se dedican a la agricul-tura, contribuyendo con su esfuerzo y su trabajo colectivo a la producción de alimentos básicos para la población" (descendants are Mexican by birth, work in agriculture, and collectively contribute to produce basic foodstuffs for the [Mexican] population).[62] These agreements highlighted that Mennonites were

---

60 Isaak Dyck, Telegram to Lic. Augusto Gómez Villanueva, Jefe Departamento de Asuntos Agrarios y Colonización, April 1973, Ejido Niño Artillero Collection, Archivo General Agrario, Mexico City.

61 Bergen, *La Batea*, 4.

62 "Acuerdo sobre Inafectabilidad Agrícola relativo al predio rústico denominado Lote 12 de la Colonia Menonita Número 4, La Batea, ubicado en el Municipio de Som-brerete, Zac. (Registrado con el número 10700)," *Diario Oficial de la Federación*, June 12, 1980, 1st section, 41–42.

now Mexicans, who were contributing to the country's economy. This reasoning obfuscated the peasants' right to land as well as the fact that the Mennonites had worked with local and federal officials, encouraging them to use force to help maintain their way of life.

## La Honda

La Honda, the Mennonites' other colony in Zacatecas, also experienced land conflict with nearby ejidos.

A powerful landowner, Roberto Elorduy, who was a friend of a Mennonite leader in Durango, had sold the Mennonites land that was eligible for redistribution.[63] Mennonite leader Jakob K. Guenther had been worried about this in light of conflict in nearby La Batea. He expressed as much, and Elorduy reportedly responded by saying, "Life is full of struggles."[64] In spite of this, these Mennonites bought around sixteen thousand hectares in 1964.

Eleven years later, in 1975, conflict came to a head. That year, peasants who lived in areas near the La Honda Colony took advantage of the federal emphasis on land redistribution, hoping they might increase their landholdings. Initially, four or five wagons full of peasants settled nearby. As their numbers began to grow, they built homes and a school. Intending to live there permanently, they also kept livestock. Whereas the Mennonites believed this to be an occupation of land they had rightfully purchased, peasants had the opposite impression; when the J. Santos Bañuelos ejido officially petitioned to expand their ejido in 1976, they claimed that the Mennonites were illegally occupying *their* land.[65]

Mennonites in La Honda, as in La Batea, worked with local government to resolve the situation. *Presidente municipal* Antonio Herrera Bocardo, who had helped Mennonites in La Batea, urged people in La Honda to be patient. He suggested that they protest while some bureaucrats visited the colony to assess the land claim. The colony took his advice, and a large number of Mennonite women and children blocked the main road, which made an impression on the officials. As a result, the state governor acted in the Mennonites' favor, ultimately using force to remove the Mexican peasants.

On May 19, 1976, the Mennonites were told to stay indoors and pray. Armed men made their way onto the colony in trucks, and their leader proclaimed over loudspeakers:

---

63 Peter T. Bergen, *La Honda: 50 Jahre, 1964–2014,* (La Honda, Mexico, 2014), 4.

64 Bergen, La Honda, 9.

65 Enrique Moreno G., Julián Márquez E. and Esteban Saucedo, "Carta al C. Gobernador Const. del Estado,"January 9, 1976, Ejido J. Santos Bañuelos Collection, Archivo General Agrario, Mexico City.

Die Stimme war sehr klar und eindringlich, so dass die Mennoniten es weit und breit auch in den Häusern hören konnten. Er gebot diesen Menschen zu verlassen und die Mennoniten hier jetzt weiter in Ruhe zu lassen. Überdem gab der Sprecher bekannt, dass er von 30 anfange wurde hinunter zu zahlen. Schließlich 3, 2, und dann 1! Und dann rief er: „Pero ya! Ríndense!" (Jetzt, übergebt euch!) Dann ertönte eine Trompete sehr laut.

(His voice was very clear and emphatic, so that the Mennonites far and wide could hear him in their homes. He told these people to leave the Mennonites alone so that they could live here [in La Honda] in peace. Over the loudspeaker, he announced he would count down from 30. Finally, 3, 2, and then 1! And then he called: "¡Pero ya! ¡Ríndense!" [Now, surrender!] Then a trumpet sounded very loudly.)[66]

The armed men took the peasants and their goods away. The next day, soldiers stationed themselves in the place where the ejidatarios had been living. One Mennonite family remembers soldiers saying that they

hatten gemeint, dass sie sich auf etwas Furchtbares bereit gemacht hatten und dann hatten sie gesagt, dass dies noch nichts gewesen war. Die Mennoniten aber waren dankbar, alles so friedlich verlief. Denn sie gönnten ihnen nicht Böses.

(had prepared themselves for something terrible and they said that this was nothing. The Mennonites were grateful that everything had been so peaceful because they did not harbor ill will toward them.)[67]

The ejidatarios had hoped that occupying the land for which they had petitioned would ensure that it would be granted to them. The Mennonites, however, felt that since they had purchased the land, it was theirs. So they worked with local officials and accepted this use of force in order to be able to continue their way of life.

To prevent further conflict, the Mennonites in La Honda petitioned for certificates of ineligibility for land redistribution. As part of this process, multiple officials advocated on their behalf. Antonio Herrera Bocardo described the Mennonites as taxpayers who contributed to the nation's economy and as people who helped the nation by peacefully working, farming, and producing foodstuffs.[68] A bureaucrat named Fernando Ruiz Castro, perhaps one who had

---

66 Bergen, *La Honda*, 21.

67 Bergen, La Honda, 21–22.

68 Antonio Herrera Bocardo, Letter to Joel Luevanos Ponce and Arturo Medrano Cabral, Comisión Agraria Mixta, April 24, 1979. Ejido J. Santos Bañuelos Collection, Archivo General Agrario, Mexico City; Antonio Herrera Bocardo, Letter to Joel Luevanos Ponce and Arturo Medrano Cabral, Comisión Agraria Mixta, May 2, 1979, Ejido J. Santos Bañuelos Collection, Archivo General Agrario, Mexico City.

seen the protest, also lauded the Mennonites. He highlighted the community's cleanliness and its economic contribution in terms of livestock, dairy production, and industrialized agriculture;[69] he praised their education system, nutritious diet, and personal hygiene; and he pointed out that the Mennonites in La Honda saved their money in local banks in the towns of Rio Grande or Miguel Auza and that the colony paid federal and state taxes. He concluded that "debido a los reglamentos tan estrictos de su religión, no causan nunca problemas o conflictos a las Autoridades, y cuando las hay generalmente las resuelven en forma interna y pacíficamente" (given their strict religious rules, they never cause problems or conflicts with the authorities, and that when there are problems, they resolve them internally and peacefully).[70]

In October of 1979, the SRA granted Mennonite landowners the certificates that rendered their land ineligible for further redistribution, and the ejidatarios never returned.[71]

## Learning from a Long View of Capitalist Expansion

At various points between the 1920s and the 1980s, the Mexican government appeared to have resolved land disputes through land redistribution to ejidatarios, by granting certificates of ineligibility for land redistribution to Mennonite farmers and by sending armed officials to employ force to resolve situations in the Mennonites' favor. As we saw in Santa Rita and in La Batea, conflict has often arisen over specific pieces of land that have access to water.

These examples are the result of the Mennonite colonies privileging separation from the rest of society through an agricultural lifestyle. Moreover, the way that the Mennonites colonies have explicitly or implicitly lived out federal goals in terms of agricultural policy has led to visible prosperity for some Mennonites in Mexico.[72] In the process, the way many Mennonite colonies are structured in Mexico has prevented others from achieving the same level of prosperity. In other words, the Mennonite colonies in Mexico have engaged in capitalist

---

69 Fernando Ruiz Castro, Report on the Colony in What Was Known as the La Honda Hacienda, n. d., Ejido J. Santos Bañuelos Collection, Archivo General Agrario, Mexico City.

70 Castro.

71 Herrera Bocardo, Letter, May 2, 1979; "Acuerdo sobre Inafectabilidad Agrícola, relativo al conjunto de predios rústicos denominado Fraccionamiento La Honda, ubicado en el Municipio de Miguel Auza, Zac.," *Diario Oficial de la Federación*, October 1, 1979, 2nd section, 12–13.

72 Francisco J. Llera, Ángeles López-Nórez, Lucina Arroyo, Elizabeth Bautista, Gisel Valdez, Tania Amaya, "Cultura de Trabajo Colaborativo y Desarrollo Local. Análisis sobre las Actividades Emprendedoras Colaborativas en Grupos Menonitas y No-Menonitas en Chihuahua, México," *Cultura científica y tecnológica* 14, no. 63 (2017): 16–35.

expansion and are one of many groups from within or outside of Mexico that have colonized parts of the country, displacing others in the process.

We would do well to learn from these examples and engage in reparations to counter our own participation in these systems and to right our relationships with our neighbors.

# Acompañamiento en la compra de tierras en El Tabacal

La historia bíblica enfatiza el rol integral que juega la tierra en el proceso de convertirse en el pueblo de Dios. Sin tierra no hay shalom.[1]

Luis Acosta

## Introducción

El Equipo Menonita del Chaco argentino[2], continuó la tarea misionera iniciada en 1942 por los obreros fraternales de la Junta Menonita de Misiones (Mennonite Board of Missions, MBM), actualmente Red Menonita de Misión (Mennonite Mission Network, MMN).

Durante el período de 1995-2014, el Equipo Menonita estuvo integrado por familias misioneras de EE.UU. (Horst, Wigginton, Kingsley, Friesen), a las que se sumaron una familia de Alemania (Paul) y tres de Argentina (Acosta, González Zugasti y Oyanguren). En la actualidad la tarea de acompañamiento a las comunidades indígenas del Chaco sigue a cargo de la familia Oyanguren de Argentina.

Como parte de las tareas del Equipo en su acompañamiento a las iglesias y comunidades indígenas de las provincias del Chaco y Formosa, enfocadas principalmente en la enseñanza y difusión de la Biblia en las iglesias autóctonas, también —a través de algunos miembros del equipo— se participó activamente en

*Luis Acosta es argentino, casado con Mónica Barroso y padre de Marcos y Débora. Completó estudios de Agrimensura en su ciudad natal, Tucumán y el Bachillerato en Teología en el Instituto Bíblico Buenos Aires. Integró el Equipo Menonita desde 1995 al 2015 con dedicación a la enseñanza bíblica, a acompañar la lucha por las tierras, y coordinó la traducción del AT a la lengua Toba.*

1 Willis Horst, Ute Mueller Eckhardt, y Frank Paul: *Misión sin conquista. Acompañamiento de comunidades indígenas autóctonas como práctica misionera alternativa* (Buenos Aires: Kairos, 2005), 262. Existen varias reimpresiones y una segunda edición actualizada en 2011.

2 Para mayor información sobre la historia, visión y misión del Equipo Menonita, ver el libro *Misión sin conquista*.

el proceso de lucha por la recuperación de las tierras tradicionalmente ocupadas por familias y comunidades toba, wichí y mocoví.

En 1995, Luis Acosta, en su calidad de agrimensor, fue convocado por Mike Wigginton, para sumarse a un grupo de organizaciones indígenas, varias ONG y representantes de distintas iglesias que conformaban lo que dieron en llamar: Mesa Coordinadora Provincial. Este espacio promovía el diálogo con el gobierno provincial, con el objetivo de que se cumpliera el mandato constitucional de titular las tierras reservadas para las comunidades indígenas. Para colaborar con Luis en esa tarea se sumó en 1996 Andrea Velardez, asistente social, con apoyo del Comité Central Menonita, CCM (Mennonite Central Committee, MCC).

## Aproximación a la realidad mocoví

En la provincia del Chaco conviven tres etnias aborígenes: toba, wichí y mocoví. La etnia mocoví es la de menor población y la más impactada negativamente por el proceso de colonización iniciado a comienzos del siglo xx. El pueblo mocoví fue presionado y su territorio reducido cuando el ejército los expulsó de sus tierras para que fueran ocupadas por la migración europea.

El pueblo mocoví, en su lengua llamada *moqoit*, está localizado en el sur del Chaco, distribuido en veinticinco asentamientos[3] y en Santa Fe (Ver el mapa con distribución de asentamientos en la provincia del Chaco). El total de la población que se reconoce perteneciente y/o descendiente, de la primera generación del pueblo mocoví, en Santa Fe y el Chaco, consideradas en conjunto, es de 12 145[4] habitantes aproximadamente.

Los mocoví pertenecen al grupo lingüístico guaycurú, junto con los pilagás, tobas, y otros pueblos de la región. Actualmente la mayoría vive en comunidades con identidad propia, en la periferia de las ciudades o zonas rurales. Aunque existen localidades con presencia importante de asentamientos, como en el Departamento O'Higgins, San Lorenzo y Mayor Fontana, no adquieren características de «territorio», pues viven en pequeñas superficies, la mayoría en zonas rurales. Antiguamente era un pueblo predominantemente cazador y recolector, habilidades que muchos mocoví todavía tienen, a pesar de haberse modificado sus antiguas condiciones de vida. Su economía es de subsistencia. La mayoría trabaja como peones rurales, hacheros, cosecheros y empleados en aserraderos y municipalidades, de manera temporal. Los que disponen de tierras realizan mini cultivos de algodón, hortalizas, maíz y otros, de acuerdo a los requerimientos del mercado y a sus posibilidades.

---

3 Mercedes Silva: *Memorias del Gran Chaco*. Segunda Parte. (Resistencia, Chaco: Ediciones de Nuestra Cultura, 1998), 231-32.

4 De acuerdo con la Encuesta Complementaria de Pueblos Indígenas (ECPI) 2004-2005. Instituto Nacional de Estadísticas y Censos.

A pesar de los cambios culturales, y de las presiones etnocidas, se identifican como mocoví por sus formas de ser, pensar y actuar. Muchos hablan su idioma y actualmente está surgiendo un movimiento de recuperación o reconstrucción cultural.

Los mocoví piensan que su vida y cultura son importantes, desean perpetuar su identidad a través de sus hijos, aspiran a tener un buen trato, quieren retener el habla de su lengua dentro de sus familias. Opinan que el castellano debe ser aprendido en la escuela para poder hacer trámites, notas, tener nociones contables e integrarse sin problemas a la sociedad blanca. Desean relatar su propia historia, pero en su idioma, para que las costumbres heredadas de sus antepasados no se pierdan.

En palabras de Juan José Manito, cacique de la colonia mocoví El pastoril (1975):

«Lo que no se conoce no se ama, lo que no se ama no se protege y lo que no se protege no se rescata. Debemos rescatar el olvido, recuperar las memorias de nuestros antepasados. La historia de nuestros pueblos originales, desde el lejano ayer hasta el hoy. Incorporar las lejanas historias y también el presente de los pueblos indios, describir cómo se los discrimina y cómo viven nuestros hermanos».

## Fundamentación del proceso

Como dice Kalisch[5] al referirse a la autogestión reflexiva, esta: «parte de la propia estructura y dinámica cultural comunitaria; la incorporación de toda la comunidad en el proceso reflexivo siempre da una idea más cabal de las posibilidades y perspectivas de continuidad de la acción. De este modo, en su diseño, ejecución y evaluación aparece como protagonista principal la comunidad, no sólo el líder o promotores o maestros... La autogestión reflexiva significa no pasar por encima todo este proceso que está entre iniciativa resultado; *la meta no es el objetivo sino el caminar, el andar, el proceso*».

La importancia de la participación de la comunidad en las decisiones que afectan a las mismas tiene en Argentina un reconocimiento expresado en el Artículo 75, inciso 17 de la Constitución Nacional: «Corresponde al Congreso . . . Asegurar su participación en la gestión referida a sus recursos naturales y a los demás intereses que los afecten»[6]; y el Art. 37 de la Constitución de la Provincia del Chaco: «El Estado les asegurará la participación en la protección, preservación, recuperación de los recursos naturales y de los demás intereses que los

---

5 Hannes Kalish, *Hacia el protagonismo propio: Base conceptual para el relacionamiento con comunidades indígenas* (Filadelfia, Paraguay: Pro Comunidades Indígenas, 2000), 53.

6 Ver Constitución de la Nación Argentina: http://servicios.infoleg.gob.ar/infolegInternet/anexos/0-4999/804/norma.htm.

afecten y el desarrollo sustentable»[7]. Si bien existe un reconocimiento formal por parte del Estado, en la práctica, en la mayoría de los casos, no se respetan estos derechos.

Las mismas comunidades indígenas de Argentina, expresaron su pensamiento en las conclusiones del Programa de Participación Indígena[8], llevado a cabo en el año 1997, donde exigieron tener plena participación en:

- la regulación normativa del dominio;
- los planes, programas y/o proyectos de desarrollo en el área indígena;
- la gestión referida a sus recursos naturales y/o programas sociales;
- lo referido a tierra, agua, subsuelo, aire, y demás;
- la elaboración de proyectos nacionales, provinciales, municipales, etc., para comunidades indígenas.

Pero, como señala Luis M. de la Cruz[9], «la participación indígena se dará en los tiempos y espacios propios del sujeto de participación».

En virtud de estos fundamentos se decidió iniciar un proceso participativo y de toma de decisiones conjuntas para la compra de tierras en beneficio de familias de la comunidad mocoví de El Tabacal, y solicitar al CCM la flexibilidad necesaria para la implementación del proyecto y la rendición de cuentas de los fondos ofrecidos.

## El proceso

En febrero de 1998, el Equipo Menonita recibía del CCM un ofrecimiento de fondos adicionales por $ 10 000 USD, y pedía propuestas en cuanto al uso de esos fondos. A partir de ese ofrecimiento comenzaron los contactos entre el CCM y el Equipo Menonita.

Una de las comunidades, que el Equipo estuvo visitando por varios años, es la comunidad mocoví (*moqoit*) de El Tabacal, cuyas pocas familias que la componen fueron reubicados por el estado provincial del Chaco en una área pequeña, muy poco favorable para la vida de las familias de la comunidad.

Por eso el equipo decidió apoyar la iniciativa de, con esos fondos, procurar la compra de algunas hectáreas de tierras en la misma zona, para la ubicación de

---

7 Ver Constitución de la Provincia del Chaco: https://argentina.justia.com/provinciales/chaco/constitucion-de-la-provincia-de-chaco/seccion-primera/capitulo-iii/#articulo-37.

8 PPI, Programa de Participación de los Pueblos Indígenas, Foro Nacional, Conclusiones finales, (Buenos Aires: Programa de Participación de los Pueblos Indígenas, Agosto-Setiembre de 1997), 13.

9 Luis María de la Cruz, «Asuntos de Indígenas, Agencias, y Organizaciones de Ayuda», Formosa, Febrero de 2000, 76.

algunas de las familias de la comunidad que estuvieran en las peores condiciones en cuanto a su acceso a la tierra y los recursos naturales.

Ante la oportunidad de contar con fondos para comprar tierras, y la necesidad real de la comunidad de incrementar la disponibilidad de tierras, se nos planteaban dos posibles alternativas para el proceso: 1) asumir nosotros la gestión directa de la compra de las tierras para entregarlas a la comunidad, que se convertiría de este modo en una receptora pasiva del proyecto; o 2) iniciar un proceso participativo de diálogo y toma de decisiones de la comunidad, en el que se sintieran parte como actores principales para alcanzar el objetivo.

El 18 de febrero de 1998, Willis Horst, en una carta[10] dirigida a Linda Shelly y Alden Braul, respondía al ofrecimiento:

> Saludos para ti, Linda, y para Alden.
>
> Gracias por pensar en nosotros con respecto a la posibilidad de fondos adicionales para las cuestiones de las tierras indígenas.
>
> Nos llegó en un momento muy oportuno, ya que la familia Acosta estuvo de visita en la ciudad de Formosa ayer y hoy, por lo que pudimos hablarlo de inmediato.
>
> Luis propuso inmediatamente utilizar este dinero para la compra de tierras en beneficio de una comunidad mocovita a la que ha estado acompañando durante algún tiempo y se encontró con varios impasses. Hay iniciativa local, aparentemente hay tierra disponible en la zona, existe la posibilidad y la voluntad de sacar un título comunal. Qué bendición podría ser esto. Parece que el Señor se ha movido a tiempo.
>
> Le he pedido a Luis que escriba un breve resumen de esta propuesta y se lo envíe por correo electrónico en uno o dos días. Consideramos hacer uso de los $ 10 000 que se necesitan para llevar a cabo este proyecto.

---

10 Traducida de la carta original en inglés: "Greetings to you, Linda and to you, Alden. Thanks for thinking of us in regards to the possibility of additional funds for Indigenous Land Issues. This came at a very good time, since the Acosta family was visiting in Formosa City yesterday and today; thus we were able to talk it over right away.

Luis immediately proposed using this money for a land purchase to benefit a Mocovi community he has been accompanying for some time, and encountered a number of impasses. There is local initiative, there is apparently land available in the area, there is the possibility and the willingness to take out a communal title. What a blessing this could be. It seems the Lord has moved in good timing.

I have asked Luis to write up a short summary of this proposal and e/mail it to you in the next day or two. We would envision making use of as much of the 10,000 as needed for this project to see it through."

Linda Shelly en ese tiempo era Directora del CCM para América Latina, y Alden Braul era Director del Programa del CCM en Bolivia.

Por su parte, Luis y Andrea respondieron a CCM con la siguiente propuesta el 20 de marzo de 1998:

> La comunidad de El Tabacal se encuentra ubicada en la zona sur de la provincia del Chaco, a unos 40 km de Sáenz Peña, y a unos 210 km de Resistencia, la ciudad capital. La comunidad esta integrada por unas veinte familias que pertenecen a la etnia mocoví y ocupan en la actualidad 48 has aproximadamente, dentro de un lote de 100 has donde también viven algunas familias no indígenas.
>
> Esta comunidad es una de las más pequeñas entre las comunidades mocoví, por lo que incluso una pequeña porción de tierra que se pudiera comprar sería de ayuda.
>
> A estas familias, de cinco a ocho integrantes por familia, se van continuamente agregando nuevas familias que no disponen de tierra para ubicarse.
>
> Esta comunidad cuenta con una iglesia indígena perteneciente a la Iglesia Evangélica Unida, que se encuentra en una etapa de crecimiento y desarrollo armónico. Hay en la comunidad un ambiente de armonía y unidad.
>
> Las familias de la comunidad obtienen sus recursos fundamentalmente de la cosecha del algodón, y en algunos casos de la siembra y venta de su producción algodonera en pequeña escala.
>
> Esta comunidad, como la mayoría de la comunidades indígenas de la provincia, no tiene resuelto el acceso a las necesidades básicas de alimentación, salud y vivienda.
>
> Hemos tenido una relación casi continua con la comunidad, acompañando su reclamo por las 52 has que ocupa un comerciante de la zona y que el gobierno se niega a devolverles.
>
> Oscar Villalba, un líder de la comunidad, participa activamente en la lucha por la tierra y viaja a menudo con nosotros a las reuniones donde se trata el tema.
>
> Además:
>
> No tenemos experiencia previa en la compra directa de tierras.
>
> No queremos crear expectativas en la comunidad de El Tabacal hasta tener la certeza de la disponibilidad del dinero.
>
> Queremos manejar todo el asunto con la participación y junto a la comunidad involucrada.
>
> No quisiéramos ir a la comunidad con un proyecto «que viene de arriba».
>
> Por ello, les proponemos el siguiente cronograma:

1. Que MCC nos confirme la disponibilidad del dinero y su acuerdo en cuanto al destino que se le dará.

2. Nosotros comenzaremos a trabajar junto con la comunidad en la preparación de los detalles del proyecto.

3. El MCC recibe el proyecto elaborado.

4. El MCC envía el dinero.

5. Nosotros, junto a la comunidad, realizamos la compra y los trámites de la titulación en el plazo previsto.

Respondiendo a una solicitud de ampliación de la información, Luis y Andrea escribieron el 30 de septiembre de 1998:

Tal como habíamos solicitado, el dinero que ustedes nos ofrecieron de $10 000, hemos estado trabajando junto a la comunidad mocoví de El Tabacal para la compra de tierras.

Los hermanos de El Tabacal pusieron mucho entusiasmo y fe en que de esta manera se iba a poder resolver un conflicto de larga data. En el mismo lote de 100 has donde ellos viven y ocupan unas 40 has, un señor comerciante de nuestra ciudad, José Filipchuk, recibió del gobierno una adjudicación en venta de 52 has. Esta tremenda injusticia siempre fue una herida en la comunidad y la relación de este hombre con la comunidad mocoví siempre fue muy tensa, y, si bien nunca llegaron a la violencia, hubo conflictos donde el hombre blanco una vez más impuso sus deseos sobre los derechos de los indígenas.

El gobierno, a nuestro pedido, todavía no ha entregado el título de estas tierras al Sr. Filipchuk, quien tiene solamente adjudicación en venta. Él ha cumplido todos los requisitos formales, pero, debido a la presión de la comunidad indígena, se logró que no se le entregara el título.

Desde hace meses, y por pedido de los hermanos indígenas, tanto el gobierno como nosotros hemos intentado conversar con este hombre, a fin de manifestarle nuestro deseo de comprar las mejoras que él introdujo en el terreno.

En varias oportunidades, en forma evasiva evitó el dialogo con nosotros y con el gobierno. Pero, a pesar de eso los hermanos no querían avanzar en buscar otras tierras, ya que estas están en el mismo lote que ocupan y reconocen como propias. Finalmente, hace unas dos semanas, funcionarios del gobierno lograron hablar con el Sr. Filipchuk. Él manifestó su voluntad de acceder a la venta de las mejoras, pues no tiene interés particular en las tierras y sólo las mantiene para que un sobrino suyo pueda trabajar en ellas.

Ayer hubo un giro inesperado en la situación, ya que murió el Sr. Filipchuk de manera misteriosa, según los periódicos. Aparentemente esto complicaría mucho la situación, pues debería esperarse la resolución del juicio de sucesión, pues este hombre es casado y con hijos. Los funcionarios del gobierno dicen que esto puede llevar mucho tiempo.

No quisiéramos con este problema afectar ni al CCM ni a los hermanos indígenas, por lo que se solicita al CCM la posibilidad de enviarnos el dinero de todas maneras, ya que con el dinero a nuestra disposición podríamos lograr un mejor precio.

Sabemos que esta no es la política del CCM, pero en este caso les pedimos una excepción, pues no queremos que ese dinero se pierda. Esperamos, con los otros temas financieros en los que el CCM nos apoya, haber generado algún nivel de confianza que permita esta excepción a las reglas.

No tenemos duda de que la mejor ayuda que podemos brindar a los hermanos de El Tabacal, es lograr para ellos y sus hijos más y mejores tierras que abran un horizonte de esperanza para estos hermanos que han sufrido tanto las injusticias, el desprecio y la pobreza.

Linda Shelly escribió el 25 de octubre de 1998:

Muchos saludos! Gracias, Luis, por la información que nos has mandado.

Estamos haciendo el deposito de $10 000 con MBM. Puedes estar en comunicación con ellos para conseguir los fondos.

Nos alegra que estén casi por finalizar la compra de la tierra. Favor de mandarnos un informe al comprar la tierra. Nos gustaría recibir un pequeño análisis de cómo afecta la vida de la comunidad y sus esperanzas para el futuro.

Luego de las comunicaciones recibimos el dinero y se comenzó junto a la comunidad el proceso de búsqueda para la compra de las tierras.

El 14 de junio de 2000 concretaron la transferencia de la adjudicación en venta de la parcela 18 del lote 88, de 2 has, por un valor de $ 700, ubicada en el mismo asentamiento de El Tabacal. La adjudicación se encontraba a nombre del Sr. José Eduardo Díaz, y en acuerdo realizaron los trámites correspondientes para presentarlos en el Instituto de Colonización de la provincia, y desde allí procedieron a la adjudicación y titulación de la parcela en favor de los aborígenes.

En la comunidad se reunieron para decidir quienes ocuparían la tierra; en acuerdo se les entregó a dos familias mocoví, a nombre de Bernardino Arrieta y Brígida Salteño, quienes recibirán un título individual, porque es la manera en que la tierra fue repartida entre las demás familias. Por Resolución del Instituto de Colonización de la provincia, se adjudicó en propiedad la parcela 18 a las dos familias mocoví designadas.

El 25 de julio se realizó el acta de transferencia de derecho de la parcela 5, circunscripción V, lote 82, de 5 has, por un valor de $2 500, de la Colonia Nicolás

Avellaneda, Departamento O'Higgins, perteneciente al Sr. Ramón Oel Barco, en favor de las familias mocoví de El Tabacal.

El 10 de agosto se realizó el acta de transferencia de derecho de la Unidad Económica núm. 2, subdivisión del lote 82, de 4 has, por un valor de $2 800, de la Colonia Nicolás Avellaneda, Departamento O'Higgins, perteneciente al Sr. Orlando de Jesús Peña, en favor de las familias mocoví.

El 10 de octubre se realizó el acta de transferencia de derecho de la Unidad Proyectada núm. 2, subdivisión del lote 2, de 7 has, por un valor de $2 000, de la Colonia Juan Bautista Alberdi, Departamento San Lorenzo, perteneciente a la Sra. Alicia Olinda Muñoz, en favor de las 26 familias Mocoví de la comunidad de El Tabacal.

El 18 de octubre de 2001 se concretó la transferencia de derechos de un terreno con sus mejoras dentro de la planta urbana de la Municipalidad de La Tigra, que pertenecía al Sr. Claudio Néstor García, la parcela 24, manzana 51, circunscripción V, de 400 m2 de sup. por un valor de $ 2 000, en favor de los miembros de la comunidad de El Tabacal.

La Reforma de la Constitución de la provincia del Chaco de 1994, estableció la obligatoriedad del estado provincial de realizar la titulación, en forma comunitaria, de las tierras reservadas para las comunidades. La titulación de las tierras por título comunitario le confiere a las mismas las garantías de ser indivisibles, imprescriptibles e intransferibles. A pesar de estas ventajas, en el caso de pequeñas parcelas, las comunidades —en varios casos— han optado por un título individual en favor de la familia ocupante.

El proceso de titulación de esas tierras, a pesar del largo tiempo transcurrido, sigue en proceso, pero las mismas ya fueron ocupadas por familias de la comunidad y hacen uso efectivo de ellas.

## Evaluación del proceso

Esta experiencia de acompañamiento a una comunidad indígena, en la búsqueda y compra de tierras, lo definimos acá como un «proceso», en oposición al término usualmente utilizado de «proyecto», ya que, como muestra esta misma experiencia, el acompañamiento a los procesos de las comunidades indígenas no cuadran dentro de la mentalidad occidental de proyecto. Los tiempos, las formas y las relaciones que se dan en el proceso son diferentes por tratarse de una relación diferente.

El acompañar en estos casos significa respetar los tiempos y las formas propias de las comunidades indígenas para resolver las situaciones y conflictos que puedan presentarse.

Desde un punto de vista occidental hubiera sido más sencillo dirigir el proceso nosotros mismos, buscando y comprando las tierras y diciéndoles: «acá tienen, estas tierras son para ustedes».

En cambio, en consonancia con el pensamiento del Equipo Menonita, de una presencia no dirigista, preferimos ayudar a desarrollar las potencialidades de los líderes de la comunidad, promoviendo el protagonismo propio.

El costo en este caso, es en tiempo, como queda manifestado en el cronograma del proceso. Les llevó tres años de idas y venidas para que la comunidad pudiera buscar y resolver qué tierras comprar y cómo hacerlo. El saldo de $2 000 que quedaba, les llevó casi un año para determinar el destino de ese dinero. Finalmente, por consenso, la comunidad decidió comprar un terreno con una vivienda en el pueblo más cercano, para así tener un lugar propio donde las personas de la comunidad pudieran hospedarse cuando viajaran para trámites legales o por cuestiones de salud.

Este proceso participativo permitió incrementar la confianza de Oscar Villalba para desenvolverse en el mundo «blanco», ya que él en todos los casos fue la persona que llevó adelante las negociaciones y concretó la operación. Nuestro rol en cada caso se redujo a realizar el pago a la persona involucrada y pedir los comprobantes necesarios, y a cumplimentar, junto a Oscar, los requisitos legales de la compra.

Si bien no todos los integrantes de la comunidad participaron directamente en las decisiones y acciones, se sintieron valorados y respetados al ser considerados en sus opiniones, tal fue el caso de las mujeres y los ancianos de la comunidad, cuyo pensamiento normalmente no se toma en cuenta en otros proyectos.

En resumen, se compraron 18 has de tierras rurales, aptas para el cultivo, en beneficio de diez familias, y un terreno con mejoras para beneficio de toda la comunidad.

Agradecemos especialmente al CCM por la paciencia, y el haber respetado nuestra manera de resolver y acompañar el proceso para un mejor uso del dinero donado.

Andrea Velardez y Luis Acosta
    Equipo Menonita
    Chaco, Argentina
    1998-2001

## COMUNIDADES MOCOVÍ DE LA PROVINCIA DEL CHACO

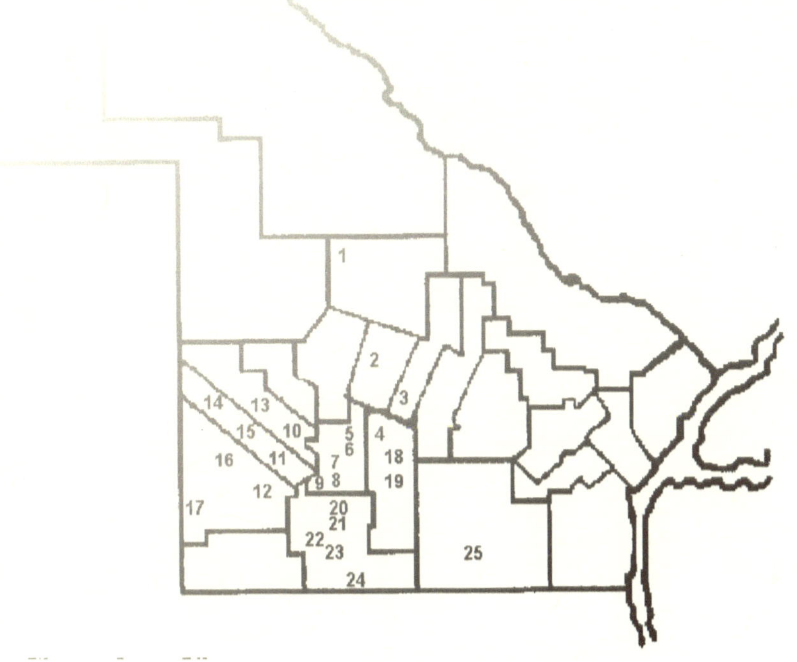


1. Raíz Chaqueña

2. Sáenz Peña

3. Colonia Aborigen, Chaco

4. Lote 16, Villa Berthet

5. Lote 12, La Tigra

6. El Tabacal

7. San Bernardo

8. Lote 3, Col. D. Matheu

9. Lote 138, Col. D. Matheu

10. Lote 40, Col. J. Lavalle

11. Las Tolderías

11a. San Lorenzo

12. Mesón de Fierro

13. Las Breñas

14. Larrea

15. Charata

16. General Pinedo

17. Gancedo

18. Lote 14, 19, V. Berthet

19. Lote 8, Samuhu

20. Villa Ángela

21. El Pastoril

22. Pegouriel

23. La Avanzada

24. Las Avispas

25. La Sabana

# Seeing Samaritans

## Subversive Othering in Kenyan-Somali Relations

Peter M. Sensenig

Over the past three decades, the Somali civil conflict, exacerbated at times by military intervention on the part of majority-Christian nations,[1] has contributed to the international displacement of two million Somalis, mostly to neighboring countries.[2] Thousands of Somalis have also relocated to the United States and Canada, many of them received by Mennonite congregations in the United States, thus furthering the scope of deep Somalia-Mennonite relationships first initiated by Mennonite missionaries in Somalia in 1953.[3] But the most sustained Mennonite interaction with Somalis is no longer on the part of North Americans; rather, Kenya Mennonite Church is now best situated to act as neighbors, particularly toward the nearly half a million Somali migrants who have settled in Kenya over the past several decades.[4] The stories here demonstrate the profound challenges of hospitality across faiths, particularly when political struggles mix with religious identity. It is clear that Mennonites, both in Kenya and in North America, must respond to the reality that Somalis have become their neighbors in new ways. It matters what language is used to de-

*Peter M. Sensenig has served in Zanzibar, Tanzania, with Eastern Mennonite Missions (EMM) since 2015. A member of EMM's Christian-Muslim Relations Team, he has taught ethics and peacebuilding at the Zanzibar Interfaith Center and in Somaliland, Ethiopia, and the United States. He has a PhD in Christian Ethics from Fuller Theological Seminary (Pasadena, CA), and is the author of* Peace Clan: Mennonite Peacemaking in Somalia *(Eugene, OR: Pickwick, 2016).*

1 Mary Harper, *Getting Somalia Wrong? Faith, War and Hope in a Shattered State* (New York: Zed, 2012), 5–13, 198.

2 Phillip Connor and Jens Manuel Krogstad, "5 Facts about the Global Somali Diaspora," *Pew Research Center*, June 1, 2016, https://www.pewresearch.org/fact-tank/2016/06/01/5-facts-about-the-global-somali-diaspora/.

3 Peter M. Sensenig, "Somali Refugees Received by Mennonite Congregations in Pennsylvania, US: Two Case Studies," in *People Disrupted: Doing Mission Responsibly among Refugees and Migrants*, eds. Jinbong Kim et al. (Littleton, CO: William Carey Library, 2018).

4 Connor and Krogstad, "Global Somali diaspora."

scribe that reality, what stories are told to make sense of it, and the ways in which we locate ourselves in those stories.

I begin with a brief description of the relationship between Kenyan Mennonites and Somali Muslims within the broader context of Kenya's interfaith challenges. I then describe two identities that Kenyan Christians have ascribed to Somalis—*shifta* and Samaritan—and the movement from the former to the latter. I conclude by arguing that although identifying others as Samaritans has some shortcomings, it is an example of religious othering that plays a positive subversive role in articulating a missiology in the context of displacement. Central to this argument is the position that understanding Jesus's interactions with and representation of Samaritans leads to the following responses: (1) challenging religious assumptions, (2) inviting repentance, and (3) promoting mutuality between hostile groups.

## I. Kenyan Mennonites and the Interfaith Context

Multiple high-profile incidents of interfaith conflict and violence over the past four decades have put Kenya consistently in the news. Three major terrorist attacks in the country—in 1980, 1998, and 2002—prefaced the the escalation of terrorist activity that began in 2011. This more recent wave, which has included dozens of grenade attacks on hotels, churches, bus stations, and other public places, has been conducted by al-Shabaab, an extremist group that controls the area across the border as well as most of rural southern Somalia, imposing a strict Islamic code and drafting young men to fight in response to the Kenyan military presence in Somalia. The most infamous of these attacks were the 2013 massacre at the Westgate Mall and the 2015 attack on Garissa University College, which killed 67 and 148 people, respectively. In Garissa, the attackers specifically targeted Christians, as al-Shabaab has done in numerous other instances in Kenya.[5] In retaliation, the Kenya Defense Forces have regularly rounded up noncombatants from Kenya's ethnic Somali population as a form of collective punishment, so that Somali Kenyans in northern areas say they fear their own country's military more than they do al-Shabaab.[6]

With each incident of terror the tension increases, and the response of Christians and Muslims to the hostility has not been coordinated well, even among

---

5 David K. Tarus and Gordon L. Heath, "Introduction," in *Christian Responses to Terrorism: The Kenyan Experience*, eds. Gordon L. Heath and David K. Tarus (Eugene, OR: Pickwick, 2017), 4–6.

6 Max Bearak, "In Kenya's Battle against al-Shabab, Locals Say the Military Is Fighting Terror with Terror," *Washington Post*, November 3, 2019, https://www.washingtonpost.com/world/africa/in-kenyas-fight-against-al-shabab-villagers-say-the-military-is-fighting-terror-with-terror/2019/11/02/52d68f24-ef4d-11e9-bb7e-d2026ee0c199_story.html.

organizations that emphasize peacemaking, such as the Program for Christian-Muslim Relations in Africa (PROCMURA) and the National Council of Churches in Kenya. PROCMURA has good relationships with Muslim leaders in the Supreme Council of Kenya Muslims (SUPKEM)—with Sheikh Ibrahim Tullab and Aisha Fathi, a lecturer in Kisumu—but the team leader describes these Muslims as "common guests in consultations," reflecting the reality that these are Christian initiatives into which Muslims are invited as guests.[7]

A major part of the challenge of interfaith peacemaking is that Kenya has received many thousands of refugees from Somalia over the past quarter century. Many have ended up in refugee camps—in particular Dadaab in northeastern Kenya, which is home to a third of a million Somali refugees, making it the largest refugee camp in the world. An additional estimated sixty thousand have made their home in the Nairobi neighborhood of Eastleigh.[8]

The influx of Somali Muslims into this majority-Christian city has turned it into a contested space marked by "mutual suspicion, intolerance, negative ethnicity, job insecurity, real or perceived marginalization, discrimination, and security-related issues."[9] The truth of this hit home for me one day when I facilitated a workshop with Somali community leaders in Eastleigh in an attempt to understand and address the impact of the actions of Kenyan security forces in the neighborhood. Young Somali men, who lived in overcrowded and under-resourced conditions and faced regular harassment from police, jokingly referred to themselves as "Walking ATMs" because they could be stopped and relieved of their cash by the police at any time. It is difficult to imagine the impact of this kind of trauma; if the purported intention of these operations is to combat radicalization, they are having the exact opposite effect.

---

7 Joy Wandabwa, Nairobi Team Leader, Program for Christian-Muslim Relations in Africa, interview by author, June 11, 2017, Nairobi, Kenya.

8 Although Kenyan Mennonite congregations planted in Mombasa and along the coast constitute a growing point of contact with Muslims, to date the most important connections with Muslims for Mennonites and other Christians have often taken place in the Nairobi neighborhood of Eastleigh. In particular, the Eastleigh Fellowship Center (EFC)—established by Eastern Mennonite Missions in 1977 as a community center for Somalis and now operated by the Kenya Mennonite Church—brings Muslims and Christians together for language learning, sports, and other activities. On a single day at EFC, for example, one might observe a Somali community meeting, an English class, a basketball coach training session, and private tutoring all happening at the same time. EFC has also been host to interfaith dialogues, workshops on interfaith relations, and peace projects such as Mennonite Central Committee-sponsored peace clubs.

9 Willem Jansen, "Mapping This Book," in *Mapping Eastleigh for Christian-Muslim Relations*, eds. C. B. Peter et al. (Limuru, Kenya: Zapf Chancery Publishers Africa, 2013), 7.

In addition to these issues, the historical connection between Somali Islam and Sufism is being challenged by the inroads made in Eastleigh by the revivalist Wahhabi movement. The radical expressions of this form of Islam, added to pressures of economic and social insecurity, contribute to a sense that faith is "high stakes" for Muslims in Eastleigh.[10]

One expression of this intensity of religious feeling is the open-air preaching (*mihadhara*)—public events aimed at inviting Christians to embrace Islam. The sermons often follow the argumentative style of the South African polemicist Ahmed Deedat, and the format is informal, featuring Christians who have converted to Islam but who have little formal training. In some cases, sermons take the form of "debates" between Muslim and Christian polemicists, with the clear goal of dominating the other side with one's arguments.[11]

Peacebuilding requires a different approach. Esther Mombo describes the critical role of dialogue in building a peaceful society; beyond mere tolerance, dialogue is "frank exploration and self-criticism in a joint forum. It is also an attempt to give respect by listening carefully to the views of the neighbor regardless of the tensions that might arise."[12] Sometimes what is called "dialogue" in Kenyan Christian circles, however, actually consists of Christians talking among themselves about Islam, without the personal links that build trust. When such "dialogue" is practiced in the absence of the religious other or in the mode of trying to win the debate, the results are deeper distrust rather than peaceful relationships.

Yet in spite of high-profile incidents of violence, open competition, and negative press and perceptions, there is hope that transformative relationships between Muslims and Christians are spreading in Kenya. The work of peacebuilding is almost always low-profile and slow to gain momentum, but it manifests itself in surprising ways.

One such surprise occurred in December 2015 when al-Shabaab militants stopped a bus in northern Kenya, ordered the passengers off the bus, and demanded that the Muslims and Christians separate. One year earlier, in November 2014, a similar incident had occurred in which al-Shabaab had stopped a bus with sixty passengers—half Muslims and half Christians—on their way to

---

10 Willem J. E. Jansen, "Mapping the Contexts of Eastleigh," in *Mapping Eastleigh for Christian-Muslim Relations*, eds. C. B. Peter et al., 16–19.

11 Joseph Wandera, "Mapping Eastleigh as a Public Platform: The World of Street Preachers," in *Mapping Eastleigh for Christian-Muslim Relations*, eds. C. B. Peter et al., 26–33.

12 Esther Mombo and Samson M. Mwaluda, "Relationship and Challenge in Kenya and East Africa," *Transformation: An International Journal of Holistic Mission Studies* 17, no. 1 (January 2000): 38.

Nairobi from northern Kenya. After al-Shabaab separated the Christians from the Muslims, they shot the Christians to death.

So when attackers again stopped a bus at Mandera near the Somali border a year later and asked the passengers to divide along religious lines, surely the previous tragedy was in everyone's mind. The Muslim women quickly shared their Islamic garments (*hijab* and *buibui*) with the Christian women so that the attackers could not determine their religious identity. The militants then asked the men to disembark, but the Muslim men, in turn, refused to separate along religious lines. Sabdow Salah Farah, one of the Muslim passengers who was injured in the attack, recounted, "We started quarrelling with them and told them they were not doing the right thing. We then asked them to kill everyone in the bus or leave us alone."[13]

It was risky for all of them, as al-Shabaab's reputation for brutal killing was well established. But the Muslims protected their Christian neighbors, and one Muslim man even lost his life in the attack. David Zarembka writes, "What is amazing about this story is that all the Muslims—without consultation ahead of time—had to agree to this rescue plan with all the men putting their lives on the line. If some had backed out or if there had been uncertainty or dissention among them, the plan would not have worked."[14]

This incident represents a new benchmark for neighborliness, reflecting the best in both faith traditions—to love and obey God and to love and protect one's neighbor. It should prompt curiosity in Christians about the religious motivations for such astonishing charity in their Muslim compatriots. It also poses a real-life parable of the sort that Jesus might tell Christians today, culminating in the question, "Who were neighbors to those who fell into the hands of the robbers?" (Luke 10:36). The answer, of course, is the religious other, whom Jesus posits as the character in the story worth emulating.

## II. Shifta or Samaritan? Somalis in the Kenyan Christian Imagination

I draw a connection to the parable of the Good Samaritan in the Muslim-Christian bus incident because some Kenyan evangelical Christians themselves are, in fact, making this connection. Faced with the challenge of a religious minority whose roots are in a neighboring country, they have identified two categories of people for understanding Somalis symbolically. Interestingly, both categories make an appearance in the parable of the Good Samaritan: The first is *shifta*, the

---

13 David Zarembka, "Game Changer in the War against Terror," African Great Lakes Initiative of Friends Peace Teams, Report from Kenya #368, January 1, 2016, http://david-zarembka.com/2016/11/16/368-game-changer-in-the-war-against-terror-january-1-2016/.

14 Zarembka, "Game Changer."

East African word for bandits who take advantage of the more-difficult-to-govern areas of the region, one of which is the northern Kenya area close to Somalia. The second is Samaritans, a label that some Kenyan evangelicals have started using to identify Somalis, effectively replacing the perception of them as shifta.

The history of the country shows just how significant a shift this is. When ethnic Somalis in northern Kenya attempted to secede and join the pan-Somali region in the 1960s, the Kenyan government labeled the conflict the "Shifta War" as part of a propaganda effort. By the time a ceasefire was brokered in 1967, the violence between Kenyan forces and Somali militia groups had killed thousands of people. It was in this context that Kenyans, following the agitprop of their government, began to use the epithet *shifta* not only for secessionists but for all Somalis.

That some Kenyan evangelicals have found a new label for Somalis therefore indicates a positive trajectory in the relationship between the two groups. Although the examples cited in this article are from interviews with Kenyan Lutherans, they are also relevant to Kenyan Mennonites who, like their evangelical neighbors, are forced to respond to the cultural and historical shaping of the narratives about Somalis. They have been surrounded by the same official propaganda about Somalis as shifta, aware of the violence of militant groups and of the Kenyan response, and, like Kenyan Christians in general, find themselves in closer proximity to Somali neighbors than ever before.

So what is happening as Kenyan evangelicals respond to Somalis? The interviews of US American scholar of religion Ken Chitwood with Kenyan evangelicals reveal a change in primary approach to this conflict—from open hostility to evangelization. The reasons for this shift, Chitwood contends, include demographic changes, economic pragmatism, and religious motivations, including both evangelization and peacebuilding.

Chitwood offers an example of the use of the Samaritan label as a metaphor in the context of a conversation around Acts 1:6–11, a Scripture passage in which Jesus promises the disciples that they will receive power from the Holy Spirit to be witnesses in Jerusalem, Judea, Samaria, and the ends of the earth. One Kenyan Evangelical Lutheran leader responded to this text, "Our Samaritans are the Somalis. Oh yes, we must receive power from the Spirit to reach them." This conversation took place as he and others were preparing to preach the gospel to Muslims through vision clinics co-sponsored by the Kenyan government and the Evangelical Lutheran Church of Kenya. So part of the move from shifta to Samaritan indicated here is that while Kenyan evangelicals are still seeing Somalis as other, they are also viewing them as "fair game for redemption and capable of conversion and Christian morals."[15]

---

15 Ken Chitwood, "Somalis as Samaritans: A Glimpse into Christian–Muslim Relations in Eastern Africa from the Perspective of Evangelical Kenyan Christians," *Islam*

Yet another metaphorical meaning for the Samaritan label is an emphasis on kinship and reconciliation. In the words of one Christian truck driver who was near Westgate Mall when the attacks occurred, "Somali and Kenyan Muslims are still our cousins. Borders can divide us, but we are still extended family."[16] While this Kenyan man does not use the label Samaritan here, the language of family applied across religious lines can have a particular power either to set the stage for mythically based conflict, as in the competition for the status of favored son between Isaac and Ishmael, or to shape the imagination in a peacemaking direction.[17]

A third possible meaning for Samaritan as metaphor is articulated by a Kenyan evangelical Christian who referenced the Good Samaritan parable from Luke 10 to describe Somalis as potential Samaritans. He gave the example of a Nairobi cab driver named Sa'id, whom he had observed helping a woman who had been in a car accident, noting that Somalis "may prove to be a surprising source of God's blessing."[18]

These three interpretations correspond to three prominent New Testament depictions of Samaritans: (1) The first, in Acts 1, places Samaritans as a middle ring in the outward expansion of the gospel—as part of the whole world to which Jesus commissions his followers to witness. (2) The second, in John 4, records Jesus's conversation with the Samaritan woman, in which the kinship of Jews and Samaritans—and the transcendence of the Messiah over both religious systems—is central to the discussion. (3) The third, in Luke 10, is the most powerful example of the three of what I call "subversive othering." That is, if the parable fulfils its purpose, it undermines our theological, social, and physical territoriality, ultimately transforming our relationship with the other.

## III. Is "Samaritan" a Helpful Label?

It may be clear at this point that my interest lies not simply in the fact that some Kenyan evangelicals are applying the label Samaritan to their Somali Muslim neighbors but in the deeper question of whether we should follow their example more broadly. In the context of displacement, what symbolic identities will lead to transformed relationships, greater justice, and more faithful communities of discipleship? Might we follow the example of these Kenyan Christians in seeing our Muslim neighbors as New Testament Samaritans, or in using other biblical

---

*and Christian-Muslim Relations* 28, no. 1 (2017): 70, 76.

16 Chitwood, 76.

17 Marc Gopin, *Holy War, Holy Peace: How Religion Can Bring Peace to the Middle East* (New York: Oxford University Press, 2002), 12–15.

18 Chitwood, "Somalis as Samaritans," 77.

metaphors? In order to interrogate this question, we need to explore several related questions.

## 1. Symbolism and the Religious Other

First, is it fundamentally helpful to think symbolically about the religious other? Marc Gopin points out that most religions express a felt need to exclude at some level, to create some kind of other, and to maintain boundaries. Yet othering is not just a religious phenomenon; religion is an easy target for criticism, but othering is ubiquitous human behavior. Societies exist because of the othering that holds them together, and the reason for the separation of church and state is not that othering is always wrong but that certain forms of it are. The liberal mistake, says Gopin, is to lump all forms of othering together, alienating Abrahamic believers in the process.[19]

In other words, religious othering is a fundamental feature of faith and practice, shaped by powerful metaphors and images. What we need is not to discard such metaphors altogether but to find ones that are transformative toward peace and mutuality.

## 2. The New Testament Meaning of Samaritan

Second, what does it mean to apply the New Testament label of Samaritan to a people group? The Kenyan Christians quoted above touched on three of the major New Testament Samaritan passages: the Ascension Commission in Acts 1, Jesus and the Samaritan woman in John 4, and the Good Samaritan in Luke 10. Two other passages also warrant note. Jesus includes a Samaritan in his healing ministry in Luke 17 and points out that only the foreigner said thank you. And, perhaps most significantly for modern interfaith relations, Jesus experiences Samaritan opposition at the beginning of his journey to Jerusalem (Lk 9:51–56). When the disciples wish to pray down fire from heaven to destroy the town, Jesus rebukes them. David Bosch sums these passages up this way: "All Luke's stories and parables about Samaritans give evidence to Jesus' refusal to embrace the vengeful sentiments of his compatriots."[20]

In short, the major significance of Samaritan references in the New Testament is that they represent a hostile relationship that sharpens Jesus's interactions and teachings. Samaritans indicate people who are close in belief to some Jewish groups, with lots of variations. At the same time, they represent difference, including the separate temple as a major issue—differences that were as

---

19 Gopin, *Holy War, Holy Peace*, 58–61.

20 David J. Bosch, *Transforming Mission: Paradigm Shifts in Theology of Mission*, 20th anniversary ed., (Maryknoll, NY: Orbis, 2011), 110.

much political and social as they were religious and ethnic.[21] Jesus's audience, including his disciples, must have found the parable of the Good Samaritan repulsive, since the Samaritan in the story "represents profanity; even more, he stands for nonhumanity. In terms of Jewish religion the Samaritans were enemies not only of Jews, but also of God. In the context of the narrative the Samaritan thus has a negative religious value."[22]

## 3. When the Samaritan Label Is Unhelpful

Third, how might applying the label of Samaritan in Muslim-Christian relations be *unhelpful*? One consideration is that several hundred people identifying as Samaritan live in Israel today, making it important to clarify that the symbolic label of Samaritan in the New Testament and its modern applications are not in specific reference to this present-day community.

Another consideration is posited by Chitwood, who identifies two ways in which the Samaritan label as used by Kenyan evangelicals can undermine the quest for peace with displaced Somalis and Kenyan Muslims. The first is using the label as an object for preaching, where "Samaritan" represents a lost and sinful person capable of responding to Christ. In such a case, the Somali becomes not simply the transcendent enemy but also a neighbor with whom one interacts for the purpose of conversion and redemption. Clearly, preaching is better than demonizing; yet, according to Newton Kahumbi Maina, an expert in Muslim-Christian relations at Kenyatta University, the ongoing competition in conversions and educational and political influence only exacerbates the centuries-long conflict between Somalis and Kenyans, and between Muslims and Christians.[23] As believers, we need something better than competition if we seek to build peace.

The second is that using the Samaritan label is necessarily territorial. Writing in a US American context, Al Tizon refutes the idea that a Christian nation can exist at all: "In fact, the idea of a Christian nation can only emerge out of a Christendom context, in which religion takes on a territorial dimension."[24] Christendom habits die hard, both on the right and on the left. When the Samaritan metaphor is superimposed onto this worldview, it only reinforces territorial assumptions.

---

21 Ida Glaser, *The Bible and Other Faiths: Christian Responsibility in a World of Religions* (Downers Grove, IL: InterVarsity, 2005), 162–67.

22 Bosch, *Transforming Mission*, 93.

23 Chitwood, "Somalis as Samaritans," 76.

24 Al Tizon, *Whole and Reconciled: Gospel, Church, and Mission in a Fractured World* (Grand Rapids, MI: Baker Academic, 2018), 24. For a more detailed argument on this, see Gregory A. Boyd, *The Myth of a Christian Nation: How the Quest for Political Power Is Destroying the Church* (Grand Rapids, MI: Zondervan, 2005).

The operational Christendom mentality at work in US American Christianity can also be observed in Kenya. Forces of globalization, urbanization, and displacement have put Christians in closer contact than ever before with Muslims, rendering the shifta label less useful and demanding a new metaphor. Chitwood wonders whether the change from Somalis as shifta to Somalis as Samaritans will be more of the same kind of othering—that is, operating with the assumption that to be Kenyan is to be Christian and conflating Somali with Muslim (despite the fact that around 11 percent of Kenyans are Muslims, not only those of Somali background). In that sense, the metaphor serves to prop up the narrative that Kenya is a Christian country and is part of the contestation of power in the country. For example, Kenyan evangelicals involved in an eye clinic in a Muslim neighborhood were presenting the gospel to Muslims, trying to demonstrate that good health goes along with Christian faith, and administering the program through President Uhuru Kenyatta's "Kenya Vision 2030" plan. In other words, they were "attempting to convert attendees at the clinic not only to 'the way of Christ,' but also to the way of Kenya."[25]

This is a powerful criticism, as it lays bare the underlying territoriality implicit in this sort of othering. In this case, metaphor is a mechanism for exerting control over the political, social, and economic spheres of Kenyan life. As shifta, Somalis/Muslims are incapable of integration into Kenyan space. As Samaritans, added qualifications make integration a possibility—if Somalis/Muslims convert to Christianity, adapt to Christian norms, and lose or temper the qualities that make them other. In re-imagining Somalis as Samaritans, Chitwood states, these Kenyan evangelicals are attempting to define what it means to be Kenyan for the purpose of commanding the political, social, and religious space of Kenya in contradistinction to the Somali as Samaritan.[26]

## IV. Samaritan as Subversive Othering

In light of these criticisms, what value is there in using the metaphorical label of Samaritan? Perhaps the first thing we should note is that this case study presents an opportunity for Christians in the West to learn from the African church, particularly as the displacement of Muslims makes increased interfaith contact more likely all the time. Paying special attention to interfaith practices in the Global South is important for a number of reasons. Africa, and the Global South in general, represents the growing edge of the Christian movement, and Africa is a major and unique meeting point for Muslims and Christians. New

---

25 Chitwood, "Somalis as Samaritans," 78–79.

26 Chitwood, 83.

global centers are developing, challenging assumptions about doing theology and mission.[27]

Tizon puts the shift in terms of the end of Christendom and the de-centering of the church in society: "Post-Christendom times call the nonwhite church, which has always been on the margins, to lead the way in defining the identity and mission of God's people today."[28] He emphasizes that global partnership across the colonial divide "will surely help to establish the church's credibility in the ministry of reconciliation. Postcolonial global partnership would demonstrate that the reconciliation the church offers to the world actually works!"[29]

Ghanaian theologian John Azumah makes the case that Africa is the only continent where the Christian and Muslim faiths meet each other as equals, not only in terms of numbers but also in the opportunities and challenges they face. For Christians in Africa, Muslims are not immigrants, aliens, or strangers; they are fellow citizens, neighbors, and family members. So talking about Islamic doctrine and practices is not treating Islam as a religious system. Rather, as Azumah puts it, "When we talk about these things in Africa, we talk about people. The most important thing in Africa is people, the second most important thing is people, the third most important thing is people. So, in a sense, Islam and Christianity in Africa are like two women married to one husband; they bicker, they quarrel, sometimes they fight but they just have to learn to live together. They cannot afford to see each other as enemies."[30]

Africa, including the Kenyan context where using the label of Samaritan as metaphor is being explored, matters a great deal in global Muslim-Christian relations because it offers some of the clearest examples of Muslim-Christian conflicts as well as interfaith hospitality. As the continent where Christians and Muslims coexist with struggle and with joy—as equals, neighbors, enemies, and relatives—Africa has much to teach the rest of the world.

This is true not only for Christians in general but also for Anabaptists in particular, as the first-, third-, and fifth-largest Anabaptist bodies in Africa are in the east—namely, Ethiopia, Tanzania, and Kenya, respectively.[31] That the

---

27 Philip Jenkins, *The Next Christendom: The Coming of Global Christianity* (Oxford: Oxford University Press, 2002).

28 Tizon, *Whole and Reconciled*, 30.

29 Tizon, 54.

30 John Azumah, "Toward Cordial Witness among Muslims: An African Perspective; Through the Lens of Historical Relations," November 8, 2007, Fuller Theological Seminary Missiology Lectures (podcast).

31 Mennonite World Conference Directory Statistics, available at https://www.mwc-cmm.org/sites/default/files/website_files/mwc_world_directory_2015_statistics.pdf. Baptized members are as follows: Ethiopia–255,493; DRC–235,852; Tanzania–65,456; Zimbabwe is fourth; Kenya is fifth with 37,172.

continent of Africa is home to the most members (more than a third) of Mennonite World Conference , combined with the reality that many of the countries with the most Mennonites also have large numbers of Muslims—especially along the East African coast—means that East Africa is the site of some of the most significant Mennonite-Muslim ecotones, along with India and Indonesia.

Chitwood concludes his article by asking, "Finally, what is Western Christian missionaries' and entities' interaction with, and impact on, Christian–Muslim relations and evangelical Christian discourse in Kenya?"[32] This is indeed our question, and I posit that, despite the pitfalls, applying the label of Samaritan as metaphor to Muslim neighbors is a gift that we can receive from Kenyan Christians. It is an example of religious othering that plays a positive subversive role in articulating a missiology in the context of displacement.

By the term *subversive othering,* I mean to say that the power of the metaphor sneaks up on us, surprising us with meanings that we did not intend to appropriate. This is the function of a large part of Jesus's life and teaching—to surprise, to turn expectations upside-down, to make the last first. I contend that Jesus's response to Samaritans in the Gospels makes the Samaritan metaphor a useful one in our relationship with Muslims—in Kenya or elsewhere—for three reasons: it (1) challenges religious assumptions, (2) invites repentance, and (3) promotes mutuality between hostile groups.

## 1. The Samaritan Metaphor: Challenging Religious Assumptions

Jesus directly confronted Jewish prejudice against Samaritans, casting the hero of the parable as a despised other, while portraying two Jewish religious leaders as villains. Taking the story a step further, David Bosch argues that in many of the New Testament stories, "salvation is ultimately tied to the person of Jesus. . . . He is the Samaritan, who takes pity on his Jewish archenemy."[33] Applying the Muslim-as-Samaritan metaphor, therefore, would render it something like this: Jesus is saying, effectively, "To you I am a Muslim." Notice he is not telling his Jewish hearers to convert to the Samaritan religion but rather to allow their ethical thinking to be shaped by looking beyond their religious categories.

Cathy Ross writes that the Samaritan's act of hospitality "crossed ethnic boundaries, caused him personal cost and inconvenience and saved a life. When we see the other person, we see the image of God, as well as our common humanity, which establishes a fundamental dignity, respect and common bond. The parable in Matt. 25 reminds us that we can *see* Christ in every guest and

---

32 Chitwood, "Somalis as Samaritans," 82.

33 Bosch, *Transforming Mission*, 106.

stranger."[34] The Kenyan Christians who use the Samaritan label as metaphor are demonstrating a concrete step in the direction of seeing the image of God, common humanity, and the person of Christ in their Somali neighbors.

## 2. The Samaritan Metaphor: Inviting Repentance

Jesus's shocking use of a hostile category of people to illustrate a virtuous way of being challenges the narrative of virtue-by-belonging. One of the primary ways we violate the dignity of people of other faiths is to identify behavior by some in another group and then assign that behavior as essential to the character of the group. For example, when Ethiopia, with the backing of the United States, invaded Somalia in 2006, the tanks rolled into Mogadishu on Christmas Day. With the goal of regime change, the Ethiopian military was not taking prisoners, and many civilians were killed. A British journalist recounted that as Somalis looked around at the damage and the thousands of dead, their widespread sentiment was, "This is the work of Christian Ethiopians. Muslims wouldn't do anything like this."[35]

Of course, we know that some Muslims can and do kill, just as some Christians do. The error of essentializing groups as incapable of good or evil becomes more obvious to whomever is on the receiving end of the error. This story, for example, rightly provokes protest from Christians. But it also demonstrates that we must be careful to direct our scrutiny toward ourselves even as we judge the actions of others. And we must always compare the best of our faiths as a practical way to love our Muslim neighbors as we love ourselves.

Jesus's rebuke to his disciples who wanted revenge against the inhospitable Samaritans calls us as Christians to repent for our own anger and hatred toward Muslims. Jesus then tells his disciples to turn that anger into repentance (Lk 10:13–16), after which he proceeds to relate the parable of the Good Samaritan. The connection is unambiguous: Samaritans are the clearest illustration Jesus could find of the importance of channeling the impulse of anger into the fruit of repentance.

Kenyan Christians have ample reason to feel anger toward certain Muslims who engage in acts of violence and terror, such as the Westgate and Garissa attacks that shook the country and its people to the core. The fact that some Kenyan Christians are nevertheless using the language of Samaritans to refer to Muslims means that they are locating themselves, whether intentionally or not, in a subversive narrative that draws them to transform that anger.

---

34 Cathy Ross, "Creating Space: Hospitality as a Metaphor for Mission," *Anvil* 25, no. 3 (2008): 171.

35 Eliza Griswold, *The Tenth Parallel: Dispatches from the Fault Line Between Christianity and Islam* (New York: Farrar, Straus, and Giroux, 2010), 128–30.

### 3. The Samaritan Metaphor: Promoting Mutuality between Hostile Groups

In response to the *Common Word* document written by Muslim scholars to Christians, Rowan Williams comments that in the story of the Good Samaritan, being a neighbor is a challenge that "continually comes at us in new ways. We cannot define its demands securely in advance; it demands that we be ready to go beyond the boundaries of our familiar structures of kinship and obligation, whether these are local, racial or religious."[36] Such readiness implies not simply a posture but also preparation, the hard work of building relationships of trust and mutuality.

The challenges of building such relationships should not be taken lightly. In our work in majority-Muslim contexts in East Africa, my spouse and I have been confronted daily by profound economic injustice as well as by the deep chasm between differing cultural and religious worldviews. Perhaps even here the Samaritan image has something to teach us; in Matthew 10, Jesus instructs his disciples to go not to Samaritan villages but to the lost sheep of the house of Israel, a glaring contradiction to much of the rest of the Gospel, where the good news is clearly intended for all people—Gentiles, Samaritans, and Jews.[37] Should Christians wrestle with this tension between mission to ourselves and mission among Muslims? Perhaps Jesus's reluctance to expand his ministry beyond his own people should inform our approach, give us an extra measure of care in how we present ourselves, and, most of all, infuse our presence with a deep and genuine humility. This is absolutely essential to mutuality.

It is easy for the familiarity of the Good Samaritan parable to obscure the startling fact that when Jesus is most directly asked what undergirds his ethic of neighbor love, he points to a person of a different religion. Significantly, Jesus was not supra-religious; he was a Palestinian Jew, so for him the Samaritan was as much the religious other as for his hearers. He is saying in clear language that his followers should be taught by those of other faiths, that we must learn from their examples as much as we intend to teach them.

Part of the argument here is that labels such as Samaritan that house subversive metaphors are not automatically or instantaneously transformative. We have noted that one can use the label without challenging the underlying assumptions of the status quo that Muslims are outsiders, foreigners, and/or potential—rather than actual—citizens of society. Yet this is precisely why the word *subversive* is appropriate; my contention is that if Kenyan Christians have primed themselves to see Somalis as Samaritans, when they are confronted with

---

36 Rowan Williams, "A Common Word for the Common Good," in *A Common Word between Us and You: Five-Year Anniversary Edition* (Amman, Jordan: Royal Aal Al-Bayt Institute for Islamic Thought, 2012), 202.

37 Bosch, *Transforming Mission*, 68.

extraordinary acts of kindness and sacrifice—as in the Mandera bus incident—they will connect naturally to the heart of Jesus's intended meaning for the parable. We are meant to be each other's teachers and each other's students.

Just as the Kenyan pastor above referred to Somalis as "our Samaritans," should other Christians follow this example in seeing Muslims more generally as "our Samaritans?" The answer, I propose, lies in whether we use the word *our* in a possessive, territorial, or defensive sense or whether we use the word to mean something along these lines: To us, Muslims operate as the Samaritans did for Jesus's hearers. Our Muslim neighbors help us to turn our scrutiny inward, to humble ourselves, and to repent of our sins. They present us with the challenge of learning from people who are different from us, who become our moral teachers and exemplars. Our feelings of anger may be stirred against them, and we learn from Jesus to transform these feelings into love.

It matters then that we are steeped in the parables and deeds of Jesus and that we are asking, along with Kenyan evangelicals, how we fit into the stories—and how those around us fit in as well. The examples given in this paper come from the context of Kenya, as Western Christians have much to learn from East Africans about interfaith mutuality. But the lessons are pertinent to the West as well, particularly as Muslim immigrants become our neighbors in increasing numbers. A recent significant study of US American evangelicals shows that attitudes toward immigrants, including Muslims, are shaped enormously by regularly hearing the stories of Scripture, including the parable of the Good Samaritan, in addition to sustained worship or service alongside immigrants.[38]

The dictum *You are what you eat* is spiritually true; we become the stories we live into, and they shape us in ways we are not even aware of. This is the meaning and the power of subversive othering: we think we are telling a story, but it is rather telling us, turning a mirror onto our weaknesses and making us stronger along with the other.

---

38 Ruth M. Melkonian-Hoover and Lyman A. Kellstedt, *Evangelicals and Immigration: Fault Lines among the Faithful* (New York: Palgrave Macmillan, 2019), 160.

# Journeying toward Reconciliation

Reflections on South Africa's Truth and Reconciliation Commission and Lessons for Canada in Its Post-TRC Era[1]

Andrew G. Suderman

The journey toward reconciliation is not an easy one. Any attempt to repair wrongs involves time and intentionality. Healing broken relationships takes longer still.

In Canada, the Truth and Reconciliation Commission (TRC), beginning in 2009 and coming to an end in June 2015, emerged as a way to "support Aboriginal peoples as they heal from the destructive legacies of colonization that have wreaked such havoc in their lives."[2] In particular, it sought to confront and raise awareness of the pain and suffering caused by Indian Residential Schools (IRS); a school system that served as a nefarious tool for colonization and dehumanization in a process that George Tinker describes as cultural genocide.[3] Neil Funk-Unrau provides a good summary regarding the intentions of the IRS:

> One of the most destructive expressions of the dominance of settler society over Indigenous society was the coercive imposition of an educational system designed to isolate Indigenous youth from their families, communities, and lifestyles in order to change them into exemplary Christian-Canadian citi-

---

*Andrew Suderman is Assistant Professor in Theology, Peace, and Mission at Eastern Mennonite University in Harrisonburg, Virginia, as well as Secretary for the Mennonite World Conference Peace Commission. He and his wife, Karen, served as Mennonite Church Canada Witness Workers in South Africa for seven years (2009–2016), where Andrew served as Director of the Anabaptist Network in South Africa (ANiSA). He is currently completing work on the manuscript of his book* In Search of Prophetic Theology: Anabaptist Inflections in South African Political Theology.

1 This article is adapted from Andrew Suderman's presentation at a February 26, 2015, event at Conrad Grebel University College (Waterloo, ON) coordinated by the Centre for Peace Advancement. Although the author no longer resides in South Africa, this paper was initially written while he was living there.

2 Truth and Reconciliation Commission of Canada, "Canada's Residential Schools: Reconciliation: The Final Report of the Truth and Reconciliation Commission of Canada, vol. 6," (2015), 4.

3 George E. Tinker, *Missionary Conquest: The Gospel and Native American Cultural Genocide* (Minneapolis, MN: Fortress, 1993).

zens. By isolating the children from their families, communities, and cultures, the authorities of the day were also able to more easily isolate the next generations from the lands and resources cherished by their ancestors.[4]

In seeking healing from this legacy, the Truth and Reconciliation Commission sought to establish not only a process through which the painful truth would be brought to the fore but also a foundation on which reconciliation could be built—a foundation that could establish and maintain respectful relationships.[5] Such a pursuit could establish the possibility of healing. The report stated that "reconciliation must inspire Aboriginal and non-Aboriginal peoples to transform Canadian society so that our children and grandchildren can live together in dignity, peace, and prosperity on these lands we now share."[6]

Canada and South Africa have a close relationship, learning from each other over the years. South African government officials, in the early to mid-twentieth century, visited several countries, including Canada, to learn how they "dealt with the native problem." South Africa became particularly interested in the reservation system that the Canadian and US governments employed, and they began using a similar system as one of the basic building blocks for their own system of apartheid or "separateness" that began in 1948.

Forty-five-plus years later, upon the official demise of apartheid in 1994, South Africa utilized a TRC process to confront and deal with its painful history to create the possibility of a new future in which its people could be reconciled. As South Africa learned from Canada about how to "deal with the native problem," Canada, in turn, has since gleaned insights from South Africa's TRC process in confronting its painful history of abuse against a segment of its own people—a history connected at least in part to Canada's own story.[7]

As Canada now enters its post-TRC era, it may also want to learn from South Africa's post-TRC experiences.[8] Toward that end, this paper seeks to ar-

---

4 Neil Funk-Unrau, "Small Steps toward Reconciliation: How Do We Get There from Here?," in *Buffalo Shout, Salmon Cry: Conversations on Creation, Land Justice, and Life Together*, ed. Steve Heinrichs (Kitchener, ON, and Harrisonburg, VA: Herald, 2013), 77.

5 Truth and Reconciliation Commission of Canada, "Canada's Residential Schools," 11.

6 Truth and Reconciliation Commission of Canada, 4.

7 This is not to suggest that South Africa was the first country to use a TRC process or the only one from which Canada learned. There have been many such processes in many other countries.

8 This has actually already been happening. For example, March 1–3, 2011, the Canadian TRC held a conference in Vancouver—"TRC Sharing Truth: Creating a National Research Centre on Residential Schools"—that gathered experts and survivors from places of genocide around the world to share how they engaged the public post-TRC with the

ticulate some of the challenges South Africa has faced and the lessons we can glean since the end of their formal TRC process, in the hope that these learnings will help Canada walk further along the path of confronting a painful past to reach a more hopeful future.

## South Africa's Truth and Reconciliation Commission (TRC)

Apartheid, an Afrikaans word meaning "aparthood" or "separateness," was a strict policy of racial segregation. While apartheid became law in 1948, the practice of racial separation and white European dominance had been common since the arrival of the first settlers in the seventeenth century. The official introduction of apartheid was accompanied by an evangelical zeal that justified ever-increasing forms of violence and repression in order to maintain the desired separation. Apartheid created an inherent privilege for the white minority in South Africa, with governmental policies that increasingly oppressed the majority of the population, who were considered to be "nonwhite."

This oppression became more apparent in the latter half of the twentieth century as the struggle against apartheid increased in tenacity. In the end, unfathomable atrocities were committed by both the regime struggling to maintain inherent privilege and those who fought against it.[9] After the official demise of apartheid in 1994, South Africa was left to deal with its history of violence, atrocities, and injustice. How does a country deal with such a past?

To wrestle with its painful history, South Africa established a Truth and Reconciliation Commission (TRC) in 1995. The TRC was designed as a mechanism to work toward national restoration, reconstruction, and healing. Desmond Tutu, the appointed chair, noted: "We were a wounded people, all of us, because of the conflict of the past. No matter on which side we stood, we all were in need of healing."[10]

The South African TRC confronted the gross violations of human rights with the intent of obtaining a clear and truthful understanding of the violence and dehumanization stemming from apartheid, so that forgiveness and reconciliation could potentially be possible for the nation as a whole. To paraphrase Tutu: "In order to forgive, we must know whom to forgive for what."[11] Truth

---

legacy/history and work of restorative justice. Participants included people from South Africa, Guatemala, Chile, East Timor, and Holocaust survivors, among others.

9 For accounts of these atrocities, see Antjie Krog, *Country of My Skull* (Johannesburg: Random House, 1998).

10 Staff Reporter of *The Mail & Guardian*, "Tutu: 'Unfinished Business' of the TRC's Healing," April 25, 2014, accessed February 21, 2015, http://mg.co.za/article/2014-04-24-unfinished-business-of-the-trc-healing.

11 Staff Reporter of *The Mail & Guardian*, "Tutu: 'Unfinished Business' of the TRC's Healing."

needed to be stated publicly so that reconciliation could follow. As Piet Meiring observed: "Finding truth goes far beyond establishing historical and legal facts. It has to do with understanding, accepting accountability, justice, restoring and maintaining the fragile relationship between human beings."[12]

The commission proved to be an innovative and creative way of grappling with the brokenness of South Africa's history. Indeed, it has become an example for others. The process was meaningful and eye-opening for the country. Those who were oppressed, repressed, and dehumanized by the apartheid regime were able to share their experiences, their stories, and, ultimately, their pain and suffering. They were able to regain a sense of dignity and humanity from having their past recognized. For once, they actually mattered and were heard. Whites, on the other hand, could no longer hide behind the pretense of ignorance as an excuse for the horrid cost paid for their privilege and comfort.

The TRC served several significant purposes. It provided a venue for the truth to be told about apartheid—the atrocities that it had created and justified as well as the society it had engineered.[13] The TRC provided an avenue through which victims could release what had happened to them and find their collective humanity. One victim recalls: "When I was tortured at John Vorster Square my tormentor sneered at me: 'You can shout your lungs out. Nobody will ever hear you!' Now, after all these years, people are hearing me!"[14] After a particularly difficult testimony in East London, a Xhosa mother shared the terrible events and tortures inflicted on her fourteen-year-old son and remarked about the relief she finally felt in sharing her experience and her truth: "Oh yes, Sir, it was worth the trouble [to testify]. I think that I will immediately fall asleep tonight—for the first time in sixteen years. Perhaps tonight I will be able to sleep without nightmares."[15]

The TRC also lifted the shroud of secrecy that had clouded much of South Africa's history. This was, and has continued to be, liberating. Many secrets were revealed; they no longer had to be maintained. Piet Meiring offers an example:

> On the final day of his appearance before the TRC when he had to testify to his role in the Khotso House (headquarters of the South African Council of Churches) bombing, former Minister of Police, Adrian Vlok, said: "When the final question was asked and when the legal team of the South African

---

12 Piet Meiring, "Bonhoeffer and Costly Reconciliation in South Africa," in *Bonhoeffer Consultation* (Stellenbosch, South Africa: Faculty of Theology, University of Stellenbosch, 2015), 7.

13 How much of the truth is a different and contested question.

14 Meiring, "Bonhoeffer and Costly Reconciliation in South Africa," 7.

15 Quoted in Piet Meiring, *Chronicle of the Truth Commission* (Vanderbijlpark: Carpe Diem, 1999), 371.

Council of Churches indicated its satisfaction . . . my heart sang. I got a lump in my throat and I thanked God for his grace and mercy to me."[16]

As South Africa transitioned from apartheid to its new democratic dispensation, the TRC played a particularly crucial role as—in essence—a pressure cooker valve. The apartheid system had generated so much pent-up tension and steam that a full-scale "explosion" seemed inevitable. The TRC, however, despite a significant amount of violence (especially in the lead-up to 1994), can be credited for preventing such an explosion. South Africa is often touted as an example of a relatively peaceful transition of power, and the TRC was one of the mechanisms that allowed for the relatively peaceful birth of a new nation, a new South Africa. This is surely worthy of praise.

But today, more than twenty years after the TRC's conclusion, obstacles in South Africa's journey toward reconciliation are becoming increasingly apparent. Pressure is increasing once again. The violent and repressive imagination that apartheid created still dominates. Recent violence directed at African foreign nationals—labeled xenophobia—as well as the police's ongoing use of excessive force (resulting in the killing of thirty-four striking miners at Marikana in 2012) are but two examples of this.

In the years following the TRC, two challenges have emerged regarding its process, the difficulties it has faced, and, possibly, its shortcomings. The first pertains to the meaning of "reconciliation." The second asks, Who is responsible for pursing and working toward reconciliation? It is worth, I think, paying attention to these two challenges, as I suspect they would also arise in other contexts.

## What Does "Reconciliation" Mean?

Although the TRC served a critical role in releasing pent-up steam, South Africa continues to grapple with what "reconciliation" actually means and what it practically looks like.

Notions such as "reconciliation" and "peace" carry a lot of baggage in South Africa (as they also do elsewhere[17]). These terms were often used during apartheid as a way of encouraging civility between races without substantially changing the apartheid-created social order. This had the effect of pacifying those who challenged the status quo while justifying, ironically, the violence required to maintain "the peace." For some, reconciliation encouraged living and acting together in a civilized manner but not challenging the existing social order. This

---

16 Meiring, "Bonhoeffer and Costly Reconciliation in South Africa," 7. See also Meiring, *Chronicle of the Truth Commission*, 357.

17 See, for example, the final two chapters of James H. Cone, *God of the Oppressed*, rev. ed. (Maryknoll, NY: Orbis, 1997).

approach maintained the logical inevitability of separation, inequality, and injustice.

But for others, reconciliation meant a radical altering of the apartheid-created social order so that justice and equality could exist for all. This was understood as true reconciliation and is more in line with the biblical notion of reconciliation, which shares close ties with justice.[18] It is also deeply unsettling for those who want to maintain the way things are, the status quo. A biblical understanding of reconciliation tirelessly pursues right relationships with God, with one another, and with creation. In order to make right relationships possible and a priority, it challenges and alters our ways of being and living. In South Africa, those who sought this form of reconciliation were often depicted as "disturbers of the peace."[19]

After the demise of apartheid, even those who were battle-hardened in the struggle against it and were skeptical of notions such as "reconciliation" were willing to begin talking about it. The anti-reconciliatory system had now been eliminated, at least in theory, thus making room for the possibility of true reconciliation. The positive traction of the TRC process highlighted the deep desire for reconciliation.

Unfortunately, the many different understandings of reconciliation became a stumbling block for the TRC and beyond. First, there was the question of whether justice would be integral in the pursuit of reconciliation. There were, for example, significant questions as to whether the TRC would seek retributive justice or restorative justice. The former, Tutu contended, was more characteristic of African jurisprudence.[20] The latter, which is ultimately the direction Tutu encouraged, was "not retribution or punishment, but in the spirit of *ubuntu*, the healing of breaches, the redressing of imbalances, the restoration of broken relationships. This kind of justice seeks to rehabilitate both the victim and the perpetrator, who should be given the opportunity to be reintegrated into the community he or she has injured by his or her offence."[21]

---

18 See, for example, the analysis and response that the authors of South Africa's *Kairos Document: A Challenge to the Church* provided regarding "reconciliation." See "The Kairos Document: A Challenge to the Church (1985)" in *Kairos: The Moment of Truth: The Kairos Documents*, ed. Gary S. D. Leonard (Pietermaritzburg, South Africa: Ujamaa Centre for Biblical and Theological Community Development and Research, UKZN, 2010), 15–17.

19 A recent biography of Desmond Tutu, for example, describes him as "a rabble-rouser for peace." See John Allen's *Rabble-Rouser for Peace: The Authorized Biography of Desmond Tutu* (New York: Free Press, 2006).

20 Meiring, "Bonhoeffer and Costly Reconciliation in South Africa," 9.

21 Desmond Tutu, *No Future without Forgiveness* (London: Rider, 1999), 51–52.

Megan Shore, in her book *Religion and Conflict Resolution: Christianity and South Africa's Truth and Reconciliation Commission*, notes how the transition from apartheid to democracy was based on the hope for a restoration of a moral human community.[22] "If truth-telling was supposed to act as a means of including all South Africans in a shared narrative, then reconciliation should be understood more properly as a moral process that restores relationships and fosters the moral community that was broken with apartheid."[23] The problem, Shore points out, is that reconciliation was not clearly defined.

Antjie Krog suggests there was a clash of cultural understanding regarding concepts such as "reconciliation," "forgiveness," "justice," and so forth during the TRC process. In response to criticisms of the TRC, Krog—as she considers why there was a lack of revenge killings compared to other contexts such as post-WWII Europe—argues that the TRC process and the objectives that arose from it centered on an epistemological and ontological background, and therefore on a perspective, that was different from other truth commissions. It was the first commission to *individualize* amnesty; it had public testimonies; and it allowed victims from both sides of the conflict to testify at the same forum.[24] But one of the most significant differences, she suggests, was the TRC's focus on "interconnectedness" (i.e., *ubuntu*) and the manner in which a person builds himself or herself into part of a community and vice versa.[25] This focus on interconnectedness became embedded in the process.

> Interconnectedness-towards-wholeness forms the interpretive foundation
> of it (as well as of the theology of Desmond Tutu or the politics of Nelson
> Mandela). I want to suggest that it was this foundation that enabled people to
> reinterpret Western concepts such as forgiveness, reconciliation, amnesty, justice, and so on in a new and usable way; in other words, that these concepts
> had moved across cultural borders and been infused with and energized by a
> sense of interconnectedness-towards-wholeness.[26]

Krog suggests that within the concept of interconnectedness-towards-wholeness,[27] notions such as forgiveness and reconciliation cannot be

---

22 Megan Shore, *Religion and Conflict Resolution: Christianity and South Africa's Truth and Reconciliation Commission* (Farnham, England and Burlington, VT: Ashgate, 2009), 109.

23 Shore, 109.

24 Antjie Krog, "Research into Reconciliation and Forgiveness at the South African Truth and Reconciliation Commission and Homi Bhabha's 'Architecture of the New,'" *Canadian Journal of Law and Society* 30, no. 2 (2015): 211.

25 Krog, 211.

26 Krog, 211.

27 This is Krog's English shorthand for the concept of *ubuntu*.

separated:[28] "The one begins, or opens up, a process of becoming, while the other is the crucial step in this becoming."[29] Indeed, these notions are versions of the same root word in isiXhosa.[30] "And here lies the 'newness': in the philosophy of Ubuntu, the two concepts are indivisibly intertwined, philosophically and linguistically. This means a radical departure from the general assumption that reconciliation and forgiveness are two separate and divisible processes."[31]

This new worldview led to some confusion about whether reconciliation was the projected outcome of the TRC process or whether the TRC was but the initial stage of a much longer process toward reconciliation.[32] The perception of some was that South Africa would be reconciled upon the completion of the TRC process and that life could simply move on without continuously raising the past and trudging through it. They assumed that people would, almost magically, be able to get along with one another. It would be possible, they thought, for South Africans to now forget about apartheid and move on.

In 2005, for example, the Afrikaans rock/punk song "Nie Langer" (No Longer) containing the following lyrics hit the radio waves in South Africa:

> The fact that I do not always agree
> Does not make me a racist.
> So look for the beam in your own eye
> Because: I will not say sorry anymore (x2)

---

28 Krog, "Research into Reconciliation and Forgiveness," 212.

29 Krog, 212.

30 Krog (212) explains: "The Truth and Reconciliation Commission in isiXhosa is *Ikomishoni yeNyani noXolelwaniso. Noxelelwaniso* is the isiXhosa for 'and reconciliation.' The *no-* consists of the connective *na-* (and, plus the prefix *u-* of *uxolelwaniso* [reconciliation]). *Uxolelwaniso* and the noun *uxolo* (peace) comes from the verb *ukuxola* (to become satisfied), which are being used most often as *ukuxolela* (to forgive). The verb *ukuxolelwanisa* (to see to it that forgiveness happens) is, in its turn, the origin for the noun *uxolelwaniso* (reconciliation). Thus, the word for reconciliation and forgiveness are versions of the *same* root in isiXhosa."

31 Krog, 212. Here Krog makes a very interesting and important observation. She notes that because of the interdependency between the concepts of reconciliation and forgiveness, black South African victims are now becoming increasingly angry at the lack of change and *wiedergutmachen* (literally, "To make good again" or "to restore") (Krog, 217). "Thus, and perhaps most importantly, only by identifying interconnectedness-towards-wholeness as the foundation of the TRC process is one able to understand that TRC resentment has more to do with thwarted beliefs now, because things were not made 'good,' than with the abuse of Christianity to suppress anger" (Krog, 217).

32 This paragraph is largely taken from a review that I wrote on Shore's book. See Andrew Suderman, "Megan Shore, Religion and Conflict Resolution: Christianity and South Africa's Truth and Reconciliation Commission—Book Review," *Political Theology* 13, no. 2 (2012): 260.

I will stand in the back of the line
Carry our rainbow on my sleeves
But I will NOT say sorry anymore (x2)
Stop wasting money on name changes.
There are people without houses,
Children without food
Who is now the guilty one?
I will no longer say sorry anymore (x5).[33]

The strong emotion of the song is evoked not only through the lyrics but also through repetition of the line "I will not say sorry anymore." The assumption of this song is that recognition for wrongdoing has been made, apologies have been given, and it's now time to move on. Little, if any, emphasis is placed on exploring ways in which restoration and restitution can be made so that the people of South Africa as a whole can live rightly with one another.

Cobus van Wyngaard, a young Afrikaans Dutch Reformed theologian, notes that although "white identity" as such is not mentioned in the song, the lyrics demonstrate that people in the mainline Afrikaans churches are at best unable to reimagine their identity apart from their "whiteness" and at worst contribute to the continued indebtedness to this racialized identity.[34] This mentality fails to understand or deal with the implications of apartheid at not only the emotional level but also the social, political, and economic levels along with the racial constructs that have been so closely tied to these realities in the South African context. It continues, in other words, to operate on a superficial understanding of "reconciliation."

Although the TRC lifted some of the oppressive clouds of the apartheid legacy, the problem remains that the reality experienced by most South Africans has not been foundationally altered. White privilege and racial inequality continue to dominate. In fact, the gap between rich and poor has become worse. Tutu and many others officially involved in the TRC process tried to inform the nation that the TRC should be seen as the beginning of a much longer walk toward (true) reconciliation. However, the intentionality required for true reconciliation has largely been put on the back burner, if it remains on the stove at all. Tutu notes much "unfinished business" in reweaving the fabric of South Africa's society:

---

33 Klopjag, "Nie Langer," from Album 3, as translated in Jonathan D. Jansen, *Knowledge in the Blood: Confronting Race and the Apartheid Past* (Stanford, CA: Stanford University Press, 2009), 40.

34 Cobus van Wyngaard, "Post-Apartheid Whiteness and the Challenge of Youth Ministry in the Dutch Reformed Church" in *Journal of Youth and Theology* 10, no. ½ (2011): 26–27.

> By "unfinished business" I refer specifically to the fact that the level of reparation recommended by the commission was not enacted; the proposal on a once-off wealth tax as a mechanism to effect the transfer of resources was ignored, and those who were declined amnesty were not prosecuted. . . .

> . . . Healing is a process. How we deal with the truth after its telling defines the success of the process. And this is where we have fallen tragically short. By choosing not to follow through on the commission's recommendations, government not only compromised the commission's contribution to the process, but the very process itself.[35]

The work needed for true reconciliation has not been done. Confused understandings of reconciliation have made it difficult to pursue.

## Who Will Ultimately Bring About Reconciliation?

The second significant challenge in South Africa's desire for reconciliation pertains to the question of responsibility: Whose responsibility is it to bring about reconciliation?

On October 28, 1998, Desmond Tutu presented the TRC's final five-volume report to South Africa's first elected president, Nelson Mandela. What was perhaps unexpected in Tutu's handing over of this report to Mandela were the people's and the church's assumptions and expectations that were also symbolically passed along with it—that the "ministry of reconciliation" became the responsibility of the state, not the church.

In October 2014, a reenactment of the TRC Faith Communities Hearing invited churches to share what they have been doing toward reconciliation since the original Faith Communities Hearing in 1997. In that initial hearing, almost all of South Africa's faith communities committed to dismantling apartheid and pursuing reconciliation, both in society and in their own denominations. During the 2014 reenactment, however, each church admitted it had "dropped the ball" in this effort, and each denominational body represented and articulated their substantial shortcomings in meeting their commitments. Several Christian denominations, for example, continue to be racially segregated.

Although this was a sad confession and realization, it also, ironically, proved to be quite hopeful as, at least officially, the church in South Africa began to remember and recommit itself to the pursuit of reconciliation. Many churches

---

35 Staff Reporter, "Tutu: 'Unfinished Business' of the TRC's Healing." The Khulumani Support Group, an organization established to support the victims of apartheid that were named during the TRC process, noted, for example, that "the process of providing measures for amnesty and other benefits for perpetrators has not been balanced by an equal focus on the provision of redress for victims" (Phillip de Wet, *Mail & Guardian*, November 16, 2012, accessed February 21, 2015, http://mg.co.za/article/2012-11-16-00-reparations-still-on-the-back-foot).

asked why they had assumed the state would be the agent of reconciliation. Since the original TRC in South Africa has ended, appalling violence has continued; inequality is increasing; the rich have not only maintained but also increased their wealth while the poor continue to live on scraps; the education system is failing; striking miners are gunned down by police; obscene spending is justified on the president's private property; and corruption runs rampant.[36] Why, these churches now asked, had they assumed that a neoliberal government would be the agent of reconciliation? A government, nonetheless, operating on assumptions of individual competition, on freedom *from* the other rather than communal belonging to each other, and on the myth that government is somehow neutral in ordering and structuring society.

The Apostle Paul reminds us that true peace and reconciliation do not come from those who rule but from those who seek to be part of God's new creation and humanity in the world (Eph 2:11–22; 2 Cor 5:17–21). He even suggests that it is the responsibility of the church to reveal this reality of God's new creation and humanity (Eph 3:10). One can hope that the church in South Africa may be reawakening to its biblical calling of being agents of true reconciliation. There are some hopeful sparks indicating that the church's amnesia is ending and that it may rekindle its mission of actively pursuing that which will allow people to live rightly with one another. But, as it is elsewhere, the journey toward living in right relationships will be a long and difficult one in the South African context.

## Reflections and Questions as Canada Enters Its Post-TRC Era

Just as South Africa's TRC process has been an inspiration for Canada and others, it may also be worthwhile for Canada and others to learn from South Africa's *post*-TRC era. What will "reconciliation" mean in Canada between Indigenous[37] and Settler communities? What actions should we stop now to prevent further harm to relationships? How can Settlers meaningfully apologize for the way in which we have dehumanized our Indigenous brothers and sisters? How will Settlers pursue the restoration and restitution that true reconciliation with Indigenous Peoples will require? Will we also be tempted to think that responsibility for reparation is the government's alone? How will we be a community—a people, a church—that will tirelessly seek to demonstrate God's new creation and be a witness to God's new humanity? How will this change the way we relate to and include Indigenous sisters and brothers? How can we embody a way of being that demonstrates our common humanity and belonging?

---

36 Desmond Tutu made these observations in "Tutu: 'Unfinished business' of the TRC's healing."

37 In this paper, "Indigenous" and "Aboriginal" are used synonymously, although effort has been made to be consistent in using "Indigenous Peoples" throughout when not quoting other sources.

Only time will tell how answers to these questions develop. We can, however, already see and therefore highlight some potential challenges in the Canadian context that will require careful, deliberate, and intentional action.

## Potential Challenges for the Canadian Post-TRC Process

### 1. A Clear Definition of Reconciliation

First, coming to a clear understanding of the meaning of "reconciliation" will be crucial, especially as Canada enters its post-TRC era. This is already one of the significant challenges. As reflected in the Canadian TRC report, "reconciliation" is difficult to explain since it is contextually sensitive. The report's stated understanding regarding "reconciliation" builds on the way the term has been used in reference to family violence: "[Reconciliation is] about coming to terms with events of the past in a manner that overcomes conflict and establishes a respectful and healthy relationship among people, going forward."[38]

The commission's hope for reconciliation was to establish and maintain mutually respectful relationships between Aboriginal and non-Aboriginal peoples.[39] Such an understanding must not remain at a metaphysical level, separate from physical and practical realities. It must deal with and respond to the injustices and violence of the past so that a new future can become possible. "Without truth, justice, and healing, there can be no genuine reconciliation. Reconciliation is not about 'closing a sad chapter of Canada's past' but about opening new healing pathways of reconciliation that are forged in truth and justice."[40]

Land, for example, is particularly important and contentious.[41] Today, cities and significant amount of industry has been built on large tracts of Indigenous treaty land. It is difficult to imagine these significant swaths of land returned to their rightful owners, even if that is what *should* be done. And yet to ignore the question of land is to ignore a significant element that has strained relationships

---

38 Truth and Reconciliation Commission of Canada, "Honouring the Truth, Reconciling for the Future: Summary of the Final Report of the Truth and Reconciliation Commission of Canada," (2015), 6.

39 Truth and Reconciliation Commission of Canada, 6.

40 Truth and Reconciliation Commission of Canada, "Canada's Residential Schools," 7. The ten guiding principles of truth and reconciliation (16) highlight important ways of recognizing the past while walking forward.

41 Thus the reason why "Calls to Action" #45–47 in the Final Report, for example, deal specifically with issues of land and the philosophical and legal tools used to justify the dispossession of Indigenous lands (e.g., the Doctrine of Discovery and treaties once agreed upon). See Truth and Reconciliation Commission of Canada, "Canada's Residential Schools," 230–31.

between Indigenous Peoples and Settlers, especially as the latter continue to enjoy the privilege that land provides.

Richard Twiss notes that "the loss of land, beyond dirt, relates to 'losing sacred space and place' and its influence in shaping personhood, being and identity. Land provides a sense of being from and belonging to a place."[42] Indeed, the goal of the residential schools, as the Truth and Reconciliation Commission of Canada highlights, was the assimilation of Indigenous Peoples to that of Settler society in order to obtain the land. "The Canadian government pursued this policy of cultural genocide because it wished to divest itself of its legal and financial obligations to Aboriginal people and gain control over their land and resources. If every Aboriginal person were 'absorbed into the body politic,' there would be no reserves, no Treaties, and no Aboriginal rights."[43] Thus, the question of restitution in general, and restitution as it pertains to land in particular, will—must, in fact—be a significant aspect in exploring reconciliation in the Canadian context.[44]

Furthermore, should there be a genuine desire to heal relationships between Indigenous Peoples and Settlers, the underlying racist and paternalistic perceptions and practices perpetuating separation and inequality must be addressed. The temptation in response to the realities of inequality, even among those who wish to heal such relationships, is to build relationships based on charity rather than justice. Such activity, however, portrays the provision of a helping hand while failing to restructure the social order that perpetuates the inequality.

As South African theologian John de Gruchy reminds us, restoring justice is indeed intricately linked to the possibility of reconciliation:

> Restorative justice has to do with renewing God's covenant and therefore the establishing of just power relations without which reconciliation remains elusive. It is not a justice that separates people into the good and the bad, the ritually clean or the ethnically acceptable, but one that seeks to bind them together in mutual care and responsibility for each other and for the larger society.[45]

We need to have a clear understanding about what "reconciliation" means; and it cannot be properly understood without its connection to justice.

---

42 Richard Twiss, *Rescuing the Gospel from the Cowboys: A Native American Expression of the Jesus Way* (Downers Grove, IL: InterVarsity, 2015), 65.

43 Truth and Reconciliation Commission of Canada, "What We Have Learned: Principles of Truth and Reconciliation," (2015), 6.

44 See, for example, Truth and Reconciliation Commission of Canada, "Canada's Residential Schools," 33–38, including the "call to action" #45.

45 John de Gruchy, *Reconciliation: Restoring Justice* (Claremont, South Africa: David Philip Publishers, 2002), 204.

### 2. Societal Awareness of Injustices

Second, unlike in the South African context, those who were (are) victimized in the Canadian context are a minority. Thus, whereas it was (is) not possible to ignore and sweep the ramifications of apartheid under the rug in South Africa—if for no other reason than the majority (over 80 percent) were affected negatively by apartheid—it may be easier to do so in the Canadian context. The fact that many Indigenous People continue to live on reserves means that their realities can potentially be more "hidden."[46]

The TRC report, for example, notes that "too many Canadians know little or nothing about the deep historical roots of these conflicts. This lack of historical knowledge has serious consequences for First Nations, Inuit, and Métis peoples, and for Canada as a whole."[47] Because Settlers are not confronted with the realities of inequality, the temptation might be to assume there is no problem, simply because many Settlers are able to remain blissfully ignorant. Thus, awareness regarding the injustices that Indigenous People of Canada have experienced, and continue to experience, will be an ongoing necessity if relationships between Indigenous and non-Indigenous people are to be examined and repaired.[48]

### 3. Overreliance on the Government and Maintaining the Status Quo

Third, as we saw in the South African context, there may be a temptation to portray and rely on the government at all levels as the primary agent responsible for the work toward reconciliation and reparation. The temptation might be to point the finger to the government and its policy as the primary actor in creating the situation Canada now faces. Indeed, many of the "calls to action" in the Canadian TRC report are directed at government—at all levels—to work

---

46 A news article on the Canadian Broadcasting Corporation website, for example, uses an interactive map to highlight where Indian Residential Schools were located. It recognizes that "despite the work of the TRC, which issued its final report and '94 Calls to Action' toward reconciliation in 2015, many Canadians still aren't aware of the schools that may have existed near them" ("Was There a Residential School Near You? Find Out with Our Interactive Map," accessed June 11, 2018, http://www.cbc.ca/news/indigenous/residential-school-interactive-map-beyond-94-1.4693413).

47 "Honouring the Truth, Reconciling for the Future," 8.

48 Thus the reason for the inclusion of "Education for Reconciliation" (Call to Action #62–65), "Youth Programs" (Call to Action #66), and "Museums and Archives (Call to Action #67–70) in the "Calls to Action" in the Final TRC Report. See Truth and Reconciliation Commission of Canada, "Canada's Residential Schools," 235–37.

toward change and reparations.[49] This may already be a first step on a very slippery slope.[50]

If the government does indeed represent the people of the nation, it should then be invited and expected to pay heed to the damage it has done; we should encourage, even demand, that it take responsibility for that past and seek ways to work toward change, reparation, and restitution. We must encourage the government to change the system it developed as it perpetuated unjust and paternalistic habits. We should remind it to help repair the relationships between Indigenous and non-Indigenous people. And, ultimately, we need to remind and continue to invite the government to participate in God's original intent for the world—to live rightly and justly with one another. The invitation to participate in repairing the brokenness it has caused must continually be articulated.

The temptation may, however, be for society to point the finger of blame toward the government as the sole perpetrator, assuming that it must therefore be the one to undo what has been done. This may incur at least two, and probably more, dangers. On the one hand, one might adopt the mentality that if the government does not accept or act on the suggested actions required to move toward healthier relationships with Indigenous Peoples,[51] the process toward reconciliation will become stagnant. The danger, in other words, is to lay responsibility for reconciliation on the government alone, which, as we saw in South Africa's case, inevitably becomes problematic; the responsibility can too easily become sidelined.

The second danger, intimately linked to the first, is that by assuming the government ought to take responsibility for the process of reconciliation and the needed actions for reparation, society at large is let off the hook; people do

---

49 See "Honouring the Truth, Reconciling for the Future," 319–37. This does not suggest that all "Calls to Action" are directed to various levels of government. There are other "calls" that are directed at churches, law societies, journalists and media outlets, businesses, etc. Indeed, the only two "calls to action" with fixed deadlines in "Honouring the Truth, Reconciling for the Future" (#48 and #58) are directed at churches, which highlights the significance of holding the church accountable for its past actions and calling it to work toward restitution. (I am indebted to Steve Heinrichs, Indigenous-Settler Relations Director for Mennonite Church Canada, for pointing this out to me.)

50 In this way, the book edited by Steve Heinrichs, *Wrongs to Rights: How Churches Can Engage the United Nations Declaration on the Rights of Indigenous Peoples* (Winnipeg, MB: Mennonite Church Canada, 2016), is a welcomed resource with its primary focus on challenging the church to take action and work toward restoring relationships.

51 We already saw a glimpse of this during the final press conference when Murray Sinclair presented and summarized the TRC report and the representative of the federal government would not clap or join the standing ovation for the proposals the TRC had made.

not need to take responsibility for the way in which Settlers have helped to create and maintain oppressive relations with Indigenous Peoples.

These two dangers end up being two sides of the same coin. They both enable and maintain the status quo, thus preventing the change necessary to create the possibility of right relationships. Segregation and the reserve system, along with the standard of living that has become a reality in the reserves (and elsewhere), continue to go unquestioned; sociopolitical inequality remains; and little effort is made to declare personal and/or corporate guilt, let alone reparation, for the abuses toward Indigenous People.

The TRC report, for example, already notes the way in which the Canadian government has largely ignored recommendations of the 1996 *Report of the Royal Commission on Aboriginal Peoples* to improve relationships with Aboriginal peoples.[52] The invitation for government to recognize its role in what has happened should continuously be extended, as highlighted above, encouraging practical ways of working toward repairing the violence it has perpetrated.

On the other hand, the people of Canada should be leery about placing too much hope in the government leading the way in the ongoing process of reconciliation. Martin Luther King, Jr., for example, reminds us that "freedom is never given to anybody. For the oppressor has you in domination because he plans to keep you there, and he never voluntarily gives it up. And that is where the strong resistance comes. Privileged classes never give up their privileges without strong resistance."[53] Dr. King's words remind us that governments often seek to maintain the status quo.[54] Thus, if the government decides not to make the

---

52 "Honouring the Truth, Reconciling for the Future," 7.

53 Martin Luther King Jr., "'The Birth of a New Nation,' Sermon Delivered at Dexter Avenue Baptist Church," in *The Papers of Martin Luther King Jr., Vol. 4: Symbol of the Movement, January 1957-December 1958*, eds. Clayborne Carson et al. (Los Angeles: University of California Press at Berkeley, 2000). Once again, I thank Steve Heinrichs for pointing me toward this contribution from King.

54 Or, what Jacques Rancière describes as the order of the police: that which is concerned with maintaining order and the status quo in society. Such a social order assumes certain presumptions regarding how power has been organized, places and roles that are distributed, along with the systems of legitimizing this distribution (Jacques Rancière, *Disagreement: Politics and Philosophy* [Minneapolis: University of Minnesota Press, 1999], 28). Rancière distinguishes this form of politics from an emancipatory politics that challenges and disrupts the status quo and its established logic. He describes this form of politics as "whatever breaks with the tangible configuration whereby parties and parts or lack of them are defined by a presupposition that, by definition, has no place in that configuration—that of the part of those who have no part. This break is manifest in a series of actions that reconfigure the space where parties, parts, or lack of parts have been defined" (29–30).

pursuit of reconciliation a priority, as is the case in South Africa, efforts toward reconciliation will stall if the process has relied solely on the government.

## Remembering Our Vocation

The words and exhortation of the Apostle Paul should be ringing loudly in our ears: the work toward true reconciliation is not, in fact, the responsibility or ministry of the state but of the church (2 Cor 5:18–19). In Ephesians, Paul makes the audacious claim that the church is tasked with demonstrating an alternative, visible example of how Jew and Gentile—Indigenous Persons and Settlers?—might relate to each other as a new social body in this world, witnessing to the way in which both are fellow citizens, heirs of God's household (*oikos*), and partakers of God's promise in Christ (Eph 2:19, 3:6). Paul describes this demonstration—living out and according to this vocation—as God's manifold wisdom (Eph 3:10). This suggests that it is the church's task and vocation to embody right and just relationships, both within its body and the way in which it relates to other communities.

And yet, we must stop and recognize the ways in which the church has failed to embody this vocation, and repent for the harm this has caused. Instead of participating in God's household and witnessing to another way of living and relating with others—a way of life centered around right and just relationships—the church participated in and provided the foundation for cultural genocide.[55] The recently approved Mennonite World Conference "Declaration of Solidarity with Indigenous Peoples" notes this well:

> We confess that at times the Church has denied the experience and witness to wholeness of our Indigenous sisters and brothers. There have been times when the Church has failed to recognize the dignity and cultural heritage of our Indigenous sisters and brothers. Indeed, there are times when we have forgotten that some of our Indigenous brothers and sisters also form our Church.

> We confess that the Church has benefited from the strategies of empires that have included violence, unsustainable extraction of natural resources, stolen land, colonial mission, genocide, environmental and water destruction, segregation, assimilation, imprisonment, and ongoing racial marginalization in health, housing, employment and education.

> We confess that some Anabaptists, as global migrants and settlers, have, in some places, gained access to land and benefits that have been withheld from

---

55 See Tinker, *Missionary Conquest*. The way in which the church participated in this violence toward Indigenous Peoples has already been well-documented and communicated. Alongside Tinker's work, see also Twiss, *Rescuing the Gospel from the Cowboys*.

Indigenous Peoples. And we confess that we still continue to participate in systems and mechanisms that perpetuate current economic inequality and oppression, which has often resulted in the loss and dispossession of land.[56]

The church, given the harms it has participated in and caused—in both South Africa and Canada—cannot abdicate the ways in which it can and must work toward making things right by reconciling relationships and working toward restoration and restitution. This tireless pursuit toward right and just relationships and living rightly with one another is the task of the church as it embodies and witnesses to what Paul describes as the realization of a new humanity (Eph 2:11–22); indeed, the church is called to witness this new humanity even to the principalities and powers (Eph 3:10).

Thus, especially because the church in Canada has participated in the violence toward its Indigenous Peoples, it must carry a responsibility and embody a vision for undoing the damage it has done in order to work toward reconciling the broken relationships between Indigenous and non-Indigenous peoples.

Lastly, we need to rethink and move beyond the constructed foundations for the ways in which Settlers and Indigenous Peoples have primarily understood themselves in relation to one another. As the Canadian TRC report notes, getting to reconciliation requires that

> the paternalistic and racist foundations of the residential school system be rejected as the basis for an ongoing relationship. Reconciliation requires that a new vision, based on a commitment to mutual respect, be developed. It also requires an understanding that the most harmful impacts of residential schools have been the loss of pride and self-respect of Aboriginal people, and the lack of respect that non-Aboriginal people have been raised to have for their Aboriginal neighbours.[57]

This is not to deny differences.[58] Rather, the focus needs to be on two building blocks that a reconciled relationship requires: 1) finding a common humanity to which we all belong, which then will 2) provide the foundation of dignity we all need. This may be too challenging in the Canadian context given that the church was precisely the one that forgot its calling and perpetuated the violence that sought to rid the humanity and dignity of Indigenous Peoples. But, if rec-

---

56 Mennonite World Conference, "Declaration of Solidarity with Indigenous Peoples," in *MWC General Council* (Kenya: Mennonite World Conference, 2018).

57 "Honouring the Truth, Reconciling for the Future," vi.

58 This is not to follow the United State's example in its pursuit toward "colorblindness," which perpetuates systemic and hidden racism. See Michelle Alexander's persuasive argument in *The New Jim Crow: Mass Incarceration in the Age of Colorblindness* (New York: New Press, 2010).

onciliation is to become reality, the church will need to work tirelessly toward this end. As the TRC states:

> Canadians must do more than just *talk* about reconciliation; we must learn how to *practice* reconciliation in our everyday lives—within ourselves and our families, and in our communities, governments, places of worship, schools, and work-places. To do so constructively, Canadians must remain committed to the ongoing work of establishing and maintaining respectful relationships.[59]

## Conclusion

Although the TRC process has come to an end in Canada, one can see from the South African experience that the journey toward reconciliation is far from over; it is an ongoing and lengthy one. As Canada drew on the South African example of the TRC process to work toward healing, in this post-TRC period, it may now want to be aware of and learn from the challenges that have emerged in the South African context since the end of that country's TRC process.

If we truly desire reconciliation, we will need to keep walking intentionally on the path toward it, not allowing the inevitable challenges to deter us from this noble and important quest. After all, God inaugurated the quest toward reconciliation and God has invited us to participate in it.

May God be with us as we continue this journey.

---

59 Truth and Reconciliation Commission of Canada, "Canada's Residential Schools," 17.

# Unsettling the Radical Witness of Peace

## A Decolonizing Investigation of Mennonite Migration from Russia to Manitoba in the 1870s

Hyejung Jessie Yum

This paper argues for the necessity of decolonizing the Mennonite peace witness in a settler colonial context. Using the historical case of Russian Mennonite migration to Manitoba in the 1870s, I demonstrate how the Mennonite peace witness has been complicated through migration to a settler colonial context.

When a large number of Russian Mennonites migrated to Manitoba in the 1870s to avoid perpetuating violence through military service, the change in social context in which they had previously interpreted violence added unforeseen factors to their attempt to avoid participating in further violence. In the midst of their commitment to peace, the group's immigration for the sake of radical witness ironically led them to become complicit in another form of violence toward Indigenous and nonwhite populations in Canada. European Mennonites not only became direct beneficiaries of the lands gained through unjust treaties but also experienced a sociopolitical shift from a religious minority to a racially privileged group, as white, through the racializing colonial process of nation-building. Their lack of attention to colonial violence consequently led Mennonites to become complicit in the construction and perpetuation of structural violence in Canada. Thus, I argue that peace witness in a settler colonial context requires a reinvestigation of the discourse and practice of peace, taking into account colonialism, upon which structural violence against Indigenous and racialized peoples has been built.

*Hyejung Jessie Yum, a PhD candidate at the University of Toronto, researches postcolonial Mennonite peace theology. She has been an editor of* Korean Anabaptist Journal *since 2016 and recently collaborated on the launch of Seeds of Peace, a peace ministry in the multicultural context of Toronto. A version of this article was published as "21세기 메노나이트 정체성과 인식론의 전환에 대한 필요성,"* Korean Anabaptist Journal, *Volume 19 (Winter 2019): 48–55.*

## Background

In the fall of 2015, the *Canadian Mennonite* article "These Records Are Unique" reported that a "significant historical artifact for Mennonites" had been found in the basement of the office of the Christian Mennonite Conference.[1] The important artifact was the *Privilegium,* written on July 24, 1873—an original letter of invitation from the Dominion of Canada to the Mennonites in Russia (present-day Ukraine) and legal agreement between the Mennonites and the Canadian government.[2] The *Privilegium* details Canada's guarantee to provide the Russian Mennonites with land, religious freedom, exemption from conscription, and freedom of education for their children.[3] As the article states,

> The Dominion of Canada was looking for *hardworking European farmers to settle* its *newest* province, Manitoba, which the government had *recently cleared of its indigenous inhabitants.* Between 1874 and 1880, 17,000 Mennonites left Russia. Seven thousand of them came to Manitoba. Most made the voyage in small family groupings, but one colony moved in its entirety.[4] [Italics added]

The article speaks of Mennonites' excitement over the discovery of this historical document detailing their ancestors' early immigration to Canada. What seems ironic is that while highlighting the early Mennonite immigrants' strong commitment to nonresistance against violence, the author is silent about the haunting settler colonial context behind words such as "hardworking European farmers to settle," "newest," and "recently cleared of its indigenous inhabitants."[5] This raises the question: What is required to witness to peace in a settler colonial context?

In this paper, when I investigate the historical case of Russian Mennonite migration to Manitoba in the 1870s, I am also investigating the historical back-

---

1 Manitoba Correspondent, "These Records Are Unique," *Canadian Mennonite* 19, no. 3 (November 18, 2015), https://canadianmennonite.org/stories/%E2%80%98these-records-are-unique%E2%80%99. Thanks to Tim Reimer for introducing me to this article and sharing his critical insight. The conversation with him motivated me to write this paper. Also, thanks to Jordan Balint and anonymous reviewers for reviewing this paper and providing helpful comments.

2 Erin Koop Unger, "This Lost Document Explains Why I'm Here (Probably You, Too)," Mennotoba, November 29, 2017, accessed May 01, 2019, https://www.mennotoba.com/lost-document-explains-im/. Unger reports that the 1873 *Privilegium* is kept in Mennonite Heritage Archives.

3 Manitoba Correspondent, "These Records Are Unique."

4 Manitoba Correspondent, "These Records Are Unique."

5 Mennonite pastor Tim Reimer initially raised a critical question about a colonial implication of the phrase "recently cleared of its indigenous inhabitants."

ground of the *Privilegium*. In doing so, I demonstrate how the European Mennonite peace witness through migration is complicated when settler colonialism is foregrounded.

## Settler Colonialism as Structural Violence

Canada is a settler colonial society. According to Walter L. Hixson, "Settler colonialism refers to a history in which settlers drove indigenous populations from the land in order to construct their own ethnic and religious national communities." And Canada, he says, is an example of this.[6] Unlike "conventional" colonialism, in which the colonizers come to colonies to exploit Indigenous people and resources, in settler colonialism colonizers also come to reside permanently in Indigenous lands.[7] Regarding such colonialism, James Belich argues, "It was settlement, not empire that had the spread and staying power in the history of European expansion."[8]

Settlers construct their own national identities and societies through a long period of migration and domination, displacing the Indigenous people and culture.[9] According to *Strength for Climbing*, a booklet aimed to help non-Indigenous people participate in steps toward truth and reconciliation with Indigenous people, "settler," for some, is "a political term that describes the newcomer's relationship to colonialism, and signifies that colonial settlement has never ceased."[10] To speak more specifically to the Canadian context, in her book *Exalted Subjects*, Sunera Thobani examines how Canadian national subjects have been constituted and Indigenous sovereignty has institutionally been subjugated and erased through legislation and policy-making based on racial violence for the sake of the colonial process.[11] She shows that "colonial sovereignty relies on very 'particular' kinds of violence: the founding violence of conquest;

---

6 Walter L. Hixson, *American Settler Colonialism: A History* (New York: Palgrave Macmillan, 2013), 4.

7 James Belich, *Replenishing the Earth: The Settler Revolution and the Rise of the Anglo World, 1783–1939* (New York: Oxford University Press, 2009), 23. Hixson, *American Settler Colonialism*, 5.

8 Belich, *Replenishing the Earth*, 23.

9 Hixson, *American Settler Colonialism*, 4–5.

10 Canadian Ecumenical Justice Initiatives and Mennonite Church Canada, *Strength for Climbing: Steps on the Journey of Reconciliation* (Toronto: KAIROS, 2015), 2 and 23. *Strength for Climbing* was published by KAIROS CANADA, an ecumenical organization advocating for ecological justice and human rights across Canada. The booklet acknowledges that the "resource is an adaptation of *Paths for Peacemaking with Host Peoples* (third edition), written by Steve Heinrichs, published by Mennonite Church Canada."

11 Sunera Thobani, *Exalted Subjects: Studies in the Making of Race and National in Canada* (Toronto: University of Toronto Press, 2012), 61.

the legitimating violence of transforming conquest into moral authority; and the ordinary and banal violence necessary for the maintenance of colonial sovereignty."[12] Once the colonial structure is legitimated, everyday forms of violence against the colonized people are tolerated. For example, Statistics Canada reports that the rate of homicide for Indigenous people in 2018 was "five times higher than the rate for non-Indigenous people."[13]

Johann Galtung's account of direct and indirect violence may help us clarify our understanding of structural violence. In his article "Violence, Peace, and Peace Research," Galtung explains the characteristics of (1) direct violence, such as killing or physically harming someone and (2) indirect violence, such as structural violence. With direct violence, the consequences of the violence can be referred back to specific actors. With structural violence, the actors harming others are not visible because "the violence is built into the structure and shows up as unequal power and consequently as unequal life changes."[14] By producing unequal power and opportunities through unequal distribution of resources and vice versa, structural violence results in persistent and systematic physical, economic, political, and psychological harm to victims, as the case of high rates of murdered Indigenous people attests.[15] The more stable the society appears, the more structural violence is perceived "as natural as the air," appearing to operate as "tranquil waters." By contrast, direct violence shows "tremendous fluctuations over time."

In other words, "a certain stability" is observed in structural violence, and thus it functions silently for those in the majority, as it has in Canada. Moreover, while direct violence is much more readily identifiable and can be measured through means such as death tolls in conflict and war, structural violence is constructed through sociopolitical interactions in a particular location over long processes of time.[16]

In the Canadian context, compounding issues of coloniality pertaining to "race," structural violence has simultaneously been constructed through the othering of diverse subjects in various degrees on multiple and intersectional axes of power-related factors according to gender, class, ability, sexuality, re-

---

12 Thobani, *Exalted Subjects*, 38.

13 Joel Roy and Sharon Marcellus, "Homicide in Canada, 2018," Government of Canada, Statistics Canada, November 27, 2019, accessed September 11, 2020, https://www150.statcan.gc.ca/n1/pub/85-002-x/2019001/article/00016-eng.htm.

14 Johan Galtung, "Violence, Peace, and Peace Research," *Journal of Peace Research* 6, no. 3 (1969): 170–71.

15 Roy and Marcellus, "Homicide in Canada, 2018."

16 Galtung, "Violence, Peace, and Peace Research," 173.

ligion, and so on.[17] While acknowledging these intersectional factors, I have chosen to focus particularly on racial violence and its relation to colonialism in this article.

Although early European Mennonites did not commit violence like murder or harm Indigenous people in a directly physical manner, they were complicit with structural violence under Canada's settler colonial project, from foundation to expansion and maintenance of "its" territory. And settler colonialism is not an unfortunate past event but a persistent structure that continues to shape the reality in which Indigenous peoples are harmed, exploited, and eliminated.[18] As a settler group, Mennonites in North America continue to benefit from the structure constructed under colonial influence.

Personally, as a Korean migrant Mennonite residing in Canada who grew up experiencing the pain from the colonial aftermath in the Korean Peninsula, I am ambivalent about my relation to colonialism in North America. I resist the Eurocentric colonial norms that racialize and minoritize me, but I also have benefited from my residence in Turtle Island[19] as well as from the early European Mennonite settlement and their continuous privilege in the society built upon the colonial legacy. In this sense, I acknowledge my own complicity in colonialism. Acknowledging such complicity calls Mennonites to take responsibility for our involvement in colonial violence.

In order to seek peace witness against such violence in a settler colonial context, it is necessary to analyze how structural violence has been and continues to be perpetuated through the deep-rooted colonial influence in Canada—an influence that stems from the country's original construction under colonial force. In the following sections, using the case of Russian Mennonite migration to Manitoba in the 1870s, I will demonstrate how peace witness can become complicit in other forms of violence when settler colonialism as structural violence is not considered.

## The Radical Peace Witness through Migration from Russia to Manitoba

In this section, I delve into the historical background of the Russian Mennonite migration in the 1870s in order to understand how the dominant Mennonite

---

17 Rita Dhamoon, *Identity/Difference Politics: How Difference Is Produced, and Why It Matters* (Vancouver: UBC, 2010), 91.

18 Maile Arvin et al., "Decolonizing Feminism: Challenging Connections between Settler Colonialism and Heteropatriarchy," *Feminist Formations* 25, no. 1 (Spring 2013): 8–34.

19 Turtle Island is the name that many Indigenous people call the continent of North America.

pacifist position influenced their decision to migrate to Canada. In addition, I examine the importance of nonresistant faith to early Mennonite immigrants in Canada before the Russian Mennonite migration.

In *Mennonites in Canada: 1786–1920*, historian Frank H. Epp describes how thousands of Mennonites migrated from Russia to Canada in the 1800s to seek "the special kind of liberty"— freedom from use of force in the military.[20] The Russian Mennonite migration in the 1870s was part of this major movement. Conflict with the Russian government about the use of the Russian language and military service were key influencers in their move.[21] The Tsar had decided to no longer exempt Mennonites from conscription, instead requiring universal military service as Russia faced German imperial growth:

> He [Tsar Alexsander II] announced his plans on July 16, 1870, implying at the same time that nonconformists would, within a 10-year period, be allowed to emigrate if they could not in good conscience submit to conscription. Thus, the Mennonites were being confronted with fundamental decisions.[22]

This change in conscription conditions was the decisive factor for migration and resulted in Mennonites strongly prioritizing full exemption from conscription in their deliberations regarding a new place to live. Whenever official representatives were sent to other countries to assess their suitability as a new homeland, the most significant part of the discernment was determining whether military service was required.[23] Canada and the United States—both looking for skilled European farmers for their newly settled lands—and Russia, which did not want to lose its "best agriculturalists" in the end, competed for the Mennonites.[24] According to James Urry, the Russian Mennonites regarded the United States as a risky choice because their religious rights would receive little protection there in comparison to Canada, who assured the Mennonites both lands and privileges previously accorded to them in Russia, including military exemption and permission to operate their own religious schools in German, their own language.[25]

Concurring with Urry, Epp notes that Canada consequently became the first choice for these Mennonites because Canada guaranteed benefits for pro-

---

20 Frank H. Epp, *Mennonites in Canada: 1786–1920*, vol. 1 (Toronto: Macmillan, 1979), 94.

21 Epp, 183–85.

22 Epp, 177.

23 Epp, 186.

24 Epp, 184–85.

25 James Urry, *Mennonites, Politics, and Peoplehood: Europe-Russia-Canada, 1525–1980* (Winnipeg: University of Manitoba Press, 2006), 162.

ficient farmers, such as complete exemption from military obligation and "a free grant of 160 acres of the best land in the possession of the Dominion of the Province of Manitoba, or in other parts of the Northwest Territory . . . to persons over the age of 21 years."[26] This shows that the Mennonites' strong commitment to faith against violence in military engagement was the primary reason why seven thousand Mennonites migrated from Russia to Manitoba between 1874 and 1880.[27]

Before this migration, military exemption had already been one of the major issues for early Mennonite immigrants to Canada. In a chapter titled "The Non-resistors and the Militia," Epp describes in detail how important it was to Mennonite immigrants to Canada to keep a clear religious position on nonresistance as the fundamental faith commitment of Anabaptists.[28] Their conviction of pacifism was founded on the article in their 1527 Schleitheim Confession that "identified weapons of force, such as sword, armor and the like, as un-Christian."[29] They also quoted Menno Simons, who wrote, "The regenerated do not go to war, nor engage in strife. They are the children of peace who have beaten their swords into plowshares and their spears into pruning hooks, and know of no war."[30]

As Epp explains, the Mennonite pacifist position rejecting violence, which began in the sixteenth century in the Netherlands and Switzerland, provided the fundamental conviction for the early Mennonite immigrants' move to Canada. Their strong commitment to pacifist conscience is further supported by their 1811 printing of the Dordrecht Confession, the very first document they printed in Upper Canada. Since the Dordrecht Confession's adoption by Dutch Mennonites in 1632, it had been one of "the chief instruments of the perpetuation of the pacifist conscience and the doctrine of nonresistance,"[31] and it now served to make the Mennonite immigrants' pacifist convictions clear.

At the beginning of their lives in Canada, the early Mennonite immigrants were not free to openly practice their belief in rejecting military engagement.[32] However, this tension was lessened with the enactment of the Militia Act of Upper Canada 1793 under the influence of changed laws in England and Amer-

---

26 Urry, 186.

27 Manitoba Correspondent, "These Records Are Unique."

28 Epp, *Mennonites in Canada*, 94.

29 Epp, 94.

30 Epp, 94. Epp's quotes are originally from John Horsch's article, "A Historical Survey of the Position of the Mennonite Church on Nonresistance," *Mennonite Quarterly Review* 1, no. 3 (July 1927): 10.

31 Epp, *Mennonites in Canada*, 94–95. The Dordrecht Confession was printed in English at Niagara-on-the-Lake by the Mennonite immigrants to Upper Canada.

32 Epp, 93.

ica as well as Quakers' claim to religious freedom, another group that adhered to nonconformist Christian faith.[33] After the passing of the Militia Act, Mennonites were exempt from military service, and the mass of Mennonites from Russia in the 1870s inherited this benefit. The nonresistant faith passed down from Anabaptists who had rejected the use of force in sixteenth-century Europe was evidently still important to these early Mennonite immigrants in Canada.

In modern Mennonite history and theology in North America, nonresistance has been recognized as the crucial aspect of the early Mennonite faith and the root of their peace tradition. In his representative work *Peace, War, and Nonresistance (1944)*, Guy H. Hershberger systematized nonresistance as the classic position of the Mennonite view of peace regarding conscription and warfare.[34] Theron F. Schlabach evaluates the major contribution of Hershberger's work as "offer[ing] a platform of biblical pacifism," noting that his work has often been regarded as "the definitive statement of Mennonites' pacifist thought" by many authors in the field of pacifism.[35] In connecting Mennonite nonresistance with peace, Epp cites Menno Simons's phrase "the child of peace" as he identifies Mennonites' rejection to military involvement in Russia as the primary reason for their migration to Canada in the 1870s.[36]

In a more recent historical work—*Mennonites, Politics, and Peoplehood: Europe, Russia, Canada, 1525–1980* (2006)—Urry describes Mennonite nonresistance as a "stance that rejected all forms of violence."[37] These modern historical and theological descriptions demonstrate that nonresistance has been acknowledged as the fundamental ground of the Mennonite peace tradition, although Mennonite understandings of violence and peace have changed and diversified in response to various social contexts such as the Vietnam War, the civil rights movement, and the second wave of feminism.[38] Despite the importance of non-

---

33 Epp, 94–95 and 97.

34 Guy Franklin Hershberger, *War, Peace, and Nonresistance* (Scottdale, PA: Herald, 1946).

35 Theron F Schlabach, "Guy F. Hershberger's War, Peace, and Nonresistance (1944): Background, Genesis, Message," *The Mennonite Quarterly Review* 80, Issue 3 (July 2006): 294, 296.

36 Epp, *Mennonites in Canada*, 94.

37 Urry, *Mennonites, Politics, and Peoplehood*, 256.

38 The following sources demonstrate that Mennonite understandings of peace have been transformed and diversified over time in North America: Ervin Stutzman, *From Nonresistance to Justice: The Transformation of Mennonite Church Peace Rhetoric, 1908–2008* (Scottdale, PA: Herald, 2011); Gayle Gerber Koontz, "Peace Theology in Transition: North American Mennonite Peace Studies and Theology," *Mennonite Quarterly Review* 81, no. 1 (January 2007); Leo Driedger and Donald B. Kraybill, *Mennonite Peacemaking: From Quietism to Activism* (Scottdale, PA: Herald, 1994); John Richard Burkholder and

resistance in the Mennonite peace tradition, it is necessary to recognize the complexity of the radical nonresistant practice of "peace-loving" Mennonites when taking a settler colonial context into account.[39]

## Unsettling the Radical Peace Witness in a Settler Colonial Context

In this section, by conducting a historical and social analysis in the context of Canadian nation-building, I demonstrate how Mennonites became complicit in colonial violence toward Indigenous and nonwhite people through the racializing colonial process. Then I argue that through European Mennonites' migration to a settler colonial context, their social position shifted from that of a religious and ethnic minority to a religiously and racially privileged group as white Christians. Russian Mennonite immigrants became direct beneficiaries of Canada's colonial project insofar as they became the new landlords in lands gained through unjust treaties and other acts of violence, and gained social power over time along with other preferred European immigrants.

### Colonial Complicity through the Settlement

When seven thousand Mennonites migrated to Manitoba between 1874 and 1880, the region had newly become the fifth province of the dominion of Canada and had been "recently cleared of its indigenous inhabitants,"[40] implying that Indigenous sovereignty in the territory had been weakened by Canada. This happened through treaties following the Manitoba Act of 1870. According to Louis A. Knafla, "relatively symbiotic relations" and "peaceful coexistence" between Indigenous peoples and settlers had begun to change to domination of the Indigenous peoples by European settlers through the Confederation treaties in Canada.[41] The Manitoba Act of 1870 was one instance where the sovereignty of the Métis and other Indigenous nations was significantly reduced in terms of their land ownership.

In the late 1860s, John A. McDonald, Canada's first prime minister, had a vision of making the country a bicoastal nation comparable to the United States.[42] As a part of the plan, the dominion of Canada purchased Rupert's

---

Barbara Nelson Gingerich, eds., *Mennonite Peace Theology: A Panorama of Types* (Akron, PA: Mennonite Central Committee Peace Office, 1991).

39 Urry, *Mennonites, Politics, and Peoplehood*, 10.

40 Manitoba Correspondent, "These Records Are Unique."

41 Louis A. Knafla and Haijo Westra, eds., *Aboriginal Title and Indigenous Peoples: Canada, Australia, and New Zealand* (Vancouver: UBC, 2010), 5.

42 According to Richard J. Gwyn, John A. Macdonald "was determined" to make Canada "a sea-to-sea nation" by "adding the North-West and then British Columbia to

Land—present-day Manitoba—from the Hudson Bay Company, without consent from Métis and other Indigenous groups residing in the territory.[43] Because this transaction could threaten Indigenous peoples' way of life—by negatively impacting hunting, for example—resistance arose from the Métis group, leading to the First Riel Resistance in 1869. Following the resistance, the Manitoba Act of 1870 and consecutive numbered treaties were negotiated between Indigenous peoples and the dominion of Canada until 1921.[44]

Because the traditional Indigenous economy was already declining under the influence of European settlement, the Prairie Indigenous peoples were more vulnerable to governmental negotiations than those of the Encounter era had been.[45] The treaties were ostensibly aimed at the protection of Indigenous peoples' rights and thus were accepted by Indigenous people at that time. However, because the Indigenous understandings of law, finance, and land were different from European settlers, many Indigenous treaty signers were unaware that "title to their lands was being expropriated" in "narrow terms, with much that was said left unwritten" through the treaties.[46] Moreover, not all Indigenous people were included in the treaty negotiations.[47]

In fact, during the treaty period, Canadian political leaders explicitly expressed that the presence of Indigenous peoples had been a hindrance to the Canadian government, calling it the "Indian problem." In the 2014 Sir John A. MacDonald Prize-winning study *Clearing the Plains: Disease, Politics of Starvation and the Loss of Aboriginal Life*, James W. Daschuk reveals that MacDonald and the Canadian government, in order to save the government funds, deliberately abandoned Indigenous people who faced widespread disease and starvation caused by the rapid decline of the buffalo population in the late 1870s.[48]

---

it as quickly as possible." Gwyn states that the pressure from the Métis Group caused "the trouble" with McDonald's plans for the North-West. See Richard J. Gwyn, *Nation Maker: Sir John A. MacDonald: His Life, Our Times* (Toronto: Random House Canada, 2011), 98.

43 Donald Swainson, *Sir John A. Macdonald: The Man and the Politician* (Kingston, ON: Quarry, 1989), 85–86.

44 Knafla and Westra, *Aboriginal Title and Indigenous Peoples*, 5.

45 Paulette Regan, *Unsettling the Settler Within: Indian Residential Schools, Truth Telling, and Reconciliation in Canada* (Vancouver: UBC, 2010), 158.

46 Regan, 90; Knafla and Westra, *Aboriginal Title and Indigenous Peoples*, 5–6.

47 Regan (*Unsettling the Settler Within*, 146) notes that Cree Chief Mistahimaskwa (Big Bear), who wanted to keep his people's traditional ways, was excluded from the Treaty 6 negotiations.

48 James W. Daschuk, *Clearing the Plains: Disease, Politics of Starvation, and the Loss of Indigenous Life*, electronic resource (Regina, SK: University of Regina Press, 2019), 99–101.

Daschuk argues that this was "the moral and legal failure of the crown's treaty commitment" to the clause that Canada should provide Indigenous people with relief in case of "national famine."[49] Furthermore, Indian Affairs Deputy Minister Duncan Campbell Scott expressed in a report to a parliamentary committee in 1920 his desire to eradicate the Indian problem, saying, "Our objective is to continue until there is not a single Indian in Canada that has not been absorbed into the body politic and there is no Indian question, and no Indian department."[50]

Given this history of Indigenous oppression, Paulette Regan, director of research with the Truth and Reconciliation Commission (TRC) of Canada, challenges "the peacemaker myth"—the pervasive belief that Canada, unlike the United States with its more violent domination, has maintained relatively peaceful relationships with Indigenous people through treaties and "well-intentioned (if ultimately misguided) policies designed to solve the Indian problem by civilizing and saving people seen as savages."[51] Tracing history from treaty-making to the recent discourse of reconciliation, Regan criticizes the discourse of "settlers as peacemakers" produced from the settlers' perspectives,[52] calling us to divert our attention from "Indian problem" to "settler problem."[53]

Under Canada's treaties and controlling policies, Indigenous communities have been displaced from their long-dwelling lands and their social status has noticeably been subjugated. Two years ago, in the midst of this reality, Canada celebrated the 150th anniversary of its birth.[54] As Lorenzo Veracini points out, given that a characteristic of settler colonialism is to make Indigenous people

---

49 Daschuk, 101.

50 Truth and Reconciliation Commission of Canada, *What We Have Learned: Principles of Truth and Reconciliation* (Ottawa: Truth and Reconciliation Commission of Canada, 2015), 25. The quote is originally from Library and Archives Canada, RG10, volume 6810, file 470-2-3, volume 7, Evidence of D. C. Scott to the Special Committee of the House of Commons Investigating the Indian Act amendments of 1920, (L-2)(N-3).

51 Regan, *Unsettling the Settler Within*, 14.

52 Regan, 83–110.

53 Regan, 11.

54 In 2018, Canada held a nation-wide "Canada 150" celebration. In response, there was also a counter narrative, such as #Resistance150, to remember colonial history and recognize Indigenous peoples' longer history in the continent. See Ashifa Kassam, "Canada Celebrates 150 but Indigenous Groups Say History Is Being 'Skated Over,'" *The Guardian*, June 27, 2017, accessed September 18, 2020, https://www.theguardian.com/world/2017/jun/27/canada-150th-anniversary-celebration-indigenous-groups.

refugees,[55] Canada's settler colonialism cannot easily be justified by its "relatively moderate" colonial practices from a Eurocentric perspective.

The *Canadian Mennonite* interpreted the *Privilegium of 1873* to say, "The dominion of Canada was looking for hardworking European farmers to settle its newest province, Manitoba,"[56] to replace the Indigenous population evacuated from the territory after the Manitoba Act of 1870. Mennonites, along with other European agriculturalists, were prime immigration candidates, desired by both Canadian and American governments.[57] In the end, the Mennonites' faith commitment against violence was ensured through Canada's military service exemption along with the country's guarantee of land.

The great irony of this fulfilled radical commitment is that it came at the expense and pain of Indigenous people through the violence of land deprivation. Mennonite poet Di Brandt expresses her anguish in encountering the harsh truth of the history of the land where she had grown up.[58]

> It is impossible for me to write the land. This land that I love, this wide, wide prairie, this horizon, this sky, this great blue overhead, big enough to contain every dream, every longing. . . . How I loved you, how I love you, how you keep me alive. This stolen land, Metis land, Cree land, buffalo land. When did I first understand this, the dark underside of property, colonization, ownership, the shady dealings that brought us [Mennonites] here, to this earthly paradise?[59]

As Brandt states, the Mennonites who sought to witness against engaging in violence consequently settled on the "newest province" of Canada, which had been unjustly taken from Indigenous people. Recognition of this complicity in colonial violence complicates the Mennonite radical peace witness.

---

55 Lorenzo Veracini, *Settler Colonialism: A Theoretical Overview* (Basingstoke, England: Springer, 2010), 35.

56 Manitoba Correspondent, "'These Records Are Unique.'"

57 Epp, *Mennonites in Canada*, 185.

58 Steve Heinrichs, ed., *Buffalo Shout, Salmon Cry: Conversations on Creation, Land Justice, and Life Together* (Winnipeg, MB: Mennonite Church Canada, 2013), 76.

59 Heinrichs, 76. Neil Funk-Unrau, a Mennonite scholar working for restorative justice between Indigenous people and settlers, quotes Mennonite poet Di Brandt. See Di Brandt, *So This Is the World & Here I Am in It* (Edmonton: NeWest Press, 2007), 1–2.

## Colonial Complicity in the Normalization of Whiteness

"Whiteness" does not hold its intrinsic meaning without the context to which it applies, and its meaning is constructed through particular historical, social, political, and cultural processes such as European colonization and slavery.[60] The Eurocentric racializing process of Canada's formation and growth expanded and privileged whiteness to build Canada as a white nation. Such structural violence continues to subjugate Indigenous and nonwhite people's lives in contemporary Canada. Within the broader context of settlement, European Mennonites as white settlers have been involved in this normalizing of whiteness through the racializing colonial nation-building process.

Political scientist Rita K. Dhamoon names this reality in her book *Identity/Difference Politics*, including Mennonites as one of the favored European immigrant groups who expanded whiteness in Canada:

> An account of the conditions under which whiteness is produced and transformed reveals that the authority of the two settler groups has been expanded to include immigrants who most easily fit into a racialized Euro-liberal representation of Canada. This expansion historically includes the Scots, Irish, Americans, Germans, Scandinavians, Belgians, *Mennonites* [italics added], and Icelandic people. The hierarchy that privileged (and continues to privilege) Euro-liberal values and whiteness therefore explicitly favoured (and continues to favour) specific groups, groups that have adapted and been reconstituted through processes of white Euro-Canadianization. The English (and the French) therefore created an imagined community, one that hinged on the notion of a white man's country and the erasure of indigeneity.[61]

The process of nation-building through immigration overtly and exclusively favored people who were racially represented as white, which, in turn, resulted in the production of various degrees of "otherness" for nonwhite people.[62] In other words, the privilege of one group is inevitably operationalized through the penalty of the other in the same system.[63]

This othering process has been constructed through many colonial disciplines of legitimatized control imposed upon Indigenous bodies, such as the formation of the reserve system, the administration of the residential school

---

60 Ruth Frankenberg, *White Women, Race Matters: The Social Construction of Whiteness* (Minneapolis: University of Minnesota Press, 1993), 6. Read Tobin Miller Shearer's article to see a discussion of white racial formation in a contemporary Mennonite context: Tobin Miller Shearer, "Conflicting Identities: White Racial Formation among Mennonites, 1960–1985," *Identities* 19, no. 3 (May 1, 2012): 268–84.

61 Dhamoon, *Identity/Difference Politics*, 74.

62 Himani Bannerji, *The Dark Side of the Nation: Essays on Multiculturalism, Nationalism and Gender* (Toronto: Canadian Scholars, 2010), 76.

63 Dhamoon, *Identity/Difference Politics*, 74.

system, and the exclusion of citizenship and voting rights.[64] Mennonites were involved in this process by running the residential schools, which were mostly operated by white Christian groups.[65] The Canadian state still practices colonialism through continuous refusal of Indigenous sovereignty, genocide of Indigenous cultures, denial of this colonial history, and refusal to honor treaties and land claims.[66] These colonial practices have generated a racialized Indigenous "victimized collective identity" rather than autonomous Indigenous identities founded on nationhood. This totalizing category has constructed "representations of indigeneity" as Other in the dominant discourses in Canada.[67]

The heterogeneity of Indigenous and white peoples has added further layers of complexity that extend beyond the binary dynamic of Indigenous peoples and white immigrants. Himani Bannerji notes, for instance, the particularity of ethnicities within European immigrants, such as the power differentials between British immigrants and Ukrainian immigrants. Nevertheless, she argues that the different ethnicities of European immigrants have been incorporated into whiteness through an "Anglo-Euro ethos" as the ethnicities have been replaced with "general Englishness."[68] According to Emma Batell Lowman and Adam J. Baker, despite the various degrees of heterogeneity among settler groups, their common identity as settler is based on particular and common processes and "practices of settler colonialism" in Canada.[69]

Lowman and Baker note a high level of heterogeneity culturally, geographically, and historically among Indigenous nations and peoples as well. Nevertheless, because of settler colonialism, Indigenous identity often centers on "the experience of struggling to live an 'oppositional, place-based existence'" and can generate "a critical mass" collectively to challenge "contemporary nation states."[70] As for Indigenous and nonwhite immigrant relations, racialized immigrants are often viewed as allies for solidarity against racism and white suprema-

---

64 Dhamoon, 125.

65 Melanie Kampen researched Indian Residential Schools in Canada that were run by Mennonite missionaries from the United States and supported by Mennonite churches in Canada. She mentions that the Residential Schools were also operated and taught by Mennonite conscientious objectors as alternative service. See Melanie Kampen, "The Spectre of Reconciliation: Investigating Mennonite Theology, Martyrdom, and Trauma" (PhD diss., Emmanuel College and the University of Toronto, 2019), 1.

66 Dhamoon, 125.

67 Dhamoon, 126.

68 Bannerji, *The Dark Side of the Nation*, 113.

69 Emma Battell Lowman and Adam J. Barker, *Settler: Identity and Colonialism in 21st Century Canada* (Halifax: Fernwood, 2015), 14–15.

70 Lowman and Barker, 14.

cy,[71] while some nonwhite immigrants can also be understood as brown settlers when claiming their legal and cultural entitlement in stolen Indigenous lands.[72]

Despite these complicated relations, what I want to point out here—by paying attention to the relation of Indigenous peoples and white settlers, including the early Mennonite immigrants—is this: the racializing mechanisms of social control that privilege whiteness while othering and thereby diminishing Indigenous and nonwhite people is structural violence constructed through colonialism. This structure of Canadian law, institutions, and governance continues to produce indirect and direct violence against Indigenous and racialized women and men. Indigenous women's bodies have been disciplined in particular ways through colonial laws like the Indian Act, implemented in 1876 and 1884.[73] Indigenous women's legal status, and thus their sociopolitical and economic rights, were controlled according to their marriage status with Indigenous or non-Indigenous men. Even after the Indian Act was changed in 1985, this colonial law continues to discipline Indigenous bodies while gaining legitimacy from the law in the name of protecting them.[74]

Also, discriminating discourses constructed by the colonial and legal disciplines still exert power over the reality of Indigenous people. For instance, Colten Boushie, a twenty-two-year-old Cree man of the Red Pheasant First Nation, was shot by Gerald Stanley, a white Saskatchewan farmer, in August 2016. Yet

---

71 In "Salmon and Carp, Bannock and Rice," Greer Anne Wenh-In Ng points out the complex relationship between Asian Canadian women and Aboriginal women. As visible minority groups in Canada, Aboriginal and Asian and Asian Canadian women share potential for solidarity. However, Asian and Asian Canadian women are also regarded as "oppressors" who "have benefited on a par to those of white Europeans." See Greer Anne Wenh-In Ng, ed., "Salmon and Carp, Bannock and Rice: Solidarity between Asian Candian Women and Aboriginal Women," in *Off the Menu: Asian and Asian North American Women's Religion and Theology*, ed. Rita Nakashima Brock (Louisville: Westminster John Knox, 2007), 204.

72 In "Decolonization Is Not a Metaphor," Eve Tuck and K. Wayne Yang argue that although minority literature of people of color "offers a strong critique of the myth of the democratic nation-state," its option is "to become a brown settler" in a "settler nation" at best, ultimately seeking "an investment in settler colonialism." However, considering all nonwhite people as settlers excludes the history of slavery that black people experienced. In "Slavery Is a Metaphor," Tapji Garba and Sara-Maria Sorentino critique Tuck and Yang's reduction of slavery to "forced labour" to claim "a settler-native dyad." See Eve Tuck and K. Wayne Yang, "Decolonization Is Not a Metaphor," *Decolonization: Indigeneity, Education & Society* 1, no. 1 (2012): 18; and Tapji Garba and Sara-Maria Sorentino, "Slavery Is a Metaphor: A Critical Commentary on Eve Tuck and K. Wayne Yang's 'Decolonization Is Not a Metaphor,'" *Antipode* vol. 52, no. 3 (March 17, 2020).

73 Dhamoon, *Identity/Difference Politics*, 127.

74 Dhamoon, 127.

Stanley, who was accused of the second-degree murder, was finally acquitted by a Saskatchewan jury.[75] Although the death of the young Indigenous man sparked outraged marches and vigils across Canada, such a racially discriminatory verdict continues to consolidate the colonial structures that foster everyday violence against Indigenous people.[76] This indicates that the colonial legal discipline is a form of structural violence that harmfully imposes a signification as the "should-be-or-can-be-erased others." Indigenous peoples are regarded as bodies out of place in a society asymmetrically structured by the white norm, a key axis of power in Canada.[77]

Through migration to the settler colonial context of Canada, Mennonites practiced the radical witness to avoid the direct violence of harming people physically in military service, but their very migration and settlement led to their participation in structural violence built through the racializing colonial process against Indigenous and nonwhite peoples. Furthermore, through colonial complicity, European Mennonites become a racially and religiously privileged group as white Christians.

## Toward Peace Witness in a Settler Colonial Context

The historical and social analysis of the case of the Russian Mennonite migration suggests the necessity of recognizing contextual factors in understanding and practicing violence and peace. The violence that the early European Mennonite immigrants to Canada were concerned with, for instance, can be traced back to their conviction of nonresistance as a pacifist faith, primarily constructed in a European context.[78] Without an understanding of the context in which violence occurs, even radical peace witness can lead to complicity in other forms of violence. This contradiction is explained not only by a limited understanding of peace as nonresistance but also by a lack of attention to violence deeply embedded in a settler colonial context. Even in relatively recent historical descriptions of the Russian Mennonite migration such as Urry's *Mennonites, Politics,*

---

75 Sarah Rieger, "'We're Not Disposable': Hundreds March to Reconciliation Bridge Demanding Justice for Colten Boushie," CBC, February 12, 2018, accessed September 16, 2020, https://www.cbc.ca/news/canada/calgary/colton-boushie-rally-calgary-1.4531101.

76 "'Shame on Canada': Vigils Being Held in N.S. over Verdict in Colten Boushie Case," CBC, February 11, 2018, accessed September 18, 2020, https://www.cbc.ca/news/canada/nova-scotia/colten-boushie-vigil-1.4530234.

77 Dhamoon, *Identity/Difference Politics*, 126–27.

78 The violence that the early Mennonite immigrants in Canada attempted to avoid is traced back to sixteenth-century Europe. From the beginning, Mennonite views of peace were contextually developed as responses to violence in the given context. For more details, see C. Arnold Snyder's *Anabaptist History and Theology: An Introduction* (Kitchener, ON: Pandora, 1995).

*and Peoplehood* (2006) and the article 'These Records Are Unique' in *Canadian Mennonite* (2015), there is little attention to its relation to settler colonialism in Canada.[79]

As I demonstrate the necessity of paying attention to colonial influence, I argue that peace witness in a settler colonial context requires a critical investigation of Mennonite peace theology and practice, explicitly considering structural and power-sensitive colonial violence. Given that the understanding and practice of violence and peace in Mennonite peace theology has predominantly been developed from white male perspectives, its relevance for a settler colonial context needs to be reconsidered.

In modern Mennonite theology, influential white male Mennonite scholars have taken on a minority position to claim their pacifist stance challenging Christendom theology without situating their privileged social location in North America. Emily Servant critiques Mennonite scholars such as John Howard Yoder and J. Denny Weaver, for instance, as having gentrified the margins by placing themselves as a religious minority in line with other marginalized groups—such as black, feminist, and womanist theologians—yet without actual experiences of suffering.[80] The result has been to displace the underprivileged and maintain the status quo.

To unmask who ultimately benefits from or is harmed by a theological discourse and practice of peace, the crucial question "By whom and for whom are violence and peace defined?" needs to be considered.[81] For critical theological discourses, the question "Through whose eyes and whose experiences are texts interpreted?" has long been key in liberation and contextual theologies.[82] In addressing multiple kinds of violence, this question challenges hegemonic discourses that have subjugated persons who are different from prevailing norms. It discloses power differentials deeply embedded in theological discourses situated in asymmetrical social structures, which often mask the voices

---

79 Urry, *Mennonites, Politics, and Peoplehood*; Manitoba Correspondent, "'These Records Are Unique.'"

80 Emily Ralph Servant, "The Gentrification of the Margins," *The Mennonite Quarterly Review* 92, no. 3 (2018): 404–5.

81 Feminist liberative ethicist Marilyn J. Legge emphasizes a critical question, "What is at stake and for whom?" as a theo-ethical method to uncover imbalanced power dynamics. See Marilyn J. Legge, "Necessary Considerations of Theo-Ethical Method" in *EMT 5912 Method in Theology and Ethics* (2016), Emmanuel College, University of Toronto, Toronto, ON, https://www.tst.edu/resources/coursefiles/EMT5912HS%20Methods%20in%20Theology%20and%20Ethics%20Final%20Version%20Legge%2020181.pdf.

82 Angela Pears, *Doing Contextual Theology* (London: Routledge, 2010). In this book, Pears introduces Latin, Black, Feminist, Queer, and Postcolonial theologies as contextual theology.

of the oppressed by universalizing the voice of the dominant and privileged. For an example of the power of these questions for theological discourse, take Samuel J. Steiner's *In Search of Promised Lands* about histories of Mennonite and Amish migration to Ontario. Steiner's use of the metaphor "promised lands" can be challenged by Native American scholar Robert Allen Warrior, author of "Canaanites, Cowboys, and Indians," who posits two questions—From whose perspective is the Exodus story interpreted? and Who is the liberation and salvation story in Exodus for—as he reads the story from the perspective of the Canaanites—Indigenous peoples—in the conquerors' *promised* land.[83]

Reading the Mennonite pacifist migratory history to Canada through the parallel Indigenous and Canaanite perspectives may lead us to ask how the pacifist God in Russia[84] can become the conqueror God in Canada. In this situation, from whose perspective and for whom are violence and peace interpreted? Who benefits or is harmed by the interpretation?

Mennonite feminist liberative ethicist Melanie Kampen argues, "Given that the Mennonite tradition is a Christian tradition that emerged in Europe during the rise of modernity, it should come as no surprise that white Mennonites in the Americas retain and reproduce epistemologies of oppression. . . . While Mennonite theology has been critical of some forms of state violence, it has not been anti-colonial."[85] Thus, when Mennonites, as historic peace churches, are to witness to peace in a settler colonial context, the colonial influence needs to be a key theological and ethical consideration in their discourses and practices of peace, with contextual sensitivity and recognition of privilege built upon colonial legacy.

## Conclusion

At the beginning of this paper, I raised a question derived from the silent scenes hidden behind the words "hardworking European farmers to settle," "newest," and "recently cleared of its indigenous inhabitants" in the *Canadian Mennonite* article about *Privilegium*: What is required to witness to peace in a settler colonial context?

---

83 Robert Allen Warrior, "Canaanites, Cowboys, and Indians: Deliverance, Conquest, and Liberation Theology Today," *Christianity and Crisis* 49 (1989): 261–66.

84 "Pacifist God" is a rhetorical expression about the nonresistant faith rather than a precise reference to a Russian Mennonite view of God. Mennonite historians, such as Frank H. Epp and James Urry, often link nonresistance to peace or describe it as a pacifist practice. As I discussed earlier, nonresistance has been regarded as the classic position of the Mennonite view of peace.

85 Melanie Kampen, Review of *Decolonizing Epistemologies: Latina/o Theology and Philosophy*, by Ada María Isasi-Díaz and Eduardo Mendieta, eds., *Anabaptist Witness* 3, no. 1 (2016).

By tracing the historical background of the *Privileguim* and conducting a social analysis, I demonstrated that a large number of Mennonites in the 1870s decided to migrate to Manitoba in order to avoid perpetuating violence through military service in Russia. Despite their commitment to peace against violence, migrating for their pacifist witness ironically led them to become complicit in structural violence in a settler colonial context; Mennonites became direct beneficiaries of Canada's colonial expansion and nation-building project—as new landlords and recipients of the dominance and the privilege of whiteness gained at the cost of the attempted elimination of Indigeneity in Canada.

The changing social context of migration complicated European Mennonites' decision against violence. Their peace witness, inherited from the sixteenth-century European context, was applicable to avoiding direct violence like military engagement. But their lack of attention to the contextual and power-sensitive violence ingrained in the Canadian settler colonial society resulted in their complicity in the construction and perpetuation of structural violence against Indigenous and nonwhite peoples in Canada.

From the social analysis and the theological reflection on this lived contradiction, I conclude that peace witness in a settler colonial context requires a critical investigation of structural violence and asymmetric power dynamics built upon colonial legacy. It also needs a reconsideration of theological discourses and practices of peace, taking colonial violence into account beyond dominant white Mennonite perspectives. There have been decolonizing theological works in North American Mennonite contexts. Nevertheless, given the vast and devastating influence of colonialism in North America, the amount of decolonizing research in Mennonite theology is still quite insufficient.[86]

---

86 The following sources are decolonizing theological works in North American Mennonite contexts: Steve Heinrichs, ed., *Unsettling the Word: Biblical Experiments in Decolonization* (Maryknoll, NY: Orbis, 2019); Mealnie Kampen, "The Spectre of Reconciliation: Investigating Mennonite Theology, Martyrdom, and Trauma," (PhD diss., Emmanuel College and University of Toronto, 2019); Anthony G. Siegrist, "Part of the Authority Structure": An Organizational History of Mennonite Indian Residential Schools in Ontario," *Mennonite Quarterly Review* 93, no. 1 (2019): 5-39; Elaine Enns, "Facing History with Courage: Toward Restorative Solidarity," (DMin., St. Andrew's College, Saskatoon, 2015); Steve Heinrichs, ed., *Buffalo Shout, Salmon Cry: Conversations on Creation, Land Justice, and Life Together* (Winnipeg, MB: Mennonite Church Canada, 2013).

Hopeful signs that this kind of engagement is happening can be found in the April 15, 2019, *Canadian Mennonite*, which includes articles on how Mennonites in Canada are engaging in Settler-Indigenous relations:

- "The Awakening: Indigenous Voices in Restorative Justice" workshop was held at the office of Mennonite Central Committee Saskatchewan in Saskatoon.[87]
- Toronto Mennonite United Church held a six-week video conference for a book study on *Unsettling the Word: Biblical Experiments in Decolonization*, published in 2019 with efforts of "over 60 Indigenous and Settler authors" "to wrestle with the Scriptures, re-reading and re-imagining the ancient text for the sake of reparative futures."[88]
- Across Canada, many Mennonites have advocated for Bill C-262, which "calls for the government to enshrine the UN Declaration on the Rights of Indigenous Peoples into Canadian law."[89]

In 2020, such efforts continue:

- In September, an anthology *Be it Resolved: Anabaptists & Partner Coalitions Advocate for Indigenous Justice* was published by Mennonite Central Committee Canada (MCC) and Mennonite Church Canada. This is "a collection of over 90 documents detailing commitments Anabaptists have made to Indigenous justice and decolonization since the 1960s."[90]
- In October, more than forty people across Canada are participating in an eight-week online book club for *Canada at a Crossroads: Boundaries, Bridges, and Laissez-Faire Racism in Indigenous-Settler Relations*, host-

---

87 Donna Schulz, "Workshop Challenges Participants to Move from Multiculturalism to Antiracism," *Canadian Mennonite* 23, no. 8 (April 10, 2019), https://canadian-mennonite.org/deconstruct-racism.

88 Joelle Kidd, "Readers 'Zoom' to Discuss Unsettling the Word: Online Book Study a Hit at Toronto United Mennonite Church," *Canadian Mennonite* 23, no. 8 (April 10, 2019), https://canadianmennonite.org/stories/readers-'zoom'-discuss-unsettling-word. See Steve Heinrichs, *Unsettling the Word: Biblical Experiments in Decolonization* (Winnipeg: Mennonite Church Canada, 2018).

89 Rachel Bergen, "Mennonites Advocate for Bill C-262," *Canadian Mennonite* 23, no. 8 (April 10, 2019), https://canadianmennonite.org/c262-rally.

90 Katie Doke Sawatzky, "New Anthology Documents Six Decades of Anabaptist Response to Indigenous Calls for Justice," Mennonite Church Canada, September 21, 2020, accessed October 09, 2020, https://www.mennonitechurch.ca/article/10700-new-anthology-documents-six-decades-of-anabaptist-response-to-indigenous-calls-for-justice); Katie Doke Sawatzky, *Be it Resolved: Anabaptists & Partner Coalitions Advocate for Indigenous Justice* (Winnipeg: Mennonite Church Canada, 2020).

ed by Mennonite Church Canada's Indigenous-Settler Relations.[91]

Alongside these decolonizing and restorative educational and activist efforts, decolonizing theological works is also a substantive way to bear witness to peace in a settler colonial context. These efforts will lead us to continue the long-standing Mennonite tradition for peace in our context today.

---

91 "Canada at Crossroads Online Book Club," Mennonite Church Canada, accessed October 10, 2020, https://www.mennonitechurch.ca/event/10674-2020-10-08-canada-at-crossroads-online-book-club).

# What Does Shalom Mean?

## Comparing Anabaptist and Indigenous Perspectives

Randolph Haluza-DeLay

Peacemaking, that important characteristic of Anabaptist praxis, has been increasingly referred to as *shalom* in recent years. This essay probes what might be meant by the term through comparing the book-length works on shalom of Mennonite theologian Perry Yoder and Indigenous scholar Randy Woodley. Yoder calls shalom "the Bible's word for salvation, justice, and peace."[1] Woodley argues for a conception of shalom that extends beyond the realm of humanity to include the entire "community of creation."[2] As a social scientist, I am interested in how shalom can be applied to living well together in this land. Toward this end, engaging the Indigenous perspective will be particularly helpful for non-Indigenous Mennonites to develop broader notions of discipleship, faith, and peacemaking, especially in light of both Indigenous-settler reconciliation and the global ecological crisis.[3] Yoder's approach—while a helpful treatise on shalom—remains limited to the levels of human society and existent political structure.

In the phrase "living well together in this land," ecological sustainability and social justice are intrinsically and inextricably linked, with an open-endedness in terms of working toward a just sustainability.[4] The words encourage us to figure out such questions as "Who is the implied 'we'?" or "What does 'living

*Randolph Haluza-DeLay is a social scientist who was a faculty member at two Canadian universities for twenty years. His scholarship has focused on environmental justice and religious responses to the ecological crises in the contemporary world. He can be reached at haluzadelay@gmail.com.*

This article began as a session for Mennonite Church-Alberta in a series on "Living Faithfully in the Anthropocene."

1 Perry B. Yoder, *Shalom: The Bible's Word for Salvation, Justice, and Peace* (Nappanee, IN: Evangel, 1987).

2 Randy Woodley, *Shalom and the Community of Creation: An Indigenous Vision* (Grand Rapids, MI: Eerdmans, 2012).

3 For the purpose of deliberate focus on these two specific thinkers and their eminently accessible works, this essay will not examine Jewish understandings of shalom.

4 As a term, "just sustainability" was coined by Julian Agyeman to describe a proactive and normative goal for human societies in terms of both justice and sustainability. See

well' and 'living well *together*' mean?" The components of this guiding principle—living well, together, in the land—all require attention primarily to actual lived relations. As does the concept of *shalom*. Lived relations occur in places.[5] We do not live in abstractions—or, at least, ideas and principles have to be practically enacted. As anthropologist Clifford Geertz asserts, "No one lives in the world in general."[6] And so a concept like shalom or just sustainability becomes what philosopher Charles Taylor calls a "strong evaluation"—an inescapable moral framework of values and practices that orients our relations in real time in a present that leads toward a future.

In Christian terms, we are required to evaluate: Do these actions bring about the wholeness of relations that characterizes *shalom* in the biblical narrative?[7] Shalom is the foundation of the Christian message, the intended purpose of the language about the kingdom of God. As Brueggemann writes:

> That persistent vision of joy, well-being, harmony, and prosperity is not captured in any single word or idea in the Bible; a cluster of words is required to express its many dimensions and subtle nuances: love, loyalty, truth, grace, salvation, justice, blessings, righteousness. But the term that in recent discussions has been used to summarize that controlling vision is *shalom*.[8]

Woodley will help Anabaptists be more faithful to a mission of reconciliation, primarily because he emphasizes that shalom requires decolonization and that shalom needs to be extended beyond the human portions of the entire community of creation. Yoder may value creation-care and likely would not disagree about decolonization, but he does not make these notions evident. In-

Julian Agyeman et al., *Just Sustainabilities: Development in an Unequal World* (London: Earthscan/MIT Press, 2002).

5 Even "cyber*space*" is geographically constituted. Web-based relations are only a portion of our relations. Even in the extreme case of lockdowns during the Covid-19 pandemic, relatively few people interacted to a greater extent with new people online than they did with people they already knew through workplaces, schools, homes, and so on. People also felt considerable dis-location during the pandemic. Even a practice such as ordering groceries online still requires locally available delivery, material food to arrive, and a place to consume it. Any item ordered from a "virtual" store is constructed in some other physical place. Materiality still matters.

6 Geertz, Clifford, "Afterword: No One Lives in the World in General," *Senses of Place*, eds. Stephen Feld and Keith H. Basso (Sante Fe, NM: School of American Research Press, 1996), 262.

7 Charles Taylor, *Human Agency and Language*, Philosophical Papers 1 (Cambridge: Harvard University Press, 1985). For an extended discussion, see Randolph Haluza-De-Lay et al., "That We May Live Well Together in the Land . . . : Place Pluralism and Just Sustainability in Canadian Studies," *Journal of Canadian Studies* 47, no. 3 (2014), 226–56.

8 Walter Brueggemann, *Peace* (St Louis: Chalice, 2001), 14.

stead, he focuses very specifically on the normative bases of socioeconomic and political structures and how, in God's design, such structures are intended to create shalom. Woodley significantly extends this conceptualization of shalom and perhaps challenges a reformist notion that shalom can be easily manifested within a liberal, capitalist, and Euro-Western cultural context.

## Shalom as Described by Yoder and Woodley

Yoder's *Shalom: The Bible's Word for Salvation, Justice, and Peace* and Woodley's *Shalom and the Community of Creation: An Indigenous Vision* are both short (146 and 166 pages, respectively) and eminently accessible works. Both books can and have been used for adult reading groups and university classes. Both authors are or have been college and seminary professors in the United States, and both have other identities as well that help provide a transnational perspective: Yoder is a Mennonite theologian (now retired), and Woodley is a Cherokee biblical scholar. Yoder's book, as he explains in the preface, is derived from teaching a Bethel College course in the early 1980s.[9] A few years after the course, his family spent time in the Philippines because he was concerned that "*peace is a middle class luxury,* maybe even a Western middle-class luxury."[10] Woodley's book began as a doctoral dissertation on "the Harmony Way," which he describes as a "shared life-concept that is widespread among Native Americans" and compares favorably to the concept of shalom.[11] And while there is no universal "Native American" (sic) culture, Woodley, like many Indigenous scholars, asserts that there are common Indigenous values or orientations. He believes his book represents one of the expressions of a globalizing, non-European Christianity.

Consistent with his Indigenous cultural lens, in his explication of biblical principles and narratives Woodley prioritizes place over history and orthopraxy (*good* relations instead of *right* relations) over orthodoxy (practice over doctrine). He draws on biblical exegesis and on teaching narratives from various North Indigenous communities. My experience of using the book with Canadian students in senior social science seminar courses at a Canadian Christian university was that Woodley often challenged their conception of Christianity as they had learned it, and because of this some students resisted the book. While Yoder's book is a challenge to reform existing society, Woodley's is a deeper, cultural challenge. He asks readers to alter their thinking, to—in Cree education scholar

---

9 Although Yoder's *Shalom* has been reissued (most recently in 2017), I will be using the original 1987 edition here since it was the one used for an AMBS short-course I took some ten years ago.

10 Yoder, *Shalom*, 3 (italics in the original).

11 Woodley, *Shalom*, xiii.

Marie Battiste's terminology—examine their "cognitive imperialism," a reference to European-derived ("Western") cultural ways of knowing having become the standard for knowledge and therefore education, religion, and other ways of teaching about, acting in, and knowing the world.[12]

Colonized peoples and settlers alike have marinated in the colonial ways of thinking and structuring relations between peoples. While "decolonization" can mean the revolutionary movements that removed colonial governments in the twentieth century,[13] Woodley means more by the term—reversing the Eurocentric capture of our minds, sociopolitical and economic systems, and relations between peoples. Yoder also draws heavily on the Hebrew narratives in the Old Testament but argues primarily for a more just social order. Such sociopolitical change is no easy matter, but, as shall be detailed later, it is expanded by the cultural, cognitive, and ontological transformations for which Woodley asks.

Shalom is the central message of the scriptures for both Yoder and Woodley; it is God's *true* intention for God's creation. For both scholars, *shalom* is a broad and complex term meaning all that is good, true, just, whole, and leads to wholeness and good relations between God, humans, and other-than human parts of creation. While Yoder tends to use the language of "justice," Woodley tends to use the language of "harmony." Both refer to shalom as a Hebrew term comparable to the Greek *eirēnē* and point out that the latter is often translated in the New Testament as "righteousness" but should mean justice and wholeness as well.

Shalom has three "shades of meaning" according to Yoder. "First, it can refer to a material and physical state of affairs, this being its most frequent usage. It can also refer to relationships, and here it comes closest in meaning to the English word *peace*. And finally it also has a moral sense, which is its least frequent meaning."[14] The first meaning asserts that all people should have their physical needs met. The second is wider and more positive—akin to the notion of peace as not merely the absence of war but rather as processes of maintaining an appropriate goodness in society and well-being for all. The third meaning refers to character and integrity and is foundational to the collective manifestation of shalom.

These three meanings are linked in practice. Shalom is not operating if material needs are not met, injustice exists, and moral integrity and well-being are not present. Yoder argues that the Greek term *eirēnē* in the New Testament (NT) adds a theological dimension—that shalom involves the work of Christ—

---

12 Marie Battiste, *Decolonizing Education: Nourishing the Learning Spirit* (Saskatoon: Purlich, 2013).

13 This is the entirety of the meaning of the term in Dane Kennedy, *Decolonization: A Very Short Introduction* (Oxford: Oxford University Press, 2016).

14 Yoder, *Shalom*, 10–11.

to what has so far seemed mostly sociological. It is at this point in his discussion that Yoder adds one of only two references in the book that go beyond the human or human-divine nexus: he commends Colossians 1 as the best NT expression of shalom.[15] In this passage, Christ is the source of shalom; his is the work of "making peace," and its effect is for more than humanity—it is for the entirety of the universe.

Yoder continues to clarify his understandings of both shalom and justice. Justice is basic to shalom, he says, but shalom goes deeper, certainly beyond both retributive and distributive justice. Shalom is *liberation* of any who are caught in bondage, referring to both the collective and physical as well as the spiritual dimensions of being. The material and spiritual, he notes, are inextricable in the Hebrew worldview. "Passages in the New Testament make clear that the result of the atonement is not only our personal liberation from sin's bondage into the realm of the lordship of Jesus. This liberation is also marked by the appearance of a new social order which embodies the values of Jesus' teachings and life."[16]

In several chapters, Yoder discuss the role of law, the state, and prophets (inspired critics of social structures that fail to create shalom). His discussion shows clearly the insufficiency of charity; shalom requires social systems that provide for well-being, not just charity that ameliorates societal inadequacies. According to Yoder, Jesus's message was one of social transformation, because if it were not, his "hard sayings" would be dismissible as inapplicable to the present world, and the remaining other-worldly spiritualized message would fit neither the *shalom* nor *eirēnē* meanings of the text. For Yoder, the gospel is about conversion to a new way of life—not conversion to "Jesus" but to Jesus's way of the shalomic kingdom of God.

Woodley begins with a preface that emphasizes the congruence of the Harmony Way with the biblical sense of shalom—as a "way of living" that includes "practical steps" for "specific action when the harmony or shalom is broken . . . [with] justice, restoration, and continuous right living as their goal."[17] "Words used to translate *shalem* [the "word origin of *shalom*"] in the NASB," he notes, "include close, ease, favorable, friend, friendly terms, friends, greet, greeted, health, peace, peaceably, peaceful, peacefully, perfect peace, prosperity, safe,

---

15 Particularly the Christological hymn in Colossians 1:15–21 and the following verses wherein the reconciliation wrought by "making peace" via the cross is for "all things." From this passage, I have tried to conceptualize "making peace with all creation" as an ecological imaginary (expanding Taylor's [*Human Agency and Language*] explication of a "social imaginary" as the way we imagine and then organize our relations as a society). See Randolph Haluza-DeLay, "Making Peace with All Creation," *Peace Review* 24, no. 2 (2012): 171–78.

16 Yoder, *Shalom*, 67.

17 Woodley, *Shalom*, xv.

safely, safety, secure, trusted, welfare, well, well-being, and wholly."[18] Most importantly, both shalom and Harmony Way "originate as *the* right path for living, being viewed as a gift from the Creator."[19] Shalom is the way life is meant to be, fundamentally as "right relations."

From the very beginning of his book, Woodley includes "human beings, animals, and plants" in our relationships. Shalom is "greater than the sum of its parts" (the subtitle of the first chapter), originates in God, and is universally expected of all humanity. We can tell when it is being practiced because it is "always tested on the margins of a society and revealed by how the poor, oppressed, disempowered, and needy are treated."[20]

After describing shalom, Woodley moves into a biblical exegesis that connects first and second testaments and then reframes "the kingdom of God" as "the community of all creation." This is God's "first discourse"—that all creation is connected and that "the Scriptures are written from a worldview that does not easily categorize creation into animate and inanimate realities."[21] In fact, Woodley believes "less relational views of reciprocity between humans and creation are modern misunderstandings, and they have everything to do with modern humanity's alienation from creation."[22]

These are not new thoughts; early eco-theology, even from American Evangelical perspectives, demonstrated the similarity between ancient Hebrew and North American Indigenous perspectives of the land and the interrelations of land, Creator, and humans.[23] Many critics inside and outside faith traditions have charged Christianity—*Western, European* Christianity specifically—as dominating and damaging nature, especially as the faith tradition has taken on the characteristics of modernity.[24]

In contrast to what he calls this type of Christianity's "typically anthropocentric and utilitarian orientation" that excludes most everyday material things from moral consideration, Woodley argues, "As people of faith, we should view

---

18 Woodley, 10.

19 Woodley, xv.

20 Woodley, 15

21 Woodley, 47.

22 Woodley, 51.

23 Wesley Granberg-Michaelson, *A Worldly Spirituality: The Call to Redeem Life on Earth* (San Francisco: Harper and Row, 1984).

24 Muslim scholar Seyyed Hossein Nasr refuted the universal claim about Christianity in 1968: "Neither Christian Armenia nor Ethiopia nor even Christian Eastern Europe gave rise to that science and technology which in the hands of secular man has led to the devastation of the globe." See Nasr, *Man and Nature: The Spiritual Crisis in Modern Man* (first published 1968), cited in Fazlun Khalid, *Signs on the Earth: Islam, Modernity and the Climate Crisis* (Leicestershire, UK: Kube Publishing, 2019), 20.

every drop of oil . . . [among other things] . . . with a theological eye."[25] That we do not means our religious worldview is unacceptably contained and only some things are considered worth being religious about. This would not be the way Indigenous religiosity sees the world. Nor is it biblical. Drawing on John, Colossians, Hebrews, and more, Woodley shows the gospel message as shalom for all creation, not just the human portion. Furthermore, he emphasizes the relationality of all parts of the creation, and, because of this, he valorizes the material world.

Woodley then begins to present Indigenous readings of scriptures and theological constructs. Sin, for example, is disruption of relations, and restoration of relations is what the gospel is about. The greatest disruption of relations, Woodley says, was European colonization of the Americas, resulting in a sort of permanent PTSD among Indigenous peoples and internalization of superiority among European settlers and those who came later.[26] Because of colonialism's underlying mentality and enduring societal structures, shalom requires all people to expend effort to decolonize, to "remove the systemic relationships embedded in colonialism."[27] And while this would likely correspond to Yoder's emphasis on shalom as requiring changed social structures, Yoder's silence on colonialism, specifically, as central to this needed change means that readers and shalom-seekers will miss this crucial and non-shalomic facet of the contemporary world.

Most Indigenous scholars argue that the current politics of "reconciliation" have merely shifted dialogue without substantive change to the existing power relations and other products of colonialism.[28] Decolonization needs to reach into the very center of Christian faith, even to decolonizing the way that the

---

25 Nasr cited in Khalid, 52. This is comparable to a point made by a previous Roman Catholic bishop in a pastoral letter about the Alberta oil sands. After a short summary, Bishop Bouchard concluded, "Any one of the above destructive effects provokes moral concern, but it is when the damaging effects are all added together that the moral legitimacy of tar sands production is challenged." This conclusion generated no little controversy (Nathan Kowalsky and Randolph Haluza-DeLay, "'This Is Oil Country': The Tar Sands and Jacques Ellul's Theory of Technology," *Environmental Ethics* 37, no. 1 [2015]: 75–97).

26 In my experience, it is usually around this point that some students begin to react strongly to Woodley's call for *them* to change, to decolonize, so that Indigenous peoples also can flourish and that if they do not change, reconciliation, which is at the heart of the gospel, cannot occur. It has sometimes gotten to the point where I have reminded the students that this is a Christian brother whom they are resisting and that, presumably, the Holy Spirit is active in him also.

27 Woodley, *Shalom*, 92.

28 Glen Sean Coulthard, *Red Skin White Masks: Rejecting the Colonial Politics of Recognition* (Minneapolis: University of Minnesota Press, 2014).

Bible has been used to oppress.[29] This also means recognizing, then valuing, the witness of the Holy Spirit in other, non-European cultures. Bravely, Mennonite Church Canada has allowed that "Indigenous intrusion troubles the house"[30] and, to some degree, has welcomed the intrusion by continuing to support work on Indigenous relations.

Both the pain of the colonized and the avoidance of the colonizer can become retreats into inaction. Any of those in the dominant group(s) who are unwilling to yield their own privileges (even to the point that structures once benefitting them no longer do so) cannot become true allies or agents of shalom.[31] Such yielding is the Jesus Way.

In subsequent chapters, Woodley shows other cultural differences between Euro-Western and Indigenous cultures and their ways of practicing the Christian faith, as well as the implications of these differences for Christian praxis. He concludes, "If we are to rescue our planet, which is currently bent on a trajectory of destruction, then Christians must begin to live out shalom, even by changing their own church cultures."[32] In other words, we will know when shalom is being practiced, because it will help the *entire* earth to flourish. *Cultural* change among the majority of North American Christians will be required.

This statement comes directly from discussion of being a church that actively welcomes strangers (newcomers). From an Indigenous Christian perspective, such a focus on good relations is to be carried into all social, political, ecological, and economic relations. Every being on the planet is our neighbor, and shalom flourishes when every being flourishes. The implications of this orientation confront the liberal, humanist, globalized, and capitalist social order with the need for revolutionary transformation.

---

29 Steve Heinrichs, ed., *Unsettling the Word: Biblical Experiments in Decolonization* (Winnipeg, MB: Mennonite Church Canada, 2018).

30 Steve Heinrichs, ed., *Buffalo Shout, Salmon Cry* (Kitchener, ON: Herald, 2013), 13. Courage is necessary for self-examination. Undergraduate students have indicated to me that the book unsettled their preexisting views, leaving them a little uneasy.

31 Anne Bishop, *Becoming an Ally: Breaking the Cycle of Oppression in People*, 2nd ed. (Halifax, NS: Fernwood, 2002). Many readers are challenged by Bishop's high standards for becoming true allies. Too many take solace at the intersectional orientation that we are all oppressors and we are all oppressed. That unfortunately lets them off the hook, so to speak, or lets them lay down their cross before they have traveled very far. It should be clear that we are not all oppressed or oppressors to the same degree.

32 Woodley, *Shalom*, 151. Emphasis added.

## Commonalities and Contrasts

### Commonalities

There are many commonalities between Yoder and Woodley's understandings of shalom. To begin with, both scholars conceptualize the human social relations of shalom similarly and do so in a way that befits their expertise in biblical scholarship and God's vision for the world. For both, shalom is relational, including collective or societal structures and extending into a seamless integrality of spiritual and material dimensions. For neither is shalom utopian; shalom is intended for contemporary times, although changes in attitude and social structures are required. Shalom is therefore, both scholars believe, an ongoing process.

Yoder and Woodley are also in agreement that shalom is tested on the margins by how a society takes care of its weaker, marginalized, and oppressed members. Therefore, shalom is not individual action, because social structures produce either shalom or oppression and social structures are not individualized. Both emphasize that shalom and its justice component are founded in the divine, not created through mere human effort. Shalom is formative for individual and community character and relies on moral integrity implemented in social relations at all levels, from the individual to the societal.

In addition, both Yoder and Woodley emphasize that the Euro-Western worldview does not correspond with a biblical worldview, and they critique the Euro-Western worldview via their explication of shalom. Woodley also compares the Euro-Western worldview to contemporary Indigenous worldviews. That means that he compares and draws wisdom from three worldviews in terms of the practice and characteristics of shalom. This multiplicity of perspectives is representative of the past century, in which the Christian faith has become expressed across an ever-wider swath of the world and its cultures, less encumbered by its millennium of European domination.[33]

### Contrasts

Examining the contrasts between the two authors will improve our praxis of shalom more than just highlighting their similarities. Yoder's emphasis is on sociopolitical justice, while Woodley focuses on relational harmony and rec-

---

33 Often perceived as a European religion, Christianity began in the Orient (the "Middle East") and expanded across Africa and Asia more quickly than in Europe. The faith reached China before it reached Russia and has always sought to express itself in culturally relevant ways. But it then collapsed back almost exclusively into Europe and began to be exported again as handmaiden to the expansion of European empires from the fifteenth century onward.

onciliation, which he also links to social and political relations. However, the most important differences between these two scholars are found in Woodley's extension of the community of shalom to all of the human and other-than-human worlds, and his explication of the significance of the colonial foundations of the contemporary settler nations (both of which will be expounded upon in the next section of this essay). Although Yoder mentions that the remit of shalom/*eirēnē* is for the whole universe, according to Colossians 1,[34] he touches on other-than-human relations only once more, stating, "As we order our economic lives to reflect the values of shalom, then our purchases for example are not based on economic factors alone, like price, but on moral and ecological factors as well."[35]

Yoder's concern for creation-care comes across in his conversation and teaching,[36] but readers will miss this connection because it's not evident in the text. Woodley, on the other hand, writes in such a way that one cannot miss his extension of shalom to *all* creation as a profound break with Euro-Western humanism. It is for this reason that Woodley so assertively presents an Indigenous form of Christian faith and why it becomes a corrective to Eurocentric capture of the Jesus way.

In addition, although both Yoder and Woodley address "land," unless the nonhuman ecology of a place is specified, most readers will consider only the social ecology—that is, the relations among humans and human groups. Nor does Yoder address "indigeneity," which matters because indigeneity includes a dimension of place-connectedness.[37] Land gains meaning by being a "place," full of meanings and histories and known by the people who live there.[38] In

---

34 Yoder, *Shalom*, 21.

35 Yoder, 142.

36 A decade ago I took an AMBS short course with Perry Yoder and asked specifically about whether shalom can be extended to human relations with the rest of creation. For years, Yoder has led theologically informed canoe trips, and he presented on the Hebraic view of nature at a 1995 conference. Many of these papers, but not Yoder's, were included in Calvin Redekop, ed., *Creation and the Environment: An Anabaptist Perspective on a Sustainable World* (Baltimore: Johns Hopkins University Press, 2000).

37 The same processes are operating in contemporary Palestine. Native Palestinians have resided in the land since Old Testament times, but the claim for Israel was represented as "a land without a people for a people without a land"—a standard settler-colonial narrative for acquiring, displacing, and then replacing the Indigenous population. This narrative dominates Israeli national discourses as well as Christian support for Zionism, which is astonishing since Palestinian Christians have seen themselves for centuries as children of the promise made to Abraham. Mitri Raheb, *Faith in the Face of Empire: The Bible through Palestinian Eyes* (Maryknoll, NY: Orbis, 2014).

38 See Haluza-DeLay et al., "That We May Live Well Together in the Land," 232, for a summary of social geographical and philosophical meanings of place, places, and

contrast, Woodley emphasizes place while arguing that Western Christianity valorizes history, a charge that is evident in the account of Israel that Yoder unpacks even as he addresses "land."[39] Woodley argues that Indigenous people's "view of the land" is the "most precious gift that they have to offer."[40] He hopes that non-Indigenous peoples will receive the gift, which will enable them to alter dis-located worldviews, think and act more relationally, and work for shalom in terms of healing the land and planet.

Lastly, Yoder emphasizes "kingdom," although he contrasts earthly kingdoms to a kingdom characterized by shalom. The idea of kingdom is central to Yoder's explication of shalom since he argues that a sociopolitical system is necessary for the institution of shalom. Taking a broader approach, Woodley insists we should replace "kingdom" with "community" and particularly with "community of [all] creation." He understands that the connotations of kingdom are substantially different from that of community. Among other features, "kingdom" implies far more hierarchy, law, and codified order than does "community."

## Woodley's Two Unique Aspects of Shalom

Woodley prominently presents two aspects of shalom that are not found in Yoder: (1) he extends shalom beyond the human portion to all creation, and (2) he emphasizes the ongoing, shalom-breaking role of colonialism on settlers and colonized alike. Yoder would likely not object to these two themes related to shalom, but, as noted already, clearly identifying these aspects is essential for bringing them to readers' conscious awareness. Articulation also shows that they are not inessential add-ons but aspects that significantly affect how shalom is conceptualized and brought into action.

Woodley's extension of the remit of shalom to all creation, and to seeing other created beings as part of a *community*, goes far deeper than most ecologically oriented Christians delve. Despite changing terminology from "stewardship" (a managerial emphasis) to "creation-care" in recent years,[41] Christian environmental discourse still posits fundamental differences between human and other-than-human parts of creation.

---

placelessness.

39 Woodley (*Shalom*, 111–36) writes an entire chapter on the importance of place as the relational nexus for practices of caring consistent with discipleship following the Jesus Way.

40 Woodley, 128.

41 Sabrina Danielsen, "Fracturing over Creation Care? Shifting Environmental Beliefs among Evangelicals, 1984–2010," *Journal for the Scientific Study of Religion* 52, no. 1 (2013): 198–215.

Without question, ecological degradation is deeply troubling; data on elements of global environmental change related to precipitous biodiversity loss, climate change, water shortages, ocean acidification, and ecosystem decline are more than sobering.[42] Despite decades of overwhelming evidence, existing human systems, institutions and cultural values have so far proved inadequate to reverse the downward trend. Ecological degradation links with other global concerns—and thus, damages to shalom—such as global hunger, poverty, social inequality, inadequate education, gender rights, and other Sustainable Development Goals (SDGs)—all malformations of the biblically expressed intentions for creation.

Woodley's emphasis on relationality fits what we know from both ecology and sociology. Both show all things to be in relationship with other things—we all eat, drink water, live in space, breath air, interact with other species and individuals of our own species, sometimes even through viruses or atmospheric droplets from the respirations of others! To see all things relationally—all of the pleasant and the nasty, the good parts of community and the less-preferred parts, the discourses and the power and the actions of all creatures—is very different from an atomistic vision, especially one that privileges only humanity.

There are many other streams of human-nature relations within the Christian tradition in addition to the stewardship or creation-care forms.[43] Woodley's approach fits what might be called the "partnership with nature" stream. Relationships imply mutual interaction and reaction to each relational partner. Viewing portions of nature (or even the entire planet[44]), however, as capable of action and reaction challenges the humanistic core of modernity, which constrains agency in creation exclusively to human beings. This is one of the characteristic features of "modernity"—the Western worldview that privileges human reason, rationalized social organization, technological capacity, and instrumental valuation of all non-human things. Woodley's Indigenous cultural lens finds congruence with Bruno Latour, one of the preeminent philosophers of science and modernity, who has critiqued the modernist comprehension of other-than-human nature as "objects" instead of having their own agency in interaction—his "actor-network theory/ontology."[45]

---

42 Will Steffen et al., "Trajectories of the Earth System in the Anthropocene," Proceedings of the National Academy of Sciences of the United States of America 115, no.33 (Aug 6, 2018), 8252–59, https://doi.org/10.1073/pnas.1810141115.

43 Larry Rasmussen, "Toward an Earth Charter," *The Christian Century* 108, no. 30 (1991): 964–67.

44 E.g., Bruno Latour, *Facing Gaia: Eight Lectures on the New Climatic Regime*, trans. Catherine Porter (Cambridge, UK: Polity, 2017).

45 I have tried to explain Latour's theory and methodology with focus on his recent work on the earth as reacting to human activity in Randolph Haluza-DeLay, "Anthro-

Would returning to a sense of the creatureliness of the creational community lead to different moral considerations and practical action? The problem is that this alternative way of life cannot even be tested within modernity and Euro-Western culture since their hegemony sets the epistemic and ontological conditions for discourse and ethics. It may be that those concerned about the environment "must find other ways to articulate [their] ethics because the established forms of ethics, in so far as they are representations and embodiments of modernity, will inevitably distort or exclude the values of critics who live or envisage a different form of life."[46]

Woodley's Indigenous vision provides such an alternative to modernity yet still sits within a Christian framework. His is one of several new approaches to environmental management being developed that contest basic features of the dominant, Euro-Western understanding of nature. For instance, *The Economist* begins a report with, "It sounds . . . like a 'pretty nutty' idea" before explaining that New Zealand designated the Whanganui River a legal person in 2017, three years after a similar designation for the forested area of Te Urewera.[47] Rivers and forests as "persons"? The indigenous Maori believe so and operate in relationship with river and forest as if it were so. The new legal status is another step in redrawing relations among Maori, *pakeha* (non-Maori New Zealanders), and the land.

The links between sustainability, justice, and peacemaking are being elucidated within the field of peace ecology.[48] One Mennonite environmental practitioner declares that the *Confession of Faith in a Mennonite Perspective* expresses an "ecojustice" orientation linking social justice, peace, and ecological sustainability: "The peace God intends for humanity and creation was revealed most

---

pocene as Creator, Gaia as Creature: An Extended Review of Bruno Latour," *Christian Scholar's Review* XLVIII, no. 4 (2019): 391–401.

46 Mick Smith, *An Ethics of Place: Radical Ecology, Postmodernity, and Social Theory* (Albany, NY: State University of New York Press, 2001), 25. For example, during the mid-1990s I was part of a grant-funded team writing a series of inserts for church bulletins on environmental matters. I wrote the one on endangered species called "Who is our Neighbor?" The Christian organization that sponsored the project had a lot of farmers involved. The statement about the need to treat animals with moral consideration—as our "neighbors"—led to controversy as the farmers argued they couldn't make an economic living if they did that.

47 The Economist, "New Zealand Declares a River a Person," *The Economist*, March 25, 2017, https://www.economist.com/asia/2017/03/25/new-zealand-declares-a-river-a-person.

48 "Peace ecology" is a research domain building a body of evidence that "social systems are only viable in a longer-term sense when they promote just and peaceful relations with ourselves, each other, and the biosphere itself" (Randall Amster, *Peace Ecology* [Boulder, CO: Paradigm, 2013]).

fully in Jesus Christ."[49] Such sentiments are laudable, although for shalom to be moved toward, they must obviously be backed by action. For instance, if ecojustice is to occur, notions of sustainability cannot be limited to the mainstream environmental approaches of nature conservation, lifestyle action, and policy reform. Such approaches to sustainability can actually undermine the type of shalom advocated by both Yoder and Woodley. According to the head of the Canadian ecumenical justice organization *Kairos*, environmentalists should struggle also for Indigenous sovereignty, land rights, and reparations for past wrongs.[50] Few do.[51]

This returns us to the horrific rupture of the possibilities for shalom perpetrated by colonialism in North America. Woodley asserts that correcting colonialism means that benefactors of colonialism would have to make restitution. In his analysis, the centrality of colonialism is uncomfortably present for readers. Yoder reminds readers that "the structures and institutions in place often operate to maintain the present system of stratification and exploitation," implying that systems derived from colonial times need replacement so that exploitation can be remedied rather than reproduced.[52] His silence, however, about colonialism specifically—such a profound element in the earth's human and ecological history—is deafening.

Colonialism is the domination and control of one people by another. The processes by which it operates include geographical incursion; external political control; destruction of social, spiritual, and cultural systems; economic dependence; social interaction based on racial distinctions; and inferior quality health, social, and other institutional services. Colonization involves forced subjugation by physical or symbolic violence and may lead to internalization of inferiority by the colonized.[53] Colonization affects members of dominant groups too, especially as they absorb the discourses about their superiority and beliefs about their culture's superior ways of operating.

The specific form of colonialism varied regionally; the British colony of Canada differed from the British colony of India, for instance. In the latter, a

---

49 Article 22: "Peace, Justice and Nonresistance," in *Confession of Faith in a Mennonite Perspective* (Scottsdale, PA: Herald, 1995), 81, cited in Luke Gascho, *Creation Care: Keepers of the Earth* (Goshen, IN: Mennonite Mutual Aid, 2008), 70.

50 Jennifer Harvey, "Dangerous 'Goods': Seven Reasons Creation Care Movements Must Advocate Reparations," Steve Heinrichs, *Buffalo Shout, Salmon Cry* (Kitchener, ON: Herald, 2013), 315–29.

51 Lynne Davis, ed., *Alliances: Re/Envisioning Indigenous/non-Indigenous Relationships* (Toronto: University of Toronto Press, 2010).

52 Yoder, *Shalom*, 140.

53 This description focuses on sociological processes rather than historical or political details alone.

small number of Europeans utilized a larger bureaucratic corps of Indians to control the entire land. In Canada, colonialism was (and still is) settler colonial, in which the characteristic processes noted above are present but the colonial people come to stay. In other words, they sought and still operate to displace or replace the Indigenous population.[54]

Colonialism is not just historical past; it exists still in hierarchies, privileges, wealth made from the land, and structures of all sorts of social, material, and mental constructions. Furthermore, new forms of the control of land and peoples emerge—neo-colonialisms such as economic colonialism (where political power is replaced by economic control) and environmental colonialism (where external actors use environmental practices as justification to control land).[55] Woodley details the impact and ongoing effects of Christian (sic) Europe's displacement and dissolution of Indigenous cultures in the Americas.

Because settler colonial processes replace local populations with new settlers, the settlers believe the land has been acquired. But because the Indigenous peoples have not disappeared (as they were supposed to), there cannot help but be conflict. Narratives conflict over indigeneity, rights, societal participation, and the land. Contested narratives are also contested legal claims. They are not easily resolved because of the different cultural frames (Euro-Western versus Indigenous) involved. But to do shalom means to address the effects of colonialism, and this inevitably means transformative change rather than mere moderation (reform) of existing legal and historical ideas. Similar struggles against the persistence of colonization are occurring around the world among Indigenous peoples and in places like Palestine.

Woodley could have been even more forceful in this regard. Glen Sean Coulthard argues that most contemporary efforts to decolonize are disingenuous and mostly just reproduce the systems of power they claim to be trying to modify.[56] This is especially true in terms of national and international politics (e.g., Canada's resistance to implementing the waifish United Nations Declaration on the Rights of Indigenous peoples). It is also true of land acknowledgments and other efforts at reconciliation that do not address any structural systems. Coulthard wants a more revolutionary solution, including explicitly anti-liberal and anti-capitalist ones. "For Indigenous nations to live," he says, "capitalism must die. And for capitalism to die, we must actively participate

---

54 Eva Mackey, *Unsettled Expectations: Uncertainty, Land and Settler Decolonization* (Halifax: Fernwood, 2016).

55 Blaine T. Garfolo and Barbara L'Huillier, "Economic Colonialism: The New Empire Building of the 21st Century," *Academy Of Business Research Journal* 1 (2014): 48–55. James Goodman "Is the United Nation' REDD Scheme Conservation Colonialism by Default?" *International Journal of Water* 5, no.4 (2010): 419–28.

56 Coulthard, *Red Skin, White Masks*.

in the construction of Indigenous alternatives to it."[57] Most importantly, Coulthard argues that most people—Indigenous and non-Indigenous alike—fail to recognize the way domination operates.

Kathryn Yusoff argues that colonialism and capitalism were both founded on extractive domination—extraction of natural resources from the earth and extraction of labor from African slaves and Indigenous peoples.[58] To do this, imperial modernity had to engage in classification—first "nature," then "Indigenous," and then "Black": "The human and its subcategory, the inhuman, are historically relational to a discourse of settler-colonial rights and the material practices of extraction."[59] "Race" is a foundation of the modern world because it was similar to and necessary for the extractive geologic of what has now become known as the "Anthropocene"—the dramatic impact of humanity on the planet's biosphere. More generally, the early twentieth-century sociologist W. E. B. DuBois defined whiteness as the "ownership of the Earth forever and ever."[60] Yusoff emphasizes that global ecological degradation is not a product of universal humanity (human sin?) but rather a historically precise result of particular human actors—national politicians and elites who coerced others (land, Indigenous peoples, Africans, European laborers) into the project. Yusoff's observation—"There can be no address of the planetary failures of modernism or its master-subject, Man [that is, Anthropocene degradation] without a commitment to overcoming extractive colonialism"[61]—corresponds to Woodley's argument. Clearly these analyses by Coulthard, Yusoff, and others support Woodley's reconfiguring of shalom to account for a transformation that extends even further than Yoder's version of shalom.

Since shalom is to be a comprehensive and practical (non-utopian) vision of wholeness, justice, well-being, and care for all, Woodley's orientation becomes an even more profound challenge because it not only undermines the modernist way that Christianity has become manifested (and exported around the world) but also demands an even more transformative project than Yoder envisioned. Is Christianity up to the task?

Gerda Kits, a professor at a Christian university, has recently argued that decolonization should be central to Christian higher education.[62] She builds

---

57 Coulthard, 172.

58 Kathryn Yusoff, *A Billion Black Anthropocenes or None* (Minneapolis: University of Minnesota Press, 2018).

59 Yusoff, 2.

60 W. E. B. DuBois, *Darkwater: Voices from within the Veil* (New York: Harcourt Brace, 1920), 54, cited in Yusoff, *A Billion Black Anthropocenes or None*, 26.

61 Yusoff, *A Billion Black Anthropocenes*, 50.

62 Gerda Kits, "Why Educating for Shalom Requires Decolonization," *International Journal of Christianity and Education* 23, no. 2 (2019): 185–203.

this argument on Reformed philosopher Nicholas Wolterstorff's thesis that Christian education should be "educating for shalom."[63] While I applaud the efforts, there are a few problems that the above analysis makes clear. Kits's version of decolonization does not include a politics of the land or an analysis of power relations. Rather, it is based primarily on the historical process and its impact on Indigenous peoples now, although it also recognizes that settler peoples in the present need to know and understand the historical facts. Without a politics of the land, colonialism is not displaced. Without an analysis of power, liberal multiculturalism remains uncontested. Settlers remain in control, and it is still assumed that Indigenous peoples are to fit into the current sociocultural systems of Canada.

Additionally, Kits does not provide examples of agency by Indigenous actors, and she references few Indigenous scholars. This omission is important because relationality and the presumption of reciprocity indicate that peoples can give to and learn from each other. In Kits's essay, it is not clear whether there are any gift(s) (or learnings) that non-Indigenous Christians can receive from Indigenous peoples.[64]

For both Yoder and Kits, solid steps toward expressing the features of shalom could be improved by analysis and critiques from those who have been "othered" by the dominance of Euro-Western thought and political-economic systems. For persons in dominant social categories, listening to criticisms of the existing world from subaltern others can improve scrutiny of one's own social position and relative privilege and can judge the adequacy of one's own assumptions about the good to which God calls.

## Land and Mission

Shalom is the church's mission, and, as the above comparison has shown, "land" remains a significant element of shalom. Thus, the question of colonial displacement is crucial to Indigenous-settler reconciliation. If shalom is to be practiced in real relations, it must be practiced in real places. That includes those places where Mennonites live on what the settler governments took from Indigenous

---

63 Nicholas Wolterstorff, *Educating for Shalom: Essays on Christian Higher Education* (Grand Rapids, MI: William B. Eerdmans, 2004).

64 Let me be clear—I believe the reason some students were so challenged by Woodley was because he asked them to learn from Indigenous peoples; that is, he asked them to change. Kits does express more willingness to be changed by her encounter with advocates of decolonization. Furthermore, she is writing to an audience that may already be suspicious of her project as going too far (Christian higher education), and the article argues strenuously against that view.

peoples.[65] Shalom, Yoder and Woodley both say, involves the correcting of wrongs and restoration of relations. Decolonizing the cognitive imperialism of the world order—which creates hierarchies among human groups and "races" and excludes the other-than-human right out of moral relations—is critical in an effort to address both world problems and the mission of the church. But it is not the only aspect of genuine shalom-like decolonization.

More broadly, one could ask what Woodley's emphasis on place can mean for the practice of the Christian faith in contemporary churches. "Place" is one of the most complicated terms in human geography, with a wide variety of meanings. It is fundamentally relational,[66] especially when histories and ecologies are combined with social relations among different groups of humans. Despite narratives of "nation," Euro-Western culture is profoundly inattentive to "place," especially compared to Indigenous peoples. Mennonite pastor/Cheyenne peace chief Lawrence Hart asserts that the majority of Christian worship is *placeless*, which also implies that Christians will have more difficulty embodying the vision of shalom.[67]

Real relations are embodied and emplaced, meaning that discipleship needs to "stay put" in a place for the development of the "strong ties" and deeply experienced knowing that can create the conditions for collective work for shalom. Being place-based does not guarantee good knowing, of course, but the equal risk is that abstracted knowledge can be "out-of-place." By being emplaced, we can assess our actions-guided-by-principles for their congruence with shalom in real conditions, Woodley argues.[68]

## Stepping Forward

Clearly the mission of the faithful church is to be shalom and, in concert with the Spirit, to bring about shalom in the place where we have been put. This mission is not to seek what is good only for us but for what allows everyone to flourish. And "everyone" here must be seen as the entirety of creation. We are to use our gifts—including our privileges or advantages, our resources, capital,

---

65 Decolonization in the abstract—or only in the patterns of the mind—is disembodied and deplaced. The colonial process that eliminated Papaschase land rights in South East Edmonton, Alberta, holds a great deal of implication for descendants of the Papaschase as well as for the Mennonite church and members living on the same land.

66 Haluza-DeLay et al., "That We May Live Well Together in the Land," 232, for a summary of social geographical and philosophical meanings of place, places, and placelessness.

67 Lawrence Hart, "The Earth Is a Song Made Visible: A Cheyenne Christian Perspective," Steve Heinrichs, ed., *Buffalo Shout, Salmon Cry* (Kitchener, ON: Herald, 2013), 153–61.

68 Woodley, *Shalom*, 127.

or power—in this mission that involves changing societal structures that do not embody shalom.

Probably most important, however, for those like me who are of the dominant social groups in society, is to learn to listen more than talk and to step back so others can step forward.[69] This implies the yielding of power and position to those who have not had power, position, or privilege. The redress of colonial displacement probably includes the #LandBack movement (returning land to Indigenous peoples), reparations for slavery (returning the value of some of the extracted labor from which others gained), and/or dramatic reduction in human consumption of planetary resources by those who already have lifestyles considerably beyond the majority of the world's human population. Frankly, for critics like Coulthard, decolonization is about breaking the system of exploitation and domination and building a new system. Like other advocates of place-based social systems,[70] he argues that local economies are inherently *less* exploitative, because people know each other and the land and have more accountability (or ease of revolt). Though Woodley does not go that far, some readers still find his call for change beyond what they can accept.

These examples are practical and material. Steve Heinrichs describes how *Buffalo Shouts, Salmon Cry* began as a form of "two-eyed seeing" wherein participants in the writing process would all take on and combine both dominant Canadian and Indigenous Canadian perspectives.[71] An alternative way to integration might be an attitude of mutual respect and equality enough to learn from each other, while taking on the wholeness of one's own background. That is, settlers do not need to take on Indigenous ways if they can bring some of the gifts of indigeneity to the mission of creating shalom. Settlers do need to yield some of their position—and not just the worst of the lands, as allocated reserves often were—to allow Indigenous peoples to reclaim space and make it place.

---

69 Bishop, *Becoming an Ally*.

70 For example, Michael Vincent McGinnis, ed., *Bioregionalism* (New York: Routledge, 1999) and Mike Carr, *Bioregionalism and Civil Society: Democratic Challenges to Corporate Globalism* (Vancouver: UBC Press), 2004.

71 Heinrichs, ed., *Buffalo Shouts, Salmon Cry*, 24.

Decolonization in the abstract is disembodied and deplaced. And how do we even imagine other-than-human nature to also have adequate places? The forces that would rupture shalom are powerful, so all gifts are needed in this work by which Creator called all peoples. In this regard, Woodley offers something of a conclusion:

> The way forward is both structural and relational, requiring honest historical and theological rethinking and coming to grips with the following concerns: colonialism and neocolonialism; the way current forms of capitalism resist shalom; the way racism affects our thinking and relationships; the practical implications for living on stolen land; how violence is thought to be needed in order to maintain the present system; what true reconciliation looks like.[72]

All of this is a challenge. In the midst of it, we would do well to remember that the goal is the process of "living well together in the land . . ." If the *community of all creation* is the "we" and *shalom* is equivalent to "living well," then the land is the site of our mission, and we do it *together*.

---

72 Woodley, *Shalom*, 136.

# Turning Ploughshares into Swords

## An Ethnohistory of Violence

Devon Miller

This paper explores the impact that the transformation of Indigenous landscapes by settler societies had upon the Indigenous communities who inhabited these landscapes. It broadens the scope of violence committed against humans to encompass destruction inflicted upon any aspect of the landscape as an act of direct violence. Typical models of violence concentrate on harms inflicted upon the physical, emotional, or psychological well-being of an individual or group of people. With those limits on violence, the displacement of Native communities is relegated to the realm of dispossession or destruction of property. Well-intended apologies from contemporary settlers that ignore the deeper epistemological and ontological relations humans develop over time with land serve only to extend settler colonialism, since such apologies perpetuate their own objectification of the land.

Recent scholarship addressing the encounter between governments rooted in European power structures and lands inhabited by Indigenous peoples has focused on a lineage of legal decrees set forth by ecclesiastical and political entities, known as the Doctrine of Discovery. Though the modern iteration of this series of legal pronouncements can be traced back to fifteenth-century papal bulls,[1] these orders parallel the conquest of the land of Canaan by Abraham and his descendants, found in the Hebrew scriptures. The focus of this paper is not meant to diminish the thoughtful work of those bringing attention to the Doctrine of Discovery's influence on the settlement of Indigenous lands; rather, it is an effort to create greater understanding of what the Doctrine of Discovery looked like on the ground. I contend that US settlers, including Anabaptist set-

---

*Devon Miller is the pastor of Florence Church of the Brethren Mennonite, which is located in what is now Southwest Michigan, a landscape that was inhabited by various Potawatomi bands when settlers first arrived in the early part of the nineteenth century. Devon is also a cabinetmaker and teaches courses related to cultural anthropology at Glen Oaks Community College and Goshen College.*

1 Francis Gardiner Davenport, ed., *European Treaties Bearing on the History of the United States and Its Dependencies to 1648* (Washington, DC: Carnegie Institution of Washington, 1917). This volume includes the papal bulls and other treaties that influenced and shaped early conceptions of the Doctrine of Discovery.

tlers, had little, if any, awareness of the formal theological and political decrees associated with the Doctrine of Discovery that drove settlement. Yet, it was the actions and everyday lives of these same settlers that brought the formal decrees issued by religious and political authorities into full maturity.

Key to this present research is the work of Tim Ingold,[2] a social anthropologist who challenges objective perspectives of landscape through a phenomenological approach he terms the "dwelling perspective." In the dwelling perspective, ontological conceptions of what it means to be human extend beyond the limits of the physical body to include non-human beings and places that humans interact with and inhabit. Using evidence from treaty negotiations between the US government and various Native American voices, I demonstrate the way in which the transformation of landscapes by settlers during the settlement period constituted acts of violence against Indigenous communities whose human ontologies were embedded within the landscape. This becomes an important consideration for contemporary Anabaptists when considering the role their ancestors played as key figures in the transformation of Indigenous landscapes, as well as what authentic reconciliation might look like.

## Background

Between the years 1789 and 1868, the Potawatomi Indians of the Great Lakes Region were party to an excess of forty treaties—far exceeding that of any tribe—by which they ceded much of their land to the United States government. The ratified terms of these treaties are readily available through various sources.[3] In retrospect, these documents appear to tell a story in which the Potawatomi either unwittingly gave up their land to the US government or were hoodwinked into doing so. Read this way, even with our best intentions in mind, the meta-narrative of the treaty-making process becomes one of commodification, greed, and thievery.

Plenty of evidence exists to support such views and is reinforced by the abstract language in which the treaties were written. For example, the 1821 Treaty of Chicago opens with this simple statement: "The Ottawa, Chippewa, and Pottawatomie, Nations of Indians cede to the United States government all the Land comprehended within the following boundaries."[4] The document

---

2 Tim Ingold, *The Perception of the Environment: Essays on Livelihood, Dwelling and Skill* (London and New York: Routledge, 2000).

3 George Emory Fay, *Treaties between the Potawatomi Tribes of Indians and the United States of America, 1789–1867* (Greely: Museum of Anthropology, University of Colorado, 1969); Charles J. Kappler, *Indian Treaties, 1778–1883* (New York: Interland, 1972); and United States, *United States Statutes at Large 7* (Boston: Little and Brown, 1848).

4 United States, "Articles of a Treaty Made and concluded at Chicago," August 29, 1821, *United States Statutes at Large 7* (Boston: Little and Brown, 1848): 218–21.

then proceeds to lay out the boundaries of the treaty, which encompass all of Southwest Michigan and a strip of land along the northeast border of Indiana, allowing certain reservations to be set aside for continued habitation by the Indians and for annual payments to be made to them. The treaty documents make no mention of the groundwork necessary to conclude the treaties, leaving the impression of a simple transfer of property.[5]

Such an assumption, however, leaves little room for the agency displayed in the negotiation of these treaties. Fortunately, other existing documents add texture to this story, and, at least in part, lend agency to the Indigenous communities involved in these treaty processes. Foremost among these documents are a collection referred to as *Documents relating to the negotiation of ratified and unratified treaties with various Indian Tribes,* held by the National Archives and Records Administration.[6] These documents contain the commissioners' journals of the proceedings, their reports to the war department, and other communication between the commissioners and other government officials detailing the negotiations of the treaties. Most importantly, for the purpose of this article, the journals contain speeches given by tribal leaders expressing their understanding of and desires for the land in question. It should be noted that these speeches have been filtered through the lenses of translators and the secretaries who acted as scribes. Nevertheless, they constitute a rich body of materials that are helpful in understanding the perspective of Indigenous peoples during the negotiations in which they ceded their lands.

Consequently, another aspect of the story emerges in which Indigenous peoples demonstrate their own agency, influencing the outcome of these negotiations. Out of these voices, it becomes evident that Indigenous leaders were aware of other factors at play in these negotiations besides the simple transfer of ownership, however fraudulent the treaties may have been.[7]

---

5 Though beyond the scope of this paper, it is worth noting that the interests, understandings, and strategies surrounding the treaties varied as greatly as the number of parties involved, both Native and non-Native. See Mark R. Schurr, "Archaeological Indices of Resistance: Diversity in the Removal Period Potawatomi of the Western Great Lakes," *American Antiquity* 75, no. 1 (2010): 44–60, and James M. McClurken, "Ottawa Adaptive Strategies to Indian Removal," *Michigan Historical Review* 12, no. 1 (Spring, 1996): 29–55.

6 National Record Service, National Archives Microcopy T 494 (Record Group 75), *Documents Related to the Negotiation of Ratified and Unratified Treaties with Various Tribes of Indians, 1801–1869* (Washington, DC: National Archives, 1801/1869), Roll 1.

7 The journals of these negotiations were transcribed from the National Archives Microcopy films while I was working as an ethnohistorical assistant for a firm, researching content related to the Forest County Potawatomi of Crandon, Wisconsin.

Again, I refer to the 1821 Treaty of Chicago, in which a large portion of Potawatomi lands in Southwest Michigan was ceded to the US government. The report, submitted by Commissioners Lewis Cass and Solomon Sibley, records the words of Metea, a leading spokesperson of the Potawatomi tribe, in the following manner:

> "Father [speaking to Cass],—Our country was given to us by the great spirit, who gave it to us to hunt upon—to make our cornfields upon—to dwell upon, and to make down our beds upon, when we die; and he would never forgive us should we now bargain it away. . . . We have given you a great tract of land already, but it is not enough to satisfy you. We sold it to you for the benefit of your white children, to farm, and to live upon. We have now but little left. We shall want it all ourselves. We know not how long we will live and we wish to leave some land for our children to hunt upon. You are gradually taking away the country which is our only inheritance. Treaty after treaty is called, and piece after piece is cut off from it. Neither are your children slow in taking possession of it. The ploughshare is driven through our tents before we have time to carry out our goods, and seek another habitation. We are growing uneasy. . . . I am an Indian—a red-skin, and live by hunting and by fishing, but my country is already too small, and I do not know how I shall bring up my children if I give it all away."[8]

For now, I want to focus on Metea's statement "The ploughshare is driven through our tents before we have time to carry out our goods, and seek another habitation." I will return to the rest of Metea's speech later on.

Raymond DeMallie,[9] an ethnohistorian of the Plains Sioux, warned scholars to be aware that when reading texts originating in unwritten languages, the temptation exists to understand them from within the reader's own context. Such a temptation presents itself when reading Metea's speech. Understood in Eurocentric terms, Metea expressed concern for the swiftness in which settlers were moving across the land, displacing the Potawatomi from their traditional homelands. However, Metea's earlier references to "dwell upon" and "habitation" indicate a deeper attachment to the land than can be explained by settler notions of property. Competing perceptions of the landscape persist into present-day society, perpetuating misunderstandings that give in to dominant Euro-American settler views, even in our attempts to reconcile.

---

8 "Journal of the Negotiations of the Treaty of August 29, 1821," National Archives Record Service, National Archives Microcopy T 494 (Record Group 75), *Documents Relating to the Negotiation of Ratified and Unratified Treaties with Various Tribes of Indians, 1801–1869* (Washington, DC: National Archives, 1801/1869): Roll 1.

9 Raymond J. DeMallie, "'These Have No Ears': Narrative and the Ethnohistorical Method," *Ethnohistory* 40, no. 4 (Autumn 1993): 515–38.

This paper contributes to the project of narrowing the gap between current understandings of the impact Euro-American settlers inflicted upon the Indigenous peoples and lands, and what actually happened.

## Violence

In 1969, Johan Galtung,[10] in laying out a roadmap to peace, took on the task of coming up with a clear definition of violence, since one aspect of defining peace included the absence of violence. Galtung defined violence as being "present when human beings are being influenced so that their actual somatic and mental realizations are below their potential realizations."[11] This definition was further characterized by the following distinctions: 1) physical versus psychological violence; 2) negative versus positive influences; 3) if there was an object that was harmed, causing indirect violence; 4) if there was an actor involved, leaving room for the possibility of structural violence; 5) whether the actions that caused the harm were intentional or not; and 6) manifest and latent, or unobservable violence.[12] According to Galtung's model, violence may be direct or indirect; it may be observable or unobservable; and it may be intended or unintended. These distinctions are helpful in understanding that violence may show up in unlikely places, especially when competing views of the world are at stake.

Later, Galtung added an additional element to his model of violence, which he called "cultural violence."[13] By this, he meant not violence inflicted against a culture but the way in which a culture legitimizes either personal or structural violence.

For Galtung, "ecological balance," which can be disrupted through "ecological degradation," is an important aspect of human existence.[14] Yet, even in Galtung's ecological degradation, there remains a dichotomy between humans and the environment, which stems from the Cartesian split between the mind and the body—a split that dominates Western ontologies of the human body. In such conceptions of the body, degradation of the environment affects humans only in an indirect and objective sense when the harm inflicted upon the environment impinges upon the physical, psychological, or social potential of an individual or group.

---

10 Johan Galtung, "Violence, Peace, and Peace Research," *Journal of Peace Research* 6, no. 3 (1969): 167–91.

11 Galtung, 168.

12 Galtung, 160–72.

13 Johan Galtung, "Cultural Violence," *Journal of Peace Research* 27, no. 3 (August 1990): 291–305.

14 Galtung, "Cultural Violence," 292.

Thus, we are left asking how Galtung's definition of violence would stack up against the claims made in Metea's speech. Would driving the plowshare through the tent be considered an act of violence? According to Galtung's definition, the act of plowing up Indigenous lands would be considered an indirect act of violence in that the object being harmed impinges upon Metea's potential realizations.

There is something lacking in this definition, however, that privileges Eurocentric understandings of the environment. In this dichotomy between humans and the environment, humans are only affected by the environment in an objective, indirect sense: when the environment is acted upon, the consequences affect the humans who live therein. In this view, land possesses spatial qualities, something that can be measured in terms of acres, sectioned off into neat geographical boundaries, and sold as private property, independent of human habitation. In Indigenous ways of thinking, however, human relationship is much more embedded in the environment than this. This is where Tim Ingold's[15] work becomes useful in considering the violent impact that settler agricultural practices had on Indigenous inhabitants.

## Dwelling Perspective

When Ingold conducted his research among hunter-gatherers of the circumpolar regions of Europe and North America, he noticed the interdependence of human and non-human beings' relationships within their environment. Consequently, he developed what he termed "a dwelling perspective"[16] of the way humans inhabit the world they live in. In this perspective, rather than simply residing in and building upon the environment that they live in, humans are continually shaped by and part of an ongoing story unfolding in a particular place. The landscape emerges through reciprocity between humans and their environment rather than simply as a result of the imposition of the human imagination upon the raw materials of nature. This differs from theories that see culture simply as a matter of the mind performed in thin air,[17] or which see culture inscribed upon the symbolic landscape that can be read as cultural texts.[18] In the dwelling perspective, culture becomes emplaced within a partic-

---

15 Ingold, *Perception of the Environment*.

16 Ingold, 5.

17 Setha M. Low and Denise Lawrence-Zúñiga, "Locating Culture," in *The Anthropology of Space and Place: Locating Culture*, eds. Setha M. Low and Denise Lawrence-Zúñiga (Malden: Blackwell, 2003), 1–47.

18 Denis E. Cosgrove, *Social Formation and Symbolic Landscape* (Madison, WI: The University of Wisconsin Press, 1998); Deryck W. Holdsworth, "Landscape and Archives as Texts," in *Understanding Ordinary Landscapes*, eds. Paul Groth and Todd W. Bressi

ular landscape so that over time humans embody specific ways of engaging the world in which they live, based on their environment.

The dwelling perspective departs from objective understandings of landscape that view the forms created by humans as symbols of the imagination growing out of Descartes's maxim "I think, therefore I am." According to Ingold, humans are always somewhere; they are never nowhere: "The landscape becomes part of us, just as we become part of the landscape."[19] In a sense, humans are clothed with their environment. The reciprocity between humans and the landscape is such that each is shaped by the other in an ongoing process of embodiment.

The primary concern for Ingold in favoring the process of embodiment over what he referred to as the "movement of *inscription*"[20] lies in the importance that Western thought has placed on form rather than process. The dwelling perspective focuses not on the forms within the landscape but on the processes through which forms emerge through the activities of dwelling. This process of embodiment that Ingold has in mind is rooted in and inspired by the phenomenology of Maurice Merleau-Ponty and Martin Heidegger, pushing back against the distinctions and limits created by traditional Western philosophy between not only the mind and body but also between the body and world, or nature.

By emphasizing processes and activities, Ingold added temporality to the spatial dimensions of landscape, but not in the abstract, quantitative sense. Instead, the dwelling perspective sees human activity in a particular place as the ongoing reciprocal exchange guided by the rhythms within the landscape through which the landscape is constantly being transformed and meaning is being generated. Such understandings of the relationship between humans and land are much more dynamic than the abstract conception of Eurocentric thought in which land is measured in terms of miles, sections, and acres and time is measured in terms of hours, days, months, and years. The body experiences the landscape in the rhythms and cycles of the landscape so that the younger generation is gradually incorporated into society, embodying the skills and knowledge needed to interact with the landscape. The body is continually between the past and the future, and the past informs the body how to behave in the future. Phenomenologists refer to this dance between the past and the future as "retention" and "protention."[21]

---

(New Haven, CT: Yale University Press, 1997), 44–55; Christopher Tilley, *A Phenomenology of Landscape: Places, Paths, and Monuments* (Oxford: Berg, 1994).

19 Ingold, *Perception of the Environment*, 191.

20 Ingold, 193.

21 David R. Cerbone, *Understanding Phenomenology* (Stocksfield, UK: Acumen, 2006).

Although I use the term "dance" somewhat metaphorically, in reality retention and protention are much like a dance. Dancers, if they have danced the dance before, get their cue from the music and their previous experience—retention—to know what their next step will be and where to place their foot—protention. Merleau-Ponty would credit this series of movements to the "habitual body,"[22] so that little thought is given to where one would step while being engaged with their partner. If the band suddenly disrupts the expected sequence of notes with the insertion of an unfamiliar line, the dancer likewise suddenly shifts to what Merleau-Ponty refers to as the "body of the moment."[23]

The body is suddenly brought back into focus, needing to improvise by interpreting the new lines in terms of its previous knowledge and experience. This awareness, or lack thereof, of the body in the world is what Merleau-Ponty calls "body schema"—that "bundle of skills and capacities that constitute the body's precognitive familiarity with itself and the world it inhabits."[24] Embodying relevant skills is necessary when navigating the world in which we live.

Merleau-Ponty was more interested in extending the body's experience to its surroundings than in prescribing its limits to the mind.[25] Western models of the body experience focus on stimuli entering the body through the nose, eyes, ears, mouth, or skin; these stimuli are then processed by the brain, giving the body a sense of its surroundings, which are completely separate from the body. To the contrary, Merleau-Ponty believed that the body was continually reaching out to and dependent on its surroundings. He argued that the body is continually taking its cue from the world and that those responses become a habitual part of the body's way of being-in-the-world.

To illustrate his point, Merleau-Ponty used the example of a blind person with a cane. The cane becomes an extension of the person, orienting them within the world in which they move, much like a baseball player's glove or an accomplished pianist's piano. In each case, the object becomes an extension of the person such that the person and object become entangled with each other, or the person is clothed with the object. The object becomes an essential part of the person's being. To strip away the cane, ball glove, or piano is to tear away the personhood of the blind person, the baseball player, or the pianist, respectively. Merleau-Ponty argued that humans are constantly engaged in similar ways with their entire environment.

---

22 Taylor Carman, "Merleau-Ponty and the Mystery of Perception," *Philosophy Compass* 4, no. 4 (2009): 220.

23 Carmen, 220.

24 Carmen, 200.

25 Maurice Merleau-Ponty, *Phenomenology of Perception*, trans. Colin Smith (London and New York: Routledge, 1962).

Ingold derived further inspiration for the dwelling perspective from Heidegger's essay "Building Dwelling Thinking,"[26] in which Heidegger set out to inquire into the nature of the housing crisis in Germany after World War II. Heidegger noticed that a dwelling had simply become a structure in which people lived. It did not necessarily mean that these dwellings were homes or that dwelling was taking place in them. The connection Heidegger was making between houses and homes is the connection Ingold is making between forms and processes and that Metea made between tent and habitation. In one, pre-eminence is given to houses and, in the other, to the process of making a home. All houses are forms, but not all houses are homes.

Heidegger attempted to breach this dichotomy by exploring the etymology of the words "dwelling" and "building." Understanding the philosophical difference Heidegger draws between dwelling and building is essential to understanding Ingold's dwelling perspective and is worth a foray into the etymological origins at this point.

The German words for building and dwelling are, respectively, *bauen* and *wohnen*. Heidegger explained that the Old High German word for *bauen* was *buan*, which meant *wohnen*—to remain or stay in a place, the same as the English word "dwelling." According to Heidegger, the original meaning of *bauen*, which was equivalent to *wohnen*, has been lost in the German language, but traces of it can be seen in words such as *Nachbar*, which, in English, is "neighbor"—literally "near dweller." The word *bauen* is the root for the German imperative word *bis*, or "to be," as in *ich bin*, or "I am," and *du bisht*, or "you are," so that, in essence, when someone says "I am" or "you are," they are really saying *ich wohne* and *du wohnst*, or "I dwell" and "you dwell." Thus, when Metea stated, "I am an Indian . . . I live by hunting and fishing," he was saying what it meant to be a Potawatomi Indian. To take those things away from him is to destroy his being.

In its current use, the word *bauen* still means "to build" and "to cultivate"—activities performed, as Heidegger suggested, not alongside of *wohnen* but comprising *wohnen*. So, "to build" and "to cultivate" is "to dwell" or "to be," which gets us to what philosophers, and, of late, anthropologists, refer to as being-in-the-world. But before I go there, I want to back up and address the other half of Heidegger's etymological endeavor, which, unfortunately, Ingold neglected to pursue but which reflects heavily on the idea of dwelling and of culture in general.

While Ingold spent a great deal of time aligning himself with the notion that building is at the same time dwelling, he skipped over the second part of the

26 Martin Heidegger, "Building Dwelling Thinking," in *Poetry, Language, Thought,* trans. Albert Hofstadter (New York: Harper Colophon, 2001), 201–30.

*bauen* and *wohnen* duo. What Heidegger meant by "to build, is really to dwell"[27] makes sense only when understanding what he meant by *wohnen*. And he did not disappoint in this regard as he embarked on a separate but less familiar etymology of the word. Heidegger pointed out that while both *bauen* and *wohnen* have the sense of staying in a place, or remaining—similar to the English word "dwelling"—*wohnen* adds more clearly the experience of remaining in a place. The origins of the German word *wohnen* trace back to the Gothic word *wunian*, which, according to Heidegger, means "to be at peace, to be brought to peace, to remain in peace."[28] It is worth quoting Heidegger in this regard to get the full sense of what he understands dwelling to consist of:

> The word for peace, *Friede*, means the free, *das Frye*; and *fry* means preserved from harm and danger, preserved from something, safeguarded. To free actually means to spare. The sparing itself consists not only in the fact that we do not harm the one whom we spare. Real sparing is something *positive* and it takes place when we leave something beforehand in its own essence, when we return it specifically to its essential being, when we "free" it in the proper sense of the word into a preserve of peace. To dwell, to be set at peace, means to remain at peace within the free, the preserve, the free sphere that safeguards each thing in its essence. *The fundamental character of dwelling is this sparing*. It pervades dwelling in its whole range. That range reveals itself to us as soon as we recall that human being consists in dwelling and, indeed, dwelling in the sense of the stay of mortals on the earth.[29]

I return to Heidegger's being-in-the-world, which he intended to be descriptive of human existence. In his earlier work "Being and Time,"[30] Heidegger parsed out what human existence on earth consists of based on his understanding of the German word *Dasien*, or "being there."[31] In brief, for humans to be on earth they need to be somewhere, and they arrange their world according to their way of being-in-the-world, whether as a farmer, scholar, shopkeeper, seamstress, hunter, or fisherman. Yet being-in-the-world is not just about the activities such as the cultivation and building in *bauen*; it is the caring as shown in the *wohnen* of Heidegger's being. Some have suggested that the phrase term "being-in-the-world" could be more accurately expressed as "being-well-in-the-

---

27 Heidegger, 349.

28 Heidegger, 351.

29 Heidegger, 351. Italics in original.

30 Martin Heidegger, *Being and Time*, trans. Joan Stambaugh (Albany, NY: State University of New York Press, 1996).

31 Heidegger, 13.

world."[32] In this way, the focus goes beyond the activity to include the quality of human existence in relation to the surrounding world—that is, other people, the land, plants, animals, and other ontological distinctions made by individuals or groups.

Although Indigenous scholars and theorists have not always expressed their work in these terms, they have brought increased awareness of their relationship to the world in ways that align with Ingold's dwelling perspective. A leading proponent in this regard has been the Potawatomi biologist Robin Kimmerer.[33] Kimmerer's popular work brings attention to human beings' relationship with non-human beings, such as soil, bees, plants, birds, the sky, and animals. She calls for reciprocity between humans and their non-human relatives, knowing that disruption of the cycles of giving and receiving, brought on by settler colonialism, leads to human and ecological harms.

In their article "Muskrat Theories, Tobacco in the Streets, and Living Chicago as Indigenous Land," Megan Bang et al.,[34] Indigenous scholars working in Chicago, root Indigenous knowledge in the land. In other words, the land teaches the people how to be in the world. Bang et al.'s Indigenous reimagination turned Descartes's ontological "I think, therefore I am" upside down to become "Land is, therefore we are."[35] The land becomes the basis for knowing how to live in the world and informs the people as a whole, not just the individual. Such processes help incorporate the younger generation into society, as Ingold has in mind.

Kyle Whyte, a Citizen Potawatomi environmental philosopher, refers to this transference of knowledge as "collective continuance."[36] Whyte argues that rather than being distinct from each other, human institutions such as politics, religion, food systems, kinship, and so forth are interrelated and that disrupting one of them adversely affects each of the others. Using the example of the Karuk

---

32 Jonas Holst, "Rethinking Dwelling and Building: On Heidegger's Conception of Being as Dwelling and Jørn Uzton's Architecture of Well-being," *Journal of Interdisciplinary Studies in Architecture and Urbanism* 2 (2013): 52–60.

33 See, for example, Robin Kimmerer, "Returning the Gift," *Minding Nature* 7, no. 2 (2014): 18–24.

34 Megan Bang et al., "Muskrat Theories, Tobacco in the Streets, and Living Chicago as Indigenous Land," *Environmental Education Research* 20, no. 1 (2014): 37–55.

35 Bang et al., 46.

36 See Kyle Powys Whyte, "Indigenous Food Systems, Environmental Justice, and Settler-Industrial States," in *Global Food, Global Justice: Essays on Eating under Globalization*, eds. Mary C. Rawlinson and Caleb Ward (Cambridge: Cambridge Scholars Publishing, 2015); and Kyle Powys Whyte, "Food Sovereignty, Justice, and Indigenous Peoples: An Essay on Settler Colonialism and Collective Continuance," in *Oxford Handbook on Food Ethics*, eds. Anne Barnhill et. al (Oxford: Oxford University Press, 2017), 345–66.

of the Pacific Northwest, whose society is centered around and depends on the salmon, Whyte spells out the effect that colonialism has upon such societies when the salmon population becomes decimated, adversely affecting their food system. The salmon clothes the relationships of those societies, and when the salmon is stripped away by dominant settler colonial actions, collective continuance is disrupted and relationships of trust between people and their environment are destroyed.

The same could be said about the extermination of buffalo on the Great Plains. Danielle Taschereau Mamers[37] reasons that the extermination of buffalo herds led to the collapse of entire societies that depended on their relationship with the buffalo for survival. In many cases, such societies were literally clothed with the buffalo. Indeed, much of their material culture was derived from their relationship of trust with the buffalo. Taschereau Mamers argues that such processes that reordered relationships between humans and the non-human world are sites of violence to be reckoned with within the settler colonial project.

The works of these contemporary scholars demonstrate the differences between Indigenous and settler perspectives of human relationships with the non-human world. The views of these Indigenous scholars echo Ingold's dwelling perspective in which humans live in and are dependent on a world of reciprocal relations with land and beings around them. Yet, one may ask, are these simply responses or reactions to the current political climate, or are these the result of collective continuance being upheld by Indigenous communities? Fortunately, we have access to the words of Indigenous leaders during the settlement period and how they viewed their relationship with the land.

The speech Metea made to Commissioners Cass and Sibley, mentioned earlier in this article, is one example. Metea addressed the commissioners with what it meant for his people to "dwell upon" the land. The land was not something to be sold; it was where his people were born, where they hunted, where they fished, where they farmed, and where they would die and be buried. It was given to them by the Great Spirit, who left them to care for it. Without the land, they would not even know how to bring up their children. The tent destroyed by the plowshare was more than just a house; it was a form that had emerged from the process of being "an Indian—a red-skin [who] lives by hunting and fishing."[38] Disrupting even one of these relationships of what it meant for the Potawatomi to dwell in this particular place violently disrupted all aspects of Potawatomi life.

---

37 Danielle Taschereau Mamers, "Human-Bison Relations as Sites of Settler Colonial Violence and Decolonial Resurgence," *Humanimalia: A Journal of Human/Animal Interface Studies* 10, no. 2 (Spring 2019): 10–41.

38 "Negotiations of the Treaty of August 29, 1821."

Elsewhere I have written about a speech made by Largo,[39] a Miami head-man, to Lewis Cass during the negotiations of the 1826 Treaty of Mississinewa.[40] I bring his speech up here again because of the awareness Largo expressed in terms of his people's relationship to the land and the soil. Largo, in response to the commissioner's promise that the Miami and Potawatomi would have access to better lands in Kansas if they agreed to sell and move from their lands in Northern Indiana, told the commissioner:

> "Father, when you collected us here, you pointed to us a country, which you said would be better for us where we could live. You said we could not stay here. We would perish. But what will destroy us? It is yourselves destroying us for you make the spiritous liquor. You speak to us with deceitful lips, and not from your hearts. It seems to me. You trampled on our soil and drove it away. Before you came, the game was plenty, but you drove it away. The Great Spirit made us red skins, and the soil he put us on is red, the color of our skins. You came from a country where the soil is white, the color of your skin. You point to a country for us in the west, where there is game. We saw there is game, but the Great Spirit made and put men there who have a right to that game and it is not ours."[41]

Largo mentioned three things that would harm his people: 1) deceitful promises, 2) spiritous liquor, and 3) trampling their land and driving away the game. According to Galtung's definition, only one of these destructive forces, liquor, would fall into the category of somatic harm. The deceitful lips would be a breach of trust and relationship. The third involved the Miami's relationship with the land. More than simply a pattern of subsistence, though that is certainly part of it, the people's relationship with the land, as Largo understood it, was being entangled and clothed in the soil. Their very being grew out of the land. He expressed this as their skin being the color of the soil. To read Lar-

---

39 The original article that this quote appeared in credited this quote, which spanned two pages, to Awbenawben, a Potawatomi headman. In that article, the author followed the numbered sequencing of the pages as found in the microfilm from which the notes to the negotiations were transcribed. Upon closer reading, it was discovered that the pages had been numbered out of sequence, and when placed in their proper order, the quote actually belonged to Largo.

40 D. Ezra Miller, "'But It Is Nothing Except Woods': Amish Mennonites on a Northern Indiana Settlerscape," in *Rooted and Grounded: Essays on Land and Christian Discipleship*, eds. Janeen Bertsche Johnson and Ryan Dallas Harker (Eugene, OR: Wipf and Stock, 2016), 208–17.

41 "Journals of the Negotiations of the Treaty of October 23, 1826," National Archives Record Service, National Archives microcopy T 494 (record group 75), *Documents Relating to the Negotiations of Ratified and Unratified Treaties with Various Tribes of Indians, 1801–1869*, (Washington, DC: National Archives, 1801/1869), Roll 1.

go's comments as though he were addressing matters of race would be to read his words from within a Western context, overlooking his people's relationship with the land, the responsibilities they felt toward it, and the rights they claimed in connection with it.

Another example of the differences between Indigenous and settler perspectives of human relationships with the non-human world, and perhaps even clearer, appears in a context geographically removed from the Potawatomi and Miami of the 1820s. During the 1870s, as the US government was trying to gather the Nez Perce onto reservations in the Pacific Northwest, the US General O. O. Howard met with headmen from the Nez Perce—including Chief Joseph, Ollokot, and Toohoolhoolzote—on several occasions to try to convince them to move their people, horses, and cattle onto the Nez Perce reservation. When Howard asked Joseph to give up his people's lands, he was impressed with the depth of Joseph's answer: "The Creative Power, when he made the earth, made no marks, no lines of division or separation. The earth was his mother. He was made of the earth and grew up on its bosom."[42]

The Nez Perce's response to Howard's request to give up their land is full of such replies. It was unthinkable that the belly of their mother, the Earth, should be ripped open by the hoe and plow. Such violence would only lead to the Nez Perce being separated from the lands they had inherited from their fathers. Howard told the Nez Perce leaders that calling the earth their mother was nonsense. No words are more poignant than those of the old headman Toohoolhoolzote in response to Howard's insult: "You white people get together, measure the earth, and then divide it . . . Part of the Indians gave up their land. I never did. The earth is part of my body, and I will never give up the earth."[43]

Even though such statements of various Indigenous peoples are separated by time, distance, and culture, when pieced together they begin to paint a picture of an Indigenous ontology that is distinct from that of Euro-Americans wishing to settle on Native lands. A letter from the same time period, written by an Anabaptist settler eying land to settle upon, helps draw those distinctions even more clearly.

Writing to kin back in Europe in 1839, Friedrich Hage, an Amish elder, provided a spatialized description of the land to the west of his home in Holmes County, Ohio, in anticipation of further settlement by Amish Mennonites. In his letter,[44] Hage gauged the land in terms of "two to three hundred hours dis-

---

42 Alvin M. Josephy, Jr., *The Nez Perce Indians and the Opening of the Northwest* (Boston and New York: Houghton Mifflin, 1965), 487–88.

43 Josephy, 503.

44 Friedrich Hage Collection, HM1-919SC, Mennonite Church USA Archives-Goshen (Goshen, Indiana, 1819–1997), File 7.

tance in one piece,"[45] an hour being the distance a man could walk in one hour, considered to be approximately three miles. According to this formula, the land Hage was describing included the balance of Ohio, the entire states of Illinois and Indiana, and parts of Iowa, Michigan, and Wisconsin—in essence, what had earlier made up the Old Northwest. The land, as Hage put it, had been "purchased from the Indians or wild people"[46] by the US government. By the time Hage wrote his letter, the land had undergone the scrutiny of the chains and links of the deputy surveyors and could be purchased "cheaply from [the US] government, a dollar and a quarter or two florins, fifty-seven kroners an acre."[47] The land was further gutted of any meaning through Hage's spatialized representation of these vast lands as being "nothing but woods."[48]

## Discussion

The plowshare has long been a symbol of peace for Anabaptist groups. Tilling the soil in the hinterlands of North America far removed from threats of political involvement was seen as an opportunity for Anabaptists to live out God's mandate for humans, peacefully and undisturbed. Such views are based on passages found in Isaiah's vision of a kingdom in which God's reign will cover the earth and people will "beat their swords into plowshares, and their spears into pruning hooks" (Is 2:4, NRSV). Unwittingly, the very object thought to bring peace inflicted violence upon the people of the land. The plowshare became the preferred weapon of settler colonialism.

Any attempts of reconciliation or decolonization by settlers that deal solely with the return of land to Indigenous communities serve only to perpetuate the settler colonial project. One way of working at this, as Bang et al. suggest, is through "the role of naming in learning and the ways in which naming is a site at which issues with reference between Western and Indigenous epistemologies unfold."[49] When the wrongs of settler colonialism are addressed by settler societies, for instance, even by those who wish to repair those wrongs, the harm is often spoken of in terms of land that was taken from Indigenous people and that needs to be returned. Such language perpetuates Western spatialized notions about the land. Decolonizing requires a decolonizing of the language used to discuss matters regarding reconciliation and reparations. The harms caused by the intrusion of settlers upon Native lands involved much more than deception and theft of property. When seen through the lenses of Ingold's dwelling

---

45 Hage Collection.

46 Hage Collection.

47 Hage Collection.

48 Hage Collection.

49 Bang et al., "Muskrat Theories," 13.

perspective and Native peoples' own understanding of their relationship with the land, plowing lands inhabited by Indigenous peoples must be understood as a violent act against Native personhood.

Another form in which meaningful and authentic reconciliation might take shape, keeping in mind that the land and culture are inextricably intertwined, may include collaboration with local Indigenous communities in caring for particular pieces of land. Let me explain.

In a fascinating essay called "Chief Williams v. the City of Chicago, et al: Making a Claim to the Chicago Lakefront," John Low[50] argues the validity of "The Sandbar Case" that was brought before the Supreme Court in 1914. Low, a member of the Pokagon Band of Potawatomi in Southwestern Michigan, has been a tribal lawyer for his band since the early 1980s. The case argued that all of the Chicago lakefront between the famous Michigan Avenue and the present lakeshore belonged to the Potawatomi. The reasoning behind this claim was that all that land was backfilled after the great Chicago fire. Furthermore, the Potawatomi never ceded the lakebed to the United States, so neither the City of Chicago nor the State of Illinois had a right to claim that land. In the end, though it must have made them squirm to do so, the Supreme Court rejected the argument, based on their claim that the Indians had "abandoned" the lake.

Low, not satisfied with the court's decision nearly one hundred years earlier, made it his project to discover the legal basis of the claim the Potawatomi had made. Using precedents derived from the Doctrine of Discovery, treaty laws set in place by the US government, and details from actual treaties between the United States and the Potawatomi, Low makes a compelling argument that Lake Michigan was never ceded to the United States. As part of his argument, he cites treaties in which portions of Lake Erie, Lake Superior, and the St. Clair River near Detroit were ceded by tribes to the United States. However, in all the treaties involving Chicago, the boundary specifically terminated at the lakeshore, which at that time was west of Michigan Avenue and the Gold Coast. Therefore, the valuable real estate along Chicago's lakeshore is built on sovereign Potawatomi territory.

Low is writing his article amid the debate of what should happen with the tiny airport known as Meig's Field, which is built into the lake; the question of whether water from Lake Michigan should be piped to regions in the country that lack water; and how to manage fishing rights on the lake. Recognizing the improbability of these lands being returned to the Potawatomi, he suggests ways that might offer imaginative courses of reconciliation for settler and Native communities moving forward—ways that would honor the dwelling perspec-

---

50 John Low, "Chief Williams v. the City of Chicago, et al: Making a Claim to the Chicago Lakefront," in *Native Chicago*, 2nd ed., ed. Terry Straus (Albatross, 2002), 383–98.

tive of landscape and culture put forth by Ingold. Low writes concerning the closing of places like Meig's Field and other resources:

> One can imagine development for cultural opportunities, such as a Museum of Indigenous Peoples, set as an appropriate counterpart to the nearby Field Museum. Perhaps there would also be opportunity for some kind of development for recreation, consistent with the city's overall lakefront park system. Important too would be the inclusion of the Chicago American Indian community of today, now very intertribal, into any planning and development of Northerly Island and Meig's Field.
>
> Just as important, if the Potawatomi were included in discussions about the management of Lake Michigan, one can imagine Tribal EPA's [sic] working alongside their non-Native counterparts to insure the proper regulations and use of these most precious liquid resources. One can easily assert that it is important and appropriate that the Potawatomi, whose traditions include a particular reverence and respect for the environment, be given a voice in the discussions about the future of Lake Michigan.[51]

In the end, Low resists insisting upon the Chicago lakefront being returned. Instead, he makes a plea that the Potawatomi's voice be heard in caring for the land and the lake, leaving room for imagination to take hold.

What if settlers possessing land would partner with local Native communities in managing those lands? What if farmers were to "tithe" a part of their land for the purpose of habitat restoration, managed in partnership with Native communities? Even settlers with small plots of land might explore ways to partner with Native communities to care for their land.

If Ingold's dwelling perspective is to hold any sway in broadening Galtung's definition of violence, then we are left with saying that the plowshares of Euro-American settlers were doing more than just tilling the land. Were they doing any less harm than the sword of the US government? Does it matter whether their intentions were malicious or not? If we listen to the voices of the leading spokesmen of the Miami, Potawatomi, Nez Perce, and contemporary Indigenous scholars, it is quite clear that the plowshare had chased their game away, supplanted their corn fields, and torn up the graves of their ancestors. Their way of being-in-the-world had been destroyed, or as Galtung might put it, the plowshare had become "the cause of the difference between the potential and the actual, between what could have been and what is,"[52] his very definition of violence.

However, the dwelling perspective does not stop at this naming of violence; it also offers us ways to think about reconciliation that go beyond the simple,

---

51 Low, 397.

52 Galtung, "Violence, Peace, and Peace Research," 169.

though perhaps impossible, return of land. Reconciliation, if it is to be authentic, will need to be built around partnerships and friendships, not simple economic exchange. Land that has been contested in the past might hold the means of bringing people together in the future, if we are willing.

# Whose Land Is It?

David Rensberger

## Genesis 3:14–19; Psalm 104:14–15, 20–23, 27–30; Mark 4:26–29

Years ago, my family took my mother back to Northern Indiana to visit the places she had known as a child and record her memories on video. At one point, my daughter, then in her early twenties, asked me how Mennonite farmers had dealt with acquiring land that the US government had taken from native people by force of arms. I didn't really have an answer. Truthfully, I was a little afraid of what the answer might be.

I recalled this conversation in 2017 while preparing a sermon for Land Sunday during the Season of Creation at Atlanta Mennonite Fellowship (Decatur, GA). This new liturgical season, originating in Australia, is meant to encourage celebration of God as Creator, to recognize the biblical theme of humans worshiping alongside other creatures, and to invite ethical living on earth as creatures within the creation.[1] The season, which occurs in September, has three rotating series of four weekly themes. In Series A (2017, 2020, etc.), the themes are Forest, Land, Wilderness/Outback, and River.

Marking the Season of Creation in the United States raises fundamental questions about the earth. To whom does it belong? How is it that "earth" created by God became "land" under human control? Preaching on Land Sunday immediately after Forest Sunday, I realized that the sequence reflected my own experience and the experience of many Mennonites in the Americas. *Forest gives way to land:* great forests are divided up into plots of land and sold to pioneers, who cut down the forests and farm the land. In this way, "earth" itself—the ground, the soil that simply exists as part of creation—also becomes "land" available for private ownership and exploitation.

To make this understanding of land clearer, let me quote one of my favorite sayings on the subject. It comes from Ambrose Bierce, a journalist and literary critic of the late nineteenth and early twentieth centuries, who had an eloquent

*David Rensberger is retired from teaching New Testament at the Interdenominational Theological Center in Atlanta and continues to research and write. He is a member of the Atlanta Mennonite Fellowship.*

1 The original Australian Website is https://seasonofcreation.com/. An American Website has been created more recently: http://www.letallcreationpraise.org/united-states-ecumenical/.

but acid tongue and a deep skepticism about most social institutions and conventions (including religious ones). In his collection of satirical definitions titled *The Devil's Dictionary*, Bierce defined land as "a part of the earth's surface, considered as property. The theory that land is property subject to private ownership and control is the foundation of modern society, and is eminently worthy of the superstructure."[2] That is to say, if society is filled with selfishness and violence, we can trace these evils back to the idea of turning the planet, which is common to all that lives, into "land" as a personal enclave to be endlessly enhanced, defended, and exploited. Throughout this reflection, I use "land" in something like this sense, not meaning it as a technical or scientific definition but simply wanting to contrast the soil or ground as it exists in nature with the same soil put to human use. Forests, prairies, wetlands, and other ecosystems have all, in various times and places, been turned into "land."

My wife and I both grew up on very productive farmland in Elkhart County, Indiana. But where did this land come from? The state seal of Indiana tells an interesting story about that. It shows a man chopping down trees with an ax while a buffalo jumps over a fallen trunk and flees the scene.[3] It quite literally portrays the conversion of forest to land. Hoosiers have always been clear about this. Late nineteenth-century historian William Hayden English, discussing an earlier version of the seal, wrote that it was meant "to forcibly express the idea that a wild and savage condition is to be superseded by a higher and better civilization. The wilderness and its dangerous denizens of reptiles, Indians and wild beasts, are to disappear before the ax and rifle of the ever-advancing western pioneer, with his . . . restless and aggressive civilization."[4] The process of transforming earth and forest into land was certainly "restless and aggressive"; whether the result was always "higher and better" may be debated. At any rate, the naked, dehumanizing racism that placed "Indians" in a category between reptiles and wild beasts is a grotesque reminder of how this history was written and learned in the nineteenth and twentieth centuries.

Where do Mennonites fit into this "restless and aggressive" process? In 2015, students and faculty from the Anabaptist Mennonite Biblical Seminary went on a nine–day journey following the "Trail of Death" along which the

---

2 Ambrose Bierce, *The Devil's Dictionary* (New York: Neale, 1911; repr. New York: Dover, 1958), 74, http://www.thedevilsdictionary.com/?l=#LAND_.

3 See Pamela J. Bennett and Alan January, "Indiana's State Seal—An Overview," Indiana Historical Bureau, State of Indiana (January 21, 2005), http://www.in.gov/history/2804.htm.

4 *Conquest of the Country Northwest of the River Ohio 1778-1783; and life of Gen. George Rogers Clark*, 2 vols (Indianapolis, IN: Bowen-Merrill, 1896), vol. 2, 774, https://babel.hathitrust.org/cgi/pt?id=yale.39002002554062&view=1up&seq=192. See also Bennett and January, "Indiana's State Seal—An Overview."

Potawatomi people of Northern Indiana were exiled from their homeland in the fall of 1838.[5] This tragedy took place just a few months before Mennonite settlers began arriving in the area. Around the time my father died in 1990, somebody looking through old papers found a land grant for property in Elkhart County signed by Martin Van Buren, who was President in 1838. This document brings the Trail of Death unbearably close to home for me. Mennonites came to America seeking freedom from persecution. Already famous in Europe for farming unfarmable land, they were willingly given land in what was then the West, and they willingly accepted it. By participating in this restless and aggressive act of civilizing, even the "quiet in the land," who had renounced violence as disciples of Jesus, could not help being tainted by what was done to provide a safe haven for them.

How can this history be redeemed? Can land become earth again? Can wrongs committed so long ago, now so thoroughly woven into culture and law, be repented, redeemed, or undone? Luke Gascho, writing in *The Mennonite*, offers some pointers. He relates his own history of working land taken unjustly from Ojibwe and Potawatomi peoples and his determination to take part in the work of undoing these wrongs. Gascho lives on part of the very land that one of my ancestors, Bolser Hess, laid claim to once its inhabitants had been brutally expelled. Unlike me, Gascho continues to be directly engaged with that soil, tilling his extensive garden and, until recently, serving as executive director of Goshen (Indiana) College's Merry Lea Environmental Learning Center. In this engagement, he has found a balance between the labor he puts in and the soil's own productivity; and he has looked to the biblical affirmation that Christ is the Creator as well as the Reconciler and Sustainer of all the created world (Col 1:15–21).[6] By these means, Gascho is pointing the way toward living with and within the creation, not against it.

The Season of Creation's Scripture texts offer another spiritual resource for this way of living. One of these texts for Land Sunday is Genesis 3:14–19. We tend to think of the events in that story as a curse on humanity following the fall; but the Bible doesn't actually speak of a "fall," and it is the snake and the ground who are literally cursed, not the humans. Yet why should the ground be cursed? Nothing that happened there was the fault of the earth! The "curse" means only that things the ground once easily gave to human beings now have to be wrenched from it by force. As with the forest of Indiana, created ground in

---

5 The course has continued to be offered in subsequent years: "Trail of Death: A Pilgrimage of Remembrance, Lament and Transformation," Anabaptist Mennonite Biblical Seminary, https://www.ambs.edu/academics/trail-of-death. See also http://www.potawatomi-tda.org/ptodhist.htm.

6 Luke Gascho, "Tilling Soil on Stolen Land," *The Mennonite*, May 2019, 10–12, https://themennonite.org/feature/tilling-soil-stolen-land/.

Genesis is transformed into agricultural land that must be worked. This is called a curse for the ground, but in the Genesis text only humans feel the effects. As one who has dug thistles out of cow pastures, I've experienced those effects myself (and maybe done a little cursing of my own). Yet thorns and thistles are a blessing for creatures that eat wild berries and seeds. The viewpoint in Genesis 3 is strongly human-centered: something must have gone wrong with the earth, because food no longer drops into our hands as it did in Paradise.

At the very beginning of the story of human relationships with the earth and with God, we find failure and bad consequences, a fracturing of the connection people have with the earth and other creatures. Elsewhere in the Bible, though, different perspectives emerge.[7] Psalm 104, for instance, has a considerably more benign view of the land and how people relate to its productivity than we find in Genesis 3. It is not sweating humans but God who causes plants to grow, in order "to bring forth food from the earth."[8] Wine and oil and bread, things that bring gladness and sustenance, come from the Creator's beneficence. People, like all other creatures, "look to [God] to give them their food in due season." At sunrise, "People go out to their work and to their labor until the evening"; at night, the animals go "seeking their food from God." Labor to gain sustenance is a requirement, as in Genesis, for both humans and animals. Yet, it is not seen as a curse but rather as part of the natural order overseen by God. Lions must hunt and humans must till the soil, but it is all part of seeking food from God. Creation relies on the Creator; for all their labor, humans do not become self-sustaining but remain dependent on God.

This mixed view of labor and sustenance shows up again in Jesus's parable of the Growing Seed in Mark 4. The farmer must go out and sow when it's planting time and must grab the sickle and get going again at harvest time. But in between, farmers have little control. They may weed or do pest control, irrigate or fertilize, but they can't control the weather, and they can't actually *make* the crop grow. Through this parable, Jesus taught his disciples that while they participated in God's Reign, they were not responsible for its success. We plant seeds, and we go into action when they bear fruit. But we can't control the direction or rate or quantity of growth. Like farmers, we must simply rely on God, with all the vulnerability that that entails.

Where can we find hope, both for the earth-become-land and for ourselves? One kind of hope for the earth can be recognized, rather grimly, in the fact that earth can get along just fine without us, but we can't get along without it. The damage we have inflicted on the environment over the past couple of centuries is coming home to roost, in flood and landslide, fire and famine. Ultimately, the

---

7 For my sermon, while I retained Genesis 3, I chose passages from Psalm 104 and the Gospel of Mark in place of the original Season of Creation selections.

8 Scripture quotations are from the New Revised Standard Version.

accounts must be balanced, whatever the consequences for human beings. Any hope for us cannot possibly lie in greater human control over earth. Instead, we must learn from those scriptures and other sources how to move from a stance of restlessness and aggression, autonomy and control, to a stance of creaturely vulnerability and reliance on God.

For one thing, we can listen to cultures, including America's First Nations, who have retained a better understanding of how to live in cooperation with earth rather than as its despot. From the scriptures we can learn to balance Genesis 1:28 with Psalms 104 and 148 and other texts. We must also remember that the Bible itself is rooted in "Indigenous" agrarian societies, not in post-Enlightenment Western culture. This listening to Indigenous peoples, both American and biblical, will be a humble and a humbling process, an act of repentance. Part of this path of hope is to accept our dependency, to be willingly vulnerable within the creation and before the Creator. If we can learn again to live within creation as the humans do in Psalm 104, rather than trying to live against our creatureliness like the humans in Genesis 3, we can hope to regain the balance of work and dependence that long characterized human life. Looking back to earlier, pre-Industrial Age Western societies might also help in this transformation.

All this runs right against the grain of the modern West, with our obsessive quest for control and efficiency, and our conviction that we alone knows what is best and true. Listening to people outside our own circle of certainty; accepting the reality of our identity as creatures rather than as creation's lords; being willing to waste time in inefficient practices like prayer and art—all this and more boils down to a colossal act of cultural and spiritual repentance.

To put it in terms of mission: we must take up a mission *to ourselves*. It is time to preach the gospel to ourselves, the gospel of the Christ who is "gentle and humble in heart" (Matt 11:29), the antithesis of the "restless and aggressive civilization" that we have cherished. This is the genius of the Anabaptist Reformation, to recognize that it is not enough to reshape the rituals and creeds that tie Christianity to a society that fails to embody the intentions of Jesus and his apostles. Rather, a church embedded in a "restless and aggressive civilization," land-rich but earth-impoverishing, needs to hear its own gospel all over again. Besides this mission to ourselves, could our repentance make us humble enough to accept a mission from the Potawatomi, the Hmong, the Hausa? What might they have to teach us about living as creatures among other cherished creatures of the one Creator?

Such a radical reformation begins in spiritual "re-formation," in rereading Scripture, relearning prayer, reacquainting ourselves with our own connections with God, God's children, and all God's creatures. But it must continue in new patterns of action. Gascho lays out a couple of examples of such patterns for people who still benefit from the transmutation of stolen earth into tilled land. One of these is the work of the Dismantling the Doctrine of Discovery Coalition. This group, operating in the Anabaptist spirit of love for neighbors and restoring relationships through active nonviolence, focuses on undoing the philosophical and legal framework by which European Christendom granted itself the specious right to conquer Indigenous peoples and dispossess them of their homelands.[9]

Secondly, Gascho is one of the leaders of the Mennonite Creation Care Network (MCCN). MCCN encourages the church to rediscover the Christian basis for taking care of creation, with its network of ties among creatures and the Creator; to confess what we have done wrong, both to the earth and to our human neighbors; and to put our repentance into action by restoring the planet.[10]

No one who becomes aware of these wrongs can hope to put them right all alone. An overly individualistic view of confession, repentance, and conversion has historically kept Christianity caught up in massive societal and *structural* sins. Each of us must work personally to reduce our negative impact on the earth, in the ways that we live and work, shop and drive. But movements and organizations such as those just mentioned can take us beyond individual action to participation in wider communities of redemption. As Episcopalian spiritual director Robert Morris writes, "The story is not about us; we are about the larger story of God's love for all of creation."[11]

Exactly how and why Mennonites, as much as any other settlers, took part in the transformation of created earth to owned land is for historians to answer. Yet we can see enough of that history—often in our own family stories—to realize our need to hold ourselves open to its reality and to seek a way toward its redemption. In order to do that, we must ask with real humility, "Whose land is it? To whom does the earth belong?"

---

9 See Dismantling the Doctrine of Discovery: A Movement of the Anabaptist People of Faith, https://dofdmenno.org/about/.

10 See Mennonite Creation Care Network, https://mennocreationcare.org/about/.

11 Robert Morris, "Faithfulness, Grace, and Growth," in *The Upper Room Disciplines 2020* (Nashville: Upper Room, 2019), 249.

# A Community of Creation,
# A Calling to Friendship

A Conversation between Steve Heinrichs and Adrian Jacobs

*On a sunny afternoon in Winnipeg, Steve Heinrichs and Adrian Jacobs shared a beer as they discussed the question of land reparations. Adrian is Cayuga of the Haudenosaunee Confederacy, and Keeper of the Circle for the Sandy-Saulteaux Spiritual Centre in Beausejour, Manitoba. Steve is a second-generation Settler, and Director of Indigenous-Settler Relations for Mennonite Church Canada. What follows is an excerpt of their conversation.*

**STEVE:** In 1993, the Canadian government initiated the *Royal Commission on Aboriginal Peoples (RCAP)*, the most significant inquiry into the fractured Indigenous-Settler relationship. The result was a massive five-volume report with over four hundred recommendations for justice and healing. And at the heart of those recommendations was a radical call—a call for the redistribution of land. Indigenous peoples needed enough land to secure their economic self-reliance, and they also needed land to provide for their spiritual and cultural needs. Many churches got on board and championed this Jubilee vision. But years later, very little has changed. Does this call still resonate?

**ADRIAN:** My experience of traditional people is that our values have allowed our people to adjust to the realities that we currently face. So even in the light of colonial imposition, where lands like the Dish with One Spoon territory of Southern Ontario are divided by borders and separated by the dotted and hard lines of Settler maps and laws . . . we still find ways to honor our connections, our relations, and our responsibilities to our homelands.

I think about an experience from my childhood. At Six Nations, surveyors were doing work for the Canadian Gypsum Company in order to exploit the mineral that was underneath our reserve. As little kids, we would see the surveyors go out and pound these four-foot-long, one-inch-square stakes into the ground and then mark those stakes with plastic orange markers. I had heard the resistance of my parents to this exploitation of our territory—and the gypsum mining was taking place right underneath our family's property. So us kids, we would go out and find all these steel stakes, and we would do our best to wiggle them out of the ground and throw them away. I laugh about it now. But this is the kind of thing that has happened to Indigenous peoples repeatedly over the course of five hundred years of colonization.

We have been forced to limit our officially recognized territories to what the colonial system has dictated. So when, for example, the Caledonia land conflict happened back in 2006, we knew from the 1784 Haldimand Proclamation, from the Plank Road Land claim issue, and from our previous relationships with the government that that "disputed" land was still our land. And Canada knew it as well. Even the local white people knew it! My dad would play hockey with some of these older white men, and they would say, "You know that the land they're trying to build a development on is your [Six Nations] land," even though the official position was that this is Canada's land, and the developer has the proper permits, and so on.

What I hear then in the *Royal Commission on Aboriginal Peoples* is a willingness of Indigenous peoples to compromise with Canada, saying, "What we need is more land. We've got rightful claims on this land. We aren't looking to get it all back. We've even taken efforts to buy back some of our land with our own money and have it recognized as part of our reserve. But we need more—we need a significant and fair share." Yet Canada doesn't respond. And the reason that Canada does not respond and actually return land and recognize greater reserve lands is because land forms part of their tax base. So it doesn't matter what we propose as compromise—and RCAP was a compromise—the colonial system doesn't like it, and it doesn't want to recognize it, even though we have a just claim.

People have made trillions of dollars from this land, and we've gotten crumbs. From an Indigenous understanding, the fundamental question is, "Where is the sharing of the fruit of the land?" Here in Manitoba, in Treatied territory, you have hydro dams all over the north that are wrecking the local trapping, fishing, and harvesting economies of our communities. Yet Manitoba Hydro, a provincial utility, makes plenty of income, and they turn around and sell the energy made off of Indigenous territories at bargain-basement rates to the United States. Where is the benefit that's coming to us? It's still our land. Where is the equity? We are not looking for the tables to be turned and for you to be thrown out of the land. But where is the inclusion in the wealth of this land? We took care of this land and all the other-than-human relatives. When Europeans came here, there were lots of fish, lush forests and berry patches, pristine waters. And now look! If you allowed us into the development and care of the land, then together we could find a way to care for those seven generations to come.

STEVE: As you share, Adrian, I think of the ways in which Indigenous nations were able to not only care for the more-than-human environment but also to flourish as Nations and peoples. Here we are, doing this interview in downtown Winnipeg, which, yes, has incredible grassroots Indigenous movements of beauty and resilience, but it is also Ground Zero of colonial fracture. There's a lot of Indigenous sisters and brothers, older ones and children—an overwhelming number—here who are on the blunt and deadly edge of ongoing colonial dispossession.

ADRIAN: Yes. Exactly.

STEVE: Going back to RCAP and that call for redistribution, we know that many churches advocated for Jubilee and tried to push the government of Canada. They created petitions, they did mass education efforts, they advocated and lobbied. But it didn't shift the powers. And in some churches, there was significant internal pushback against land redistribution. I'm interested in hearing what you think churches should be doing today. What does it mean for communities of faith to honor Jubilee now?

ADRIAN: I understand the challenge from the standpoint of being a pastor. You're torn between the call of the pastor to provide comfort, to help people grow, to feed and encourage them, protect them and help them be rooted in their identity. To provide comfort is a genuine pastoral concern. And yet the other dimension of life and leadership is the prophetic, where you call a community or someone out on their inequitable life. The whole idea of sin is saying that there are things you or we as a group are doing that are not right, that we must change, that we must repent of, and that we must turn from.

I was called as a pastor, and I worked with people to provide comfort. I know how truly important that is. And I have five children, and my life was about nurturing them in their identity, encouraging them, letting them know that their uniqueness is valuable, is accepted, and is needed as the gift of God inside of them. And it's when you have that spirit of your work as a pastor—the shepherding, comforting spirit—that the prophetic voice is possible for people to respond to. When the two come together, that's when we have genuine leadership. This is what Canada and what I would call the National Church has failed to do.

I say "National Church" because, in my understanding of the Scriptures, the church community represents the larger nation too. When Christ calls Ephesus to account in Revelation 2, we know that there were a bunch of congregations in Ephesus. But he refers to them as one and calls them "the Church of Ephesus." And, as in Matthew 25, where Jesus says that the nations are held to account, I believe that God will call Canada to account, and, on that day, God will call upon the Church of Canada. And there will be no "But I'm not a part of that!" And this is where my pastoral heart breaks, for when a nation is judged, everybody suffers—innocent babies, children, women, men, elders . . . the whole nation suffers when there is an accounting that is recorded in Scripture. And if God does not hold nations to account, then what is just judgment and justice anyway? Then justice is just a bunch of bullshit that means nothing. So, as a pastor and a father, I understand the prophetic witness and its consequence in the light of family. And no one wants to see their children and their community suffer. But, just like Covid-19, everybody suffers the consequences of this deadly pandemic.

Canada and every church finds it easy to be the chaplain of the status quo. But Jesus, who was the best pastor and who is the shepherd that we call on, is also the prophet in our midst who turns over the tables of the money-changers and indicts the economic system that is exploiting people's sins and vulnerabilities in order to profit themselves. Jesus says, "No more!" Where is the repentance for the love of money in the church, for the systems of greed that dehumanize people and put themselves before human dignity?

When people begin to hear about the Indigenous situation, they are floored by it, and sensitive people ask, "So what can I do?" I've often said, "Listen to our story until you are reduced to a puddle of tears, and stay there until God resurrects you." And that may not even happen in your lifetime. "And when you do stand up, you will find that you are hand in hand, not just with Indigenous peoples but also with all those who have been victimized by unjust systems."

The church is never going to be comfortable with a prophetic dimension, but the idea of being a Christian is being a martyr. It requires the death of something. Maybe not literal death but a dying of something, and you're going to feel the pain of that. And I've lived with that for sixty-four years of my life. I've lived with the idea that I'm suffering different things at different times, not because of stuff that I've done—and I've done stuff that I deserve to suffer for, and I'll take that stripe any time—but suffering that comes my way just because I am Indigenous. And as much as people say, from the other side of the equation, "But I never did that," I can say right back to them, "But I never did anything either, and I'm still suffering!"

So what do I see as the church's response? I see weeping and wailing and gnashing of teeth. I see crying and praying and repentance. I see a melting to the spirit of Jesus. That is what I think the answer is, as hard as that is and as rarely as that occurs. I just don't see much of a difference taking place otherwise. Because you've got all these programs and government plans and money, and it's still the same, and it often gets worse. And I don't know what else will change it but genuinely changed hearts. And I thought that's why Jesus came in the first place, to change us from the inside out.

STEVE: You know better than I do, Adrian, that when non-Indigenous people engage this land conversation for the first time, we often quickly jump to the questions concerning our own personal property, or, if we're privileged, what we might do with Grandma's farm or the parent's cottage that the family has inherited. But I hear you saying something different—don't jump to the property questions; you can't go there until you've actually sat with the pain. Am I hearing you right?

ADRIAN: I think that's partly right. And I should say that when it comes to sitting with pain, there's only so much one can take. In my classes, I've assigned a textbook on the Indian Residential School history. And some of the students can only read two or three pages before they need to stop. They feel it so deeply and are so burdened. And I understand that. There's an exhaustion that comes when you read seriously; you're caught up in the story and you feel really bad. And you should feel bad because that's a human response. But I know that there's limits to our energy. And I'm aware of that for myself. And that's why I write poetry and listen to music and do those things that are helpful to express the things that I'm going through.

When it comes to the land question, the thing to recognize is that there's a major difference between the colonial and native perspectives, which produces different answers and even different questions. From the colonial perspective, the answer is always litigation, court decisions, compensation, and land restoration with clear and certain boundary markers . . . a response that seeks finality and certainty. And from that colonial perspective, people are afraid that Indigenous peoples will attain some form of power. "What's going to happen to us if they are in charge?" But the reality is, they are afraid of their own system. Afraid that they will be on the receiving end of that system that preys on vulnerable peoples. So if Indigenous peoples get some power, they think they will experience what Indigenous peoples experienced and be kicked out of their homes, have their connections to the land destroyed, kept from fishing and harvesting the land, and so on.

Yet the reality and promise of Indigenous peoples is something radically different. We will share all things and teach you how to fish. We will show you how to harvest, and we will let you know how trapping can take place in order to maintain the viability and well-being of the land. We will provide the things that we need to take care of ourselves and our communities, together. Indigenous peoples have another conception of how we can be together—and the conception is, "Friends." Because that's what the Two Row Wampum—the original treaty of this land—was all about. The first row of beads describes the relationship between the Dutch and the Haudenosaunee, and it's the desire for friendship. That's what you're invited to. Not adversaries. Not debate partners. Not court adversaries. We've got to go back to what we said to you in the first place. The land is rich, the land is bountiful, the land is wild, and the land can kill you . . . but we will show you how to live, and we will show you how to harvest, and we invite you into this abundance and into this beloved community that's not just people but also the community of plants, of fish, of trees, of birds, of thunders, the community of sun and moon and stars and all the things we're inviting you to enjoy in the abundance of this land. We will share that with you again. You just need to realize that that's what we're inviting you into.

We are partakers of this land, and you don't shut us out . . . you don't shut us out of our own pharmacy, which is the land, and you don't shut us out of our own grocery store, which is the land, and don't shut us out of our own church, which is the land and the ceremonial places, and you don't shut us out from Mother Earth.

The community of creation—that's what you're being invited to! Sounds like a good idea, doesn't it? Sounds a lot like what Jesus is going to do when he comes back to this earth anyways. And if there is going to be a Jubilee, it can't be limited to some parochial limited vision, but it means something much more. It's for all the peoples and nations of the Earth.

Proceedings from the AAR/SBL
Mennonite Scholars and Friends Session:
"Migration, Borders, and Belonging"

# Past Encounter, Present Resonance

Jennifer Graber

Consider two episodes on America's southern plains. First, in 1887 Christian Krehbiel, president of the Foreign Mission Board of the General Conference Mennonite Church, brought fifteen Arapaho children from the Indian Industrial School at Halstead, Kansas, to live on his family's farm. In addition to academic lessons, Native boys received training in farm work and girls were taught domestic skills. Krehbiel emphasized the importance of "family life," but not just any kind of family; he meant the singular combination of Christian living and industriousness that characterized Mennonite families. He also contrasted his farm and the Halstead School with life on the Arapaho reservation, where the army threatened, treaties provided rations promoting "slavish dependence," and Native people lived nomadically, consulted healers, and practiced traditional rituals.[1]

One of the first Arapaho children to attend Krehbiel's school was Henry Lincoln. According to Mennonites, the Halstead experience bore fruit in Henry. He was baptized in 1890 and became part of the "Christian Six," a group of Arapaho young men who encouraged relatives to renounce their traditional ways. Here, we move to our second episode for consideration: in 1900, while still a member in good standing of Zion Arapaho Mennonite Church, Henry Lincoln led a meeting for ritual peyote ingestion.[2]

These episodes—Krehbiel's placement of Arapaho children with his Mennonite family and Henry Lincoln's participation in peyote rites while a baptized member of a Mennonite church—highlight two important patterns I observed

---

*Jennifer Graber is Professor of Religious Studies and affiliated faculty in the Program for Native American and Indigenous Studies at the University of Texas at Austin. She and her family attend Austin Mennonite Church.*

1 Henry Peter Krehbiel, *History of the General Conference of the Mennonites of North America* (Canton, OH: self-published, 1898), 307–9.

2 Christian Krehbiel Papers, folder 13, MS 10, Mennonite Library and Archives, Bethel College, Newton, KS, (hereafter MLSBC); Zion Arapaho Mennonite Church, Canton, Oklahoma, record book, CONG 104, MLSBC; Loretta Fowler, *Wives and Husbands: Gender and Age in Southern Arapaho History* (Norman: University of Oklahoma Press, 2010), 238; Omer C. Stewart, *Peyote Religion: A History* (Norman: University of Oklahoma Press, 1987), 196.

during research for my book on Kiowa Indian-American Christian encounters: First, each Christian denomination identified a *particular gift* it offered to Native peoples. These gifts not only differentiated them from other white Americans but also made them stand out among other Christians. For Mennonites, that special gift was family. Second, Native peoples, especially those affiliated with Christian schools and churches, responded in unexpected ways to these offers of Christianity through the medium of special gifts. Native worldviews—with their focus on kinship, land, and peoplehood—created forms and expressions of Christian life that missionaries had never seen before.

I'd like to reflect on these patterns using examples from my book *The Gods of Indian Country*.[3] Then I'll come back to the above examples that are part of a new project in which I'm researching the encounter between General Conference Mennonites and Arapahos.

## Pattern #1: Particular Gifts of Christian Missionary Groups

### 1. Quakers

The Society of Friends, or Quakers, emphasized two things in their work among Kiowas and other tribes in the American West: their peace testimony and their record of relating peacefully to Native peoples. They referred often to colonial Pennsylvania, where they had played leading roles in the colony's government and initiated a variety of interactions with Native nations. Over time, Quakers developed an almost mythic memory of these colonial encounters. There's no better symbol of this viewpoint than Edward Hicks's painting of "The Peaceable Kingdom." Hicks, a Quaker preacher, depicted a scene from the prophet Isaiah in the foreground: the wolf and the lamb, the leopard and the kid, the calf and the lion. Nestled behind them, another example of the peaceable kingdom, is William Penn making a treaty with the Lenape, or Delaware, Indians.

Quakers contrasted their interactions with Native people with those of other Americans, including self-proclaimed Christians. They saw settlers as selfish swindlers and quick to violence, and they considered colonial and later American officials to be corrupt leaders who rarely worked with Native people's best interests in mind. As a result, Quakers offered their services to the government soon after the American founding.

Quakers were some of the first Christian activists to arrive at the young nation's newly created reservations. In the 1790s, they initiated "civilization" programs among the Iroquois, or Haudenosaunee, of upstate New York. Of course, these weren't the first Christian *missions* to Native people; the colonial

---

3 Jennifer Graber, *The Gods of Indian Country: Religion and the Struggle for the American West* (New York: Oxford University Press, 2018).

period had many before this. But Quaker reservation work involved a new level of partnership with governmental officials. Society members sought to influence federal Indian policy, implement it on reservations, and thereby transform Native cultures in a totalizing fashion.

With this view of their mythic past, along with their success in forging government partnerships, Quakers constructed a sense of themselves as the "Indian's friend," as especially able to direct the nation's Indian policy toward a benevolent and enlightened end. They found new opportunities after the Civil War, when federal officials dispatched former generals to subdue tribal nations across the West. Quakers not only voiced opposition to this militarized approach, they also offered themselves as an alternative. They created a committee to lobby federal officials, arguing that reservations were places Native people could be persuaded to live. They also claimed their policy recommendations would result in a new era of peaceful relations.

In response to Society lobbying, President Ulysses S. Grant initiated what came to be known as the Peace Policy, and sometimes even the Quaker Policy. It assigned more than seventy reservations to Christian denominations, which then designated members to administer these sites on behalf of the federal government and their own respective religious bodies. President Grant also established a committee of Protestant leaders, including several Friends, to advise the federal Indian office. Quakers celebrated; a new era, driven by their peaceful witness, had arrived.

Before turning to Kiowa responses to the Quakers' arrival on their reservation, let me add two more examples of Christian groups vying for influence by way of their particular gifts: Roman Catholics and Baptists.

## 2. Roman Catholics

Roman Catholics, of course, had carried out missions to Native peoples dating back to the late fifteenth century. When the United States acquired lands west of the Mississippi River, they inherited a territory that, to some degree, had already been evangelized by Spanish and French Catholic missionaries. Given this extensive experience, Roman Catholics assumed they would have a special place in the government partnership to administer reservations. In fact, the Peace Policy stated that a record of mission work among a tribal nation would lead to an assignment, and in light of their record, Catholics anticipated renewed work on at least thirty reservations. To their surprise, federal officials granted them only seven. Further, the government assigned many reservations to Protestant groups who had no history of Native missions, and they refused to name a Catholic representative to the committee of churchmen advising President Grant.

In response, Catholics founded the Bureau of Catholic Indian Missions to publicize their history of Native missions to Catholic laypeople as well as federal officials. Bureau leaders claimed that Catholics had, over several centuries, baptized more than one hundred thousand Native people. Worried about reservations assigned to Protestant groups, they claimed more than eighty thousand Indians were being coerced away from their Catholic faith.

In this context of government agencies privileging Protestants, Catholics developed a somewhat surprising take on the particular gift they had to offer American Indians. To be sure, they affirmed that theirs was the one true church and the only true sacraments, but they also began to talk about religious liberty and the First Amendment to the Constitution, presenting themselves as the special protectors of Catholic Indians' religious freedom. Bureau leaders called on their coreligionists to rise up and defend "their Catholic brethren on the plains," as the "religious liberty of the Indian" was at stake. Roman Catholics viewed themselves as particularly able to defend Native people from government-sponsored prejudice.

## 3. Baptists

Baptists love the Bible. When it comes to missions, they especially love Acts 16:9–10, the Macedonian call. In the King James Version, it reads:

> And a vision appeared to Paul in the night; There stood a man of Macedonia, and prayed him, saying, Come over into Macedonia, and help us.

> And after he had seen the vision, immediately we endeavoured to go into Macedonia, assuredly gathering that the Lord had called us for to preach the gospel unto them.

Of course, these verses were cited by other Christians as well, but they appeared inordinately in Baptist mission materials. Indeed, Baptists believed themselves especially likely to receive Macedonian calls from non-Christians, and they viewed themselves as particularly adept at answering these calls.

For instance, the first Baptist missionary to live among Kiowas claimed that Cûifã gàui/Lone Wolf the Younger, an important leader, had asked him to start a school. The missionary sent letters about the request to Baptist mission circles. In short order, Baptist missionaries arrived and soon outnumbered other American Protestants on the reservation. Over time, the story about Lone Wolf's school request underwent some embellishment. According to another Baptist missionary, Lone Wolf and some of his followers appeared at church one Sunday. The Kiowa leader addressed the missionaries. "Oh, friends," he said, "will you share with us your life and light and joy and gladness? Your knowledge, your Bible—your Jesus?" This account circulated broadly in a mission pamphlet called "Lone Wolf's Appeal." It captured Baptists' sense of their special work among Native people: they heard the Macedonian call, answered it, and then told others about it.

## Pattern #2: Native Responses

I've shown how three Christian groups cultivated a sense of their particular gifts for Native missions. Now I'd like to turn to Kiowa responses to these outsiders and their offerings. Lone Wolf, again, provides a helpful example. According to Baptists, Lone Wolf wanted exactly what their nineteenth-century revivalist piety offered: joy, knowledge of salvation, and a holy book. He asked for things only Baptists made available, they said, since Quaker meetings were not known for their joy and Roman Catholics did not prioritize Bible distribution.

While Lone Wolf did look to Baptists for some things, it seems they might have mischaracterized the situation. True, Lone Wolf invited missionaries to live in his camp and start a school and he attended some of their Sunday services, but he also looked outside Baptist circles: Some children in his family went to the Methodist school. His nephew (who was like a son to him) became a Methodist minister. Other children in his family went to the Roman Catholic school, and Lone Wolf himself attended mass on occasion. According to Benedictine missionaries—the Roman Catholic order working on the reservation—Lone Wolf once stood before a statue of the Sacred Heart of Jesus and thanked the "Great Spirit" for sending priests "to teach them about Jesus." The missionaries were, reportedly, so excited that they circulated the story to supporters through their abbey's newspaper, which featured an image of the Virgin Mary standing over Indian Territory.

Lone Wolf moved not only between Christian denominations but also from the Kiowa reservation to Washington, DC. He did not go for the same reason Quakers had gone. They had wanted "civilizing programs" for Native people. Neither did he go for the purpose Roman Catholics had—to lobby for reservation assignments. He went, instead, to demand that the federal government honor its treaty with his people. He went to fight allotment, the process by which Congress mandated the breaking apart of communally held reservation lands into plots assigned to individual Native men. The "surplus" lands left over after this dispersal would then be opened to white Americans for settlement. According to Lone Wolf, this process violated an 1867 treaty and threatened to dismantle the connections binding Kiowa people to each other. Roman Catholics, remember, had argued that they were singularly committed to protecting Native people from the federal government's adverse actions. But when Lone Wolf objected to government treaty breaking, he found no Catholic allies.

To be fair, Roman Catholics did not get deeply involved in the allotment question. But Protestants did, especially the Quakers. Recall their earlier memorial to Congress, calling on Americans to take a peaceful approach to Indian nations? They had argued that federal policy be based on persuasion, that Native people be presented with appealing options meant to draw them toward "civilized" living. In the 1860s, that meant reservations that promoted farming, refigured domestic life, and transformed ritual practice. By 1890, it meant private property through the legal mechanism of allotment. Quakers ardently promoted allotment, with one Society member founding a pan-Protestant association to promote it.

As with earlier experiments to persuade Native people to accept reservation life, this one also failed. Lone Wolf never chose to farm. He never agreed to allotment. Instead, he gathered Kiowas together to support his trips to Washington. Once there, he and his nephew initiated a legal case to protect their treaty-guaranteed lands—a case they took all the way to the Supreme Court.

Lone Wolf is one of many examples of the ways Kiowas responded to Christian missions. In his experience, we see that missionaries offered things that did not necessarily resonate with his understanding of what it meant to be a people, to live in a place, and to relate to the powers present there. So how did Lone Wolf understand these things? How did his worldview affect his engagement with missionaries?

Born in the 1840s, Lone Wolf grew up celebrating Kiowas' most important annual ritual, the Sun Dance. He participated at least forty times during his lifetime. In this summer gathering, he learned how to approach powerful forces and beings: One humbled oneself before them. One asked things of them. One made vows to show the seriousness of one's request. And one fulfilled those vows when blessed with positive outcomes. These exchanges with powerful forces were made in front of one's kin. They were made on *behalf* of one's kin. They occurred in beloved places, often at the bends of rivers or at stands of trees where ancestors had gathered before.

It's quite easy to see that Baptist joy, knowledge, and books would not necessarily have been what Lone Wolf was looking for. He wanted powerful forces to hear his requests and answer them. His people would not flourish or even survive otherwise. That doesn't mean that the missionaries' God had nothing to offer him. To the contrary, a mission school provided his young relatives with English language lessons, which proved helpful in their legal case. They also received medical care from missionaries and sometimes even miraculous cures from the new and powerful figure, Jesus. Such care and cures were eagerly sought when child mortality was high.

Lone Wolf and other Kiowas also looked to missionaries as potential allies. For centuries, Kiowas had made agreements with other Native nations and European colonizers, and they approached Americans with this history in mind. Kiowas were sometimes able to make similar alliances with them, such as with the Methodist missionary who transcribed their petitions and sent them to Congress. Or the Baptist missionary who let them bury their loved ones in the church cemetery so that their relatives' remains would be safe from white settlers who might otherwise desecrate them in the rush to scoop up Oklahoma land.

When missionaries acted as allies, Kiowas fulfilled their obligations to them. And when powerful beings, including God the Father; his son, Jesus; or Jesus's mother, Mary, made good things happen, they fulfilled vows made to them. We have evidence of these acts in missionary records. For instance, a Kiowa woman vowed to hold a feast if Jesus healed her relative. When her kinsman's health improved, she delivered; to the missionary's chagrin, she killed her only head of cattle and served it up for all. At the meal, she gave a speech about her plea, her vow, and the deliverance she had experienced from Jesus. She encouraged other Kiowas to bring their petitions to him.

So Kiowas came to Christianity with a particular approach to powerful forces and with a particular way of bringing their concerns forward. Theirs was not a position that privileged joy, knowledge, or books. They emphasized places, relationships, and obligations. Their main purpose was the perpetuation of the Kiowa people in a land they loved.

This worldview was also characterized by a second pattern I observed among Kiowa Christians: religious fluidity. Remember Lone Wolf's interaction with Baptist, Methodist, and Roman Catholic missions? This was highly typical of Kiowa engagements with Christianity. Church records tell of Kiowas receiving multiple baptisms, taking communion in multiple churches, seeking healing from multiple missionaries, and sending their children to a variety of mission schools. And this fluidity was not simply between churches; it also moved outside the bounds of Christianity. Kiowa Christians were known to participate in Sun Dances, at least until the dances ended in 1890. They also continued to consult traditional healers, seek visions, and consider themselves protected by powerful animal spirits. They attended meetings for ritual peyote ingestion, and they joined the pan-Indian Ghost Dance movement.

They did this because their approach to sacred power had always been additive. As scholars have noted, being Kiowa involves assembling many pieces.[4] Sometimes these additions are metaphorical, involving new stories. But they are also quite literal. Kiowas acquired powerful *things* throughout their history. This practice started with medicine bundles created centuries ago when they lived in the Far North. When they migrated to the Northern Plains, they obtained an important object, the *Táimé*, from their Crow neighbors, who taught them about the Sun Dance. When they lost that *Táimé* in 1868, they made another. For Kiowas who affiliated with churches, coming to Jesus, Mary, or God the Father was to access more pieces and fit them into the assemblage of Kiowa life.

---

4 Luke E. Lassiter et al., *The Jesus Road: Kiowas, Christianity, and Indian Hymns* (Lincoln: University of Nebraska Press, 2002), 12.

## Arapahos and General Conference Mennonites

While my research about the encounter between Arapahos and General Conference Mennonites is only in its earliest stages, fluidity of religion similar to that of the Kiowas is evident among Arapahos. Henry Lincoln, for example, the Arapaho boy who attended a Mennonite school in Kansas and encouraged others to become Christian, was later reported to convene peyote meetings. Frank Harrington, an Arapaho teenager who worked with Mennonite missionaries to translate the Bible, also served as a leader for the Arapaho version of the Sun Dance.[5] Willie Meeks, who served as an assistant to a Mennonite pastor, joined the society of lizard doctors—men who had visions in which lizard spirits gave them powers to heal.[6] Bessie Plentybear, who attended the Krehbiel family's farm-school, married the custodian of the Arapaho's sacred wheel. In her home, she hosted supplicants who made vows before it. She and her husband were responsible for bringing the wheel to summer Sun Dances.[7] And at least some Arapaho Mennonites, including those mentioned here who attended Mennonite school and joined the Mennonite congregation, picked up and assembled many other such pieces, similar to their Kiowa neighbors.[8]

Mennonite missionaries, of course, objected to this fluidity, at least when it was visible to them. I haven't yet found evidence that they knew about Willie Meeks and his work as a lizard doctor, but they eagerly wished for an end to the Sun Dance and objected vigorously to peyote meetings. Rodolphe Petter, Mennonite missionary to the Cheyenne who shared a reservation with the Arapaho, complained that "return to heathen customs," meaning Sun Dance and peyote rituals, was common "even among the [Indian] Christians."[9]

For Petter and other Mennonite missionaries, the world of supernatural power did not consist of pieces. It had one central reality: Jesus, the world's savior. To be sure, Mennonites in the United States debated the characteristics of Christian life, including the necessity of sharing the gospel with strangers. While Old Mennonites came to missions later, the General Conference had been active in mission work since the early 1870s.[10] Like other American Chris-

---

5 Fowler, *Wives and Husbands*, 223–40.

6 Fowler, 240.

7 Fowler, 212–13.

8 Zion Arapaho Mennonite Church, Canton, Oklahoma, record book, MLSBC; Christian Krehbiel Papers, folder 13, MS 10, MLSBC. Willie Meeks's school enrollment is attested to in some records but not others.

9 Typed historical accounts of various Oklahoma Cheyenne and Arapaho mission stations, one on Cantonment by Roldolphe Petter, SA.II. 2056, MLSBC.

10 Krehbiel, *History of the General Conference of the Mennonites of North America*, 272.

tians, they quickly identified the special gift they had to offer Native people: Christian discipleship and industry learned through incorporation into Mennonite families.

Of course, missionaries used other formats to convey their gospel message: they preached in Arapaho camps, built churches, and opened schools on the reservation. But whenever they discussed Arapahos' need for Jesus, they insisted on a concurrent renunciation of Arapaho traditional ways. Such changes seemed impossible, however, when students lived among their Arapaho kin. Separation was necessary. Though many denominations in this era accomplished such separation by opening off-reservation boarding schools, the Mennonite example is intriguing for its deliberate convergence of faith, work, and *family* that took the place of boarding school. As Krehbiel claimed, Arapaho children who lived on his family farm were educated "spiritually and industrially," and his wife was "as a mother" to Arapaho boys and girls.[11]

## Learning to See All Families

As each denomination cultivated a sense of their particular gifts for Native people, they each also inflicted a particular trauma. Mennonites, for example, convinced that theirs was the only kind of Christian family, were blind to the Arapaho families in their midst. They failed to see the importance in Arapaho naming practices, which imbued children's names with particular meaning and history. They tried to stop children's initiation into communal rituals passed down by older family members. And they had little besides criticism for the way Arapaho parents and relatives fed, clothed, and raised their children.

In identifying this Mennonite blindness, I refer to not only the past but also the present and my own experience. In the last pages of *The Gods of Indian Country*, I give an account of Kiowa ceremonial dances I attended with a friend a few years ago. The experience was profoundly moving, especially as I witnessed the love and connection between Kiowa parents and children. I watched mothers fix their daughters' traditional dresses and shawls, and I saw fathers make space for their sons to sit around the communal drum. My friend brought a cradleboard made by his grandmother. In it, he placed his own grandchild. This beautiful cradle had been made with loving care at a time when Kiowa children were particularly vulnerable. On that lovely fall day, I watched a young mother strap the board to her back and carry her baby into the dance circle.

For the longest time I could not put my finger on why this event had such an effect on me, but now I understand. I grew up in an Anabaptist farm family[12]

---

11 Krehbiel, 297, 309.

12 My father grew up among the Old Order Amish. His family became Beachy Amish in his early teens. My immediate family attended a Church of the Brethren con-

that hosted children from the South Side of Chicago through the Fresh Air Program.[13] The children stayed with us, ate with us, and ran around the farm with us. For a few weeks each summer, we called them our brothers.[14] But they weren't our brothers. They had their own families. And I've only just come to realize that we never, ever asked them about their own lives, their loved ones, their schools, or their neighborhoods. That lack of interest, that erasure, is the legacy of Anabaptist/Mennonite's particular approach to peoples they evangelized. For me, that realization prompts renewed effort to ask what families I still don't see and what work of repair I can initiate.

---

gregation, while extended family on my father's side occupied the Anabaptist spectrum, including various Amish subgroups, Conservative Mennonite Conference, and what became Mennonite Church USA.

13 Tobin Miller Sherer, *Two Weeks Every Summer: Fresh Air Children and the Problem of Race in America* (Ithaca, NY: Cornell University Press, 2017).

14 Although the Fresh Air program included both girls and boys, only boys stayed with our family.

# Race, Religion, and Land in *The Gods of Indian Country*

Joseph R. Wiebe

In her book *The Story of Radio Mind*, Pamela Klassen retells an exchange between Canadian government officials and an unnamed Gitxsan elder in northwest British Columbia.[1] The officials insisted that the Indigenous community was on Canadian land. To which the elder replied, "If this is your land, where are your stories?" Klassen remarks that stories and land restitution "must be at the heart of any attempt to take responsibility for and to remedy the ways that North America came to be through the theft of Indigenous lands."[2]

Jennifer Graber's book *The Gods of Indian Country* is one such story that can help take responsibility for and remedy one of the causes of dispossession.[3] Graber tells of federal and religious strategies from 1803 to 1903 to assimilate Kiowa people. A central contribution of her story is a description of the role of race and religion in determining national belonging. While African slaves' racial otherness was construed as insurmountable for citizenship, Indigenous people were racialized differently; they could become American through cultural conversion. Graber reveals how Christians were central agents of the attempt to absorb Indigenous communities into American culture.

Graber also demonstrates that at the heart of this process has been land (i.e., territory). Rather than discuss land as something passively encountered—from which one migrates, on which one draws borders, or to which one belongs—the through-line of Graber's story is land as the fundamental broker to Indigenous-settler relations. Graber makes two arguments: first, that religion was used

---

*Joseph R. Wiebe is Assistant Professor of Religion and Ecology at the University of Alberta. His book,* The Place of Imagination: Wendell Berry and the Poetics of Community, Affection, and Identity, *was published by Baylor University Press (Waco, TX) in 2017. His current work is on decolonial religious environmental ethics.*

1 Pamela E. Klassen, *The Story of Radio Mind: A Missionary's Journey on Indigenous Land* (Chicago: University of Chicago Press, 2018). Klassen is quoting from J. Edward Chamberlin, *If This Is Your Land, Where Are Your Stories? Finding Common Ground* (New York: Penguin Random House, 2004).

2 Klassen, *Radio Mind*, 7.

3 Jennifer Graber, *The Gods of Indian Country: Religion and the Struggle for the American West* (New York: Oxford University Press, 2018).

as a means for land acquisition and cultural transformation (which is a polite way of saying dispossession and cultural genocide); second, that Indigenous peoples—specifically Kiowa in her narrative—used "religion" to enact and protect their sovereignty as a defense against these efforts.

To understand both the formation of American land as we know it today and nineteenth-century American religious history, we must look to Indigenous peoples. Typically, the history of land and religion has placed settlers at the center and Indigenous peoples at the margins; Graber instead places Indigenous people and their territory at the center to retell this history.

The specific story Graber tells is how Quakers and other Christian "friends of the Indian" participated in this imperial project of land acquisition and Indigenous assimilation through activities geared toward making the place and people amenable to government aims and policies. The political background, of course, is the forced removal of Indigenous people. Graber's story, though, also calls attention to figures like Jedidiah Morse—a geographer and minister who outlined what a "friend of the Indian" consisted of. Graber quotes Morse, who described Indigenous people as "neglected and oppressed" and who argued it was therefore the responsibility of Americans—specifically Christian Americans—to improve Indigenous communities for the benefit of the entire nation. The polemical context for defining friendship was forced removal. Friendship came to be defined through arguments and protests against Jackson's Indian Removal Act. Both Jackson and "friends of the Indian" claimed to be acting out of humanitarian motivations. While friends objected to removal, they nevertheless shared the same vision for political and religious organization of the place referred to as Indian Territory.

It is on this point I want to make two observations intended both to show how the story Graber tells is helpful for contemporary efforts of decolonization and to move the conversation forward. First, by foregrounding the good intentions and seemingly charitable vision of both political and religious colonial agents, Graber analyzes the complexity of colonial powers to see the various ways people fit in. This capacity is a good reason to read her book in a Mennonite context; we settler Mennonites have a tendency to hold on to aspects of our identity and history so as to disassociate ourselves from colonialism. But this can only be achieved when the account of colonialism in mind is overly simplistic. The more complex the account, the more we discern just how capacious colonialism is. In other words, recognizing how pervasive colonialism is disabuses us from tendencies of disassociation and leads to acknowledging that we fit into that narrative, we have a part we play.

I am left wondering: where does Graber and her scholarship fit in the narrative of colonialism? More reflection on her positionality woven throughout the book would have helped locate Graber's work within the current flows of colonialism and efforts of decolonization. How is her positionality reflected and brought out or changed through her research—telling the stories, looking through the ledgers and calendars? Graber mentions her relations, but they only appear in the acknowledgments and epilogue. What would it look like to weave these into the story she tells? How would explicitly interconnecting her positionality with the archival documents affect the work—the kind of knowledge it produces and for whom it could be given? Here is an opportunity to decolonialize academia in general and religious studies in particular; instead, Graber continues the practice of playing off personal relationships and experiences as color commentary to the bare facts of the events research methods uncover. Indigenous scholars refuse to do this in favor of Indigenous methods and traditional knowledge and routinely express how the peer-review process is prejudiced against their approach to academia.[4]

Second, Graber argues that "our histories mirror nineteenth-century policy goals in which white Americans occupy the center and Native people dwell on the periphery."[5] American religious history needs more Indigenous voices. Graber balances the scales by bringing in Indigenous sources to describe Kiowa ceremony and community life—a risky undertaking that she handles deftly. And yet, the analytical framework for Kiowa religion is largely constructed through white-settler scholars. There is a sense in which the center-periphery issue Graber mentions in her field is reiterated in the theoretical underpinnings of the book's interpretive lens. Indigenous scholars, including Kiowa writers, are in the footnotes and bibliography but don't noticeably affect how Kiowa religion is understood in the text.

For example, Kiowa understood and practiced religion, according to Graber, as "rites for engaging sacred power."[6] In Graber's narration, Kiowa turned to religion for sacred power to provide protection, but in 1833 these rituals "were

---

4 For a conversation with Indigenous scholars on this topic, see "The Politics of Citation: Is the Peer-Review Process Biased against Indigenous Academics?" CBC Radio, posted February 23, 2018, https://www.cbc.ca/radio/unreserved/decolonizing-the-classroom-is-there-space-for-indigenous-knowledge-in-academia-1.4544984/the-politics-of-citation-is-the-peer-review-process-biased-against-indigenous-academics-1.4547468. See also Heather Castleden et al., "'I Don't Think That Any Peer Review Committee . . . Would Ever "Get" What I Currently Do': How Institutional Metrics for Success and Merit Risk Perpetuating the (Re)production of Colonial Relationships in Community-Based Participatory Research Involving Indigenous Peoples in Canada," *The International Indigenous Policy Journal* 6, no. 4 (2015); Jackie Street et al., "Is Peer Review Useful in Assessing Research Proposals in Indigenous Health? A Case Study," *Health Research and Policy Systems* 7, no. 2 (2009); Elaine Coburn et al., "Unspeakable Things: Indigenous Research and Social Science," *Socio* 2 (2013): 331–48.

5 Graber, *Gods of Indian Country*, 14.

6 Graber, *Gods of Indian Country*, 12.

not enough" "to ensure health and safety."[7] In one particular encounter that became known as the Cutthroat Massacre, Osage killed many Kiowa and also captured two children, a medicine bundle, and the *Táimé*.[8] In 1834, during an American-instigated parlay between Kiowa and Osage, one of the children and the *Táimé* were returned. Graber notes that while Americans focused on their own involvement in the negotiations to work toward a treaty, Kiowa oral traditions gave primary agency to the child who was returned. It was "not through an American-brokered truce, but because she implored a medicine bundle" that the girl gained "new powers from a buffalo," which she transferred to Kiowa warriors upon her return.[9] "This story" Graber writes, "captures something about the Kiowas' strength, as well as their adaptability."[10]

While Graber's framework shows how strength and adaptability are qualities internal to the community, it doesn't further connect these qualities to Kiowa sovereignty or nationhood. Jenny Tone-Pah-Hote, a Kiowa scholar at University of North Carolina whose work Graber cites, narrates the event as one of the "acts of diplomacy in the shifting political landscape of the plains [that] shaped the history of the Kiowa nation."[11] Expressive culture, such as dances and art, communicate the importance of the relations that form their nationhood, which is composed of less politically defined structures and more "familial and community life, where maintaining an understanding of Kiowa identity centre[s] on individuals related to one another."[12] In other words, drawing on and interacting with sacred power through expressive culture such as ritual and art communicates Kiowa identity through relationality, which is the basis for sovereignty and governance.

For Tone-Pah-Hote, tying expressive culture to diplomacy, religion to relationality, is how Kiowa both navigated and survived the assimilation era as well as set the "foundation for the spread of intertribal movements in which Kiowas would participate" in the twentieth century.[13] The framework for understanding nineteenth-century Kiowa identity and nationhood through religion sets the stage for understanding contemporary Kiowa resistance, survivance, and flourishing through dance, art, and material culture. Again, it's not that these Kiowa-voiced dynamics and connections aren't present in the book; it's that

---

7 Graber, 33.

8 Graber (3) defines *Táimé* as "the sacred object at the center of Kiowa Sun Dance practices . . . [It is] considered a mediator between the sun and the people."

9 Graber, 43–44.

10 Graber, 44.

11 Jenny Elizabeth Tone-Pah-Hote, *Envisioning Nationhood: Kiowa Expressive Culture, 1875–1939* (Minneapolis: University of Minnesota Press, 2009), 9.

12 Tone-Pah-Hote, 6.

13 Tone-Pah-Hote, 9.

they're just peripheral. Without their centrality, settler religious scholars are still tempted to view ritual acts such as the one that preceded the Cutthroat Massacre as a "failure" because it didn't effect a specific cause; that is, it is tempting to view the act as superstitious.

Religion determines belonging, but whether that belonging is vicious or virtuous—whether it engenders habits and character qualities that deteriorate or foster one's tradition—is determined by relationships. Put differently, to say that religion determines belonging is to say that religion expresses primary, political attachments. Graber's book tells a story about settler colonialism that helps us understand how religion as a force and expression of relationality has been both an agent of colonialism as well as a tool for decolonization. The term "friend" as a form of political belonging continues to be used in settler-Indigenous alliances, so Graber's book is both a window into the past as well as an analytical resource for understanding contemporary relationships.

One group in Manitoba, Canada, for example, call themselves Friends of Shoal Lake 40.[14] They are a group working with Shoal Lake 40 First Nation for access to clean drinking water—a resource that was polluted as a result of its provision to Winnipeg.[15] One awareness-raising campaign the group held was to create stencils of stories from the Nation and use water to fill out the message on concrete sidewalks during summer. Surely it's good to get the perspective and experience of Shoal Lake 40 First Nation's members to form the basis of their advocacy, but is getting community members to tell their stories for the public appropriate? The First Nation members have already given Winnipeg clean drinking water; haven't they given enough? The members of Friends of Shoal Lake 40 that I know were keenly aware of this dynamic.

Whether or not engagement and advocacy are an example of extraction or justice won't be determined through an abstract interpretive framework; rather, it will be determined by relationships. Friends of Shoal Lake 40 is a case that reminds us to be vigilant in the political function of friendship; relationships like the ones in this case, as Graber's book shows, need to be scrutinized. This example is also a reminder that the function of academic conversations and scholarship is up for grabs and open to interpretation, but if it's rooted in explicit positionality and relationship, it will have the potential to participate in decolonization.

---

14 See their Facebook page: https://www.facebook.com/friendsofSL40/.

15 For the history of Shoal Lake 40 in colonialism and the lack of accessible clean drinking water, see Adele Perry, *Aqueduct: Colonialism, Resources, and the Histories We Remember* (Winnipeg: ARP, 2016).

# The US/Mexico Borderlands in the Mennonite Imagination

Felipe Hinojosa

My quest to research and write on Latina/o religious politics began in the Mennonite church. While that might seem like a stretch to some, for me it was an easy choice. I grew up in that church, visiting and getting to know white Mennonites throughout the Great Plains and the Midwest in countless church conferences during the summers. I knew where the archives were, where to find the best Amish bakeries, and which books I should be reading.

It also helped that back in 2006 when I started working on my book, *Latino Mennonites: Civil Rights, Faith, and Evangelical Culture*,[1] no one had written a book on Latina/o activists and preachers in the Mennonite church. Sure, I was familiar with Rafael Falcón's *The Hispanic Mennonite Church in North America*[2] and José Ortiz and David Graybill's *Reflections of an Hispanic Mennonite*.[3] But Falcón's book is an encyclopedic review of Hispanic leadership in the (Old) Mennonite Church, and Ortiz and Graybill's is a more personal narrative on the life and work of the Rev. José Ortiz. While both books delve into the marginalization that Latina/os have faced in the Mennonite Church, they leave out the details of the moments when religious faith clashed with civil rights politics—moments that are so central to the Latina/o religious experience, especially during the 1960s and 1970s.

In addition, very little had been written on white Mennonites' attitudes about and perceptions of Latina/os as a nonwhite minority. In fact, more had

*Felipe Hinojosa is an associate professor in the Department of History at Texas A&M University and the director of the Carlos H. Cantú Education and Opportunity Endowment. He is the author of* Latino Mennonites: Civil Rights, Faith, and Evangelical Culture *(Baltimore, MD: Johns Hopkins University Press, 2014) and* Apostles of Change: Latino Radical Politics, Church Occupations, and the Fight to Save the Barrio *(Austin, TX: University of Texas Press, 2021).*

1 Felipe Hinojosa, *Latino Mennonites: Civil Rights, Faith, and Evangelical Culture* (Johns Hopkins University Press, 2014)—written first as a dissertation in graduate school.

2 Rafael Falcón, *The Hispanic Mennonite Church in North America: 1932–1982* (Scottdale, PA: Herald, 1986).

3 José Ortiz and David Graybill, *Reflections of an Hispanic Mennonite* (Intercourse, PA: Good Books, 1989).

been written and published on Mennonites in Latin America—from Mexico to Puerto Rico to Argentina—than on Latina/o Mennonite communities in Chicago, South Texas, and New York City. Sadly, that continues to be the case. Just walk into any Mennonite history library and you'll know what I am talking about.

My book, *Latino Mennonites*, addresses this oversight by focusing on the Latina/o communities in the United States, specifically in Chicago, South Texas, Puerto Rico, and New York. I organized the book in this way for two reasons: (1) In each instance, white Mennonites crossed urban and rural borders that were foreign to them; whether they traveled from Elkhart, Indiana, to the streets of Chicago or the cotton fields of Texas, in each case Mennonites were out of their element. (2) From each of these communities emerged many of the Latina/o preachers and activists who rose to leadership in the 1960s and 1970s.[4]

This essay is not as much a recap of these two pieces as it is personal reflections on how these missionary border crossers—white Mennonites—imagined the US/Mexico borderlands and how they reflected those images and perceptions back onto an eager audience. The years since the publication of *Latino Mennonites* have only confirmed for me just how important the US/Mexico borderlands and the people who reside there are to the continued development of Mennonite and Anabaptist studies.

To understand the history of (Old) Mennonite missions with Latina/os in the United States and Latin America, we can begin with Mennonite missionaries T. K. Hershey[5] and William G. Detweiler. In the spring of 1936, Hershey and Detweiler loaded their Ford V-8 and drove from their homes in Pennsylvania to the US/Mexico borderlands. There they surveyed the Southwest from Texas to California in hopes of beginning a mission to the Mexican population.

The two missionaries documented their journey well, creating a goldmine of information that still sits at the Mennonite Church USA archives in Elkhart, Indiana, untouched for the most part by Mennonite historians.[6] In small notebooks, they wrote down their impressions, places they stopped to eat, obser-

---

4 *Latino Mennonites* does not go in-depth to cover the work of more conservative Latina/o Mennonites in Lancaster Conference, for example, nor does the book cover communities in Florida. The book also stops in 1982, right at the moment when a new wave of leadership—more Latin American in orientation—began to take on important leadership positions in the United States. Some saw this new wave as a progressive step forward, but others viewed it as a move away from the more radical politics of Latina/o Mennonites from the United States.

5 The work of T. K. Hershey in Argentina and (later) of his son Lester in Puerto Rico was a significant part of the mission to Latinos across the Americas.

6 See the T. K. Hershey collection at the Mennonite Church Archives in Elkhart, Indiana. I should note that before Hershey and Detweiler set out on their journey, mis-

vations about the landscape, and notes about the abundance of agriculture in Texas.

After traveling more than seven thousand miles, Hershey and Detweiler decided that the South Texas region (just south of San Antonio), where a "good class of Mexicans"[7] resided, represented the ideal spot for their mission work. The two men never elaborated on what exactly they meant by a "good class of Mexicans," but I suspect they saw this population of mostly poor Mexican farm workers as quiet and docile—in other words, easy targets for religious conversion.

The South Texas region where Hershey and Detweiler began their missionary work had a violent and contested history, including routine killings and displacement of Mexicans.[8] The Mexicans' main source of oppression had come from the state itself and the law enforcement under its direction—the Texas Rangers and later the US Border Patrol (established in 1924). When the US war of aggression against Mexico began in the South Texas borderlands in 1846, land theft became a central part of white identity, and the Texas Rangers lynched and killed Mexicans.

Hershey and Detweiler, without any sense of where they were or the history of the region, started small mission churches there, supposedly meeting a passive Mexican population who surrounded them with love. Their observations were typical of white populations encountering Mexicans in the West and Southwest. Curious, they tried to make sense of this new race of people who were neither fully Black nor fully Indian but a mixed race, a "brown race." The lack of clarity over Mexicans' racial identity frustrated the missionaries.[9] At the annual Mennonite Board of Missions and Charity meeting in 1943, missionary Amsa Kaufman reported that "as a class they [Mexicans] are more or less ignorant and given to vices, shooting and cutting affairs."[10] Kauffman was simply reading off of racial scripts that described Mexicans as violent—scripts whose

---

sionaries D. H. Bender and S. E. Allgyer conducted their own trip to the borderlands sixteen years earlier in March 1920.

7 Thirtieth Annual Report, Mennonite Board of Missions and Charities Annual Meeting, Belleville, PA, May 10–12, 1936, box 2, file 1, IV-6-3, Mennonite Church Archives, Elkhart, IN.

8 For more on anti-Mexican violence in Texas, see Monica Muñoz Martinez, *The Injustice Never Leaves You: Anti-Mexican Violence in Texas* (Harvard University Press, 2018).

9 Thirty-Seventh Mennonite Board of Missions and Charities Annual Meeting, Mission Board Report, 1943, box 4, file 7, IV-6-3, Mennonite Church Archives, Elkhart, IN.

10 Thirty-Seventh Mennonite Board of Missions and Charities Annual Meeting, Mission Board Report, 1943, box 4, file 7, IV-6-3. Mennonite Church Archives, Elkhart, IN.

histories were born out of colonialism, land theft, and state-sanctioned racial violence in Texas.

Concerns and questions about Mexicans as a racial group—as a brown race—extended into all areas of life. The flexibility and openness of the religious practices of Mexicans, for example, was seen as an extension of their mixed race and thus their confused sense of peoplehood. One minute Mennonites were baptizing the new believers they had welcomed into their small mission churches—very proud of their new converts—and the next, they were frustrated with those same converts attending Catholic mass or continuing to make their usual visits to the *curanderas* or *curanderos* (spiritual healers) in the community. Not sure what to think, Mennonites surmised that just as Mexicans are a mixed race people unable to govern themselves, they are also a deeply religiously confused people: "Many of these people do not know where they stand when it comes to religion," they reported to their brethren in the north.[11]

Around that same time, in the late 1930s, Mennonite Brethren (MB) missionaries arrived in the border communities of the western end of the Rio Grande Valley, in the small town of Los Ebanos, Texas. The MBs, never ones to be left behind, embarked on their own trek to the US/Mexico border. When missionary couple Harry and Sarah Neufeld arrived in the border town of Edinburg, Texas, they did what every white family did upon arriving in South Texas—they started looking for other white people. The Neufelds liked Edinburg, but they wanted to go more rural, deeper into the *ranchos* of the border region. When they stopped at the parsonage of the First Baptist Church, they were relieved to find the white pastor, who welcomed them and advised that if they dared to go to the rural border towns and villages, they would appear to the Mexican population as "foreign devils."[12]

Nothing could have been further from the truth, however; the Neufelds were welcomed and treated like royalty by the Mexican population in Los Ebanos. During the first half of the twentieth century, the town had fluid borders that allowed people to cross freely. During prohibition, it was an important crossing for bootleggers and tequileros. During the Neufelds' nearly twenty years in Los Ebanos, they lived in a two-story home that looked a lot like "little house on the prairie."

---

11 David Alwine, "Mexican Border Mission," *Gospel Herald* (March 9, 1939), accessed at the Mennonite Church Archives, Elkhart, IN.

12 Harry Neufeld, *Eight Years among the Latin Americans* (Hillsboro, KS: Center for Mennonite Brethren Studies, Tabor College, 1945), 10–11. See also my master's thesis: Felipe Hinojosa, "Yours for the Salvation of Mexican People: Race, Identity, and the Growth/Decline of Mennonite Brethren Missionary Efforts in South Texas, 1937–1971" (master's thesis, University of Texas–Pan American, 2004).

At the height of their success, in the 1960s, they left South Texas. The Neufelds had planted a number of promising churches in the Rio Grande Valley and helped start a private Christian school that became popular among the Mexican American population. Their sudden departure prompted many in the community to believe it had everything to do with the love interest of their son, Gordon. The rumor was that Gordon had fallen in love with a Mexican girl, and, well, that was simply not acceptable. Shortly after the Neufelds found out about their son's love interest, they reported to the people of Los Ebanos that God had called them to another mission. They left and never returned.

I'll never forget the night I interviewed several *hermanas* (women elders in the MB church in South Texas) after a Wednesday night church service. The pastor informed me that my best chance at interviewing these women would be to join him in the van as he dropped them off at their homes after the service. I did just that. When I posed the question about Gordon's love interest, they knew exactly what I was referring to. Some argued that the Neufelds would never allow their son to marry a Mexican girl. Other women in the van scoffed at that notion; they did not believe that the Neufelds harbored any anti-Mexican sentiment. The conversation went back and forth without much consensus. I got the sense that these *hermanas* had not settled the issue and that would be just fine with them. At the end of the day, they simply wanted me to know how much they loved the Neufelds and the churches they had planted.[13]

Eight years after being in South Texas, Harry Neufeld collected his journal entries into a small book he titled *Eight Years among the Latin Americans*.[14] The book serves as a window into Neufeld's thoughts, his sense of himself, and the kind of religious and racial superiority he believed in. A large portion of its pages are devoted to the work of *curanderos/as* (folk healers) in the small ranching communities of Los Ebanos, Chihuahua, Cuevitas, and La Grulla.[15]

---

13 In one interview, the MB pastor, Alfredo Tagle, shared with me: "He [Neufeld] told us one thing, but we all knew that the reason he left was because his son Gordon had fallen in love with a Mexican girl, and Neufeld did not believe in the mixing of the races" (Alfredo Tagle, Interview by author, tape recording, Mission, TX, September 2003). This comment by Rev. Tagle was confirmed in another conversation I had with the Rev. Ricardo Peña.

14 Harry M. Neufeld, *Eight Years among the Latin Americans* (Hillsboro, KS: Center for Mennonite Brethren Studies, Tabor College, 1945).

15 For more on Mennonite Brethren missions in South Texas, see Felipe Hinojosa, "Race, Gender, and Mennonite Brethren Religious Identity Along the Texas-Mexico Border, Part 1," *Direction* 34, no. 2 (Fall 2005): 145–58 and "Race, Gender, and Mennonite Brethren Religious Identity Along the Texas-Mexico Border, Part 2," *Direction* 35, no. 1 (Spring 2006): 162–75.

To say that Harry Neufeld was an interesting character is an understatement. A somewhat charismatic man—or at least that's the way he came across in his writings and in the documents inside the Tabor College archives—Neufeld wrote himself into the center of what reads like a superhero comic book, where Mexicans on the border were a primitive people and he was their savior. Below is a short excerpt:

> One day when the missionary made his rounds to this home to visit the patient, the mother met him with a peculiar smile and twinkle in her eye and stated in Spanish: "Now we know what is the matter with our daughter."
>
> "Is that so?" asked the missionary rather surprised, "and what might that be?"
>
> "Well," the mother said, "she has 'Susto'."
>
> "Susto, what is that?" asked the missionary.
>
> "Don't you know what 'Susto' is?" the mother asked in wonderment.
>
> The missionary, not being very well versed in the language at the time, returned to his home two miles away, got a dictionary, and found the word 'Susto' to mean fear. He then drove back to the sick child's home and announced that now he knew what 'Susto' meant.
>
> "But why do you think that the child has 'Susto'?" was his inquiry.
>
> "Well, I know, because a lady came here and said so," was her quick and triumphant reply.
>
> "When?"
>
> "Yesterday."
>
> "Who was the lady?"
>
> "I don't know that."
>
> "Have you ever seen her before?"
>
> "No, I have not."
>
> "Well, how does the lady know she has 'Susto'?"
>
> "Well," and with the typical shrug of the shoulders and protruding of the underlip of the mouth she answered, "I don't know."
>
> "And after the girl has been taken to the doctor and the missionaries money has been spent on the medicine and for gas and oil on the car to take her there, and after the missionary has been kind to you and to watch over your girl and you are going to disregard all that and believe a perfectly strange woman that she has 'Susto'? . . . I am going to ask you a favor. When that strange woman comes here to cure your daughter, don't you let her touch

this girl. Keep her out of this home and you believe what I am telling you. I will guarantee you that your daughter will get well," replied the missionary, grasping the "shield of faith."[16]

Neufeld decried traditional *curanderismo* as a false belief system but had no objections to placing himself as the new "faith healer" in the community. He loved it so much he kept writing about it. Neufeld shared many of his healing stories in reports via the *Christian Leader*, the MB church magazine.

> There is much crying in the village; a child is dying in the home of a staunch hostile Roman Catholic. Should we go there? Yes, we must! We go! We ask permission to pray. The medic has pronounced the child beyond recovery. But God hears our plea and immediately the child rallies and gets well. Rejoicing in the village? Surprise and wonderment? Yes, and not a little bit.[17]

> The girl is bleeding from the nose. Nothing will stop it. The missionary is called. Prayer is made, but the girl bleeds on. A call to the doctor is urged, but it is too far to go to one . . . What shall be done? All eyes are upon the missionary . . . all the cotton is pulled out of the nostrils and washed out . . . the bleeding recedes and the girl is better.[18]

Neufeld (MB) and T. K. Hershey (Old Mennonite) were part of a constellation of Mennonite missionaries making their way through the US/Mexico borderlands, Latin America, Africa, and India. Theirs was an emerging white Mennonite generation—still tied to their ethnic roots but more Americanized—that stitched evangelism to their increasing awareness of being white. In the process, they demonized these regions, positioned themselves as saviors, and wrote back about their experiences to an eager public across the Great Plains and Midwest that had funded this exoticism. Through their letters and magazine articles and annual conference reports, they shaped an entire generation's views on the borderlands in general and the Mexican population in particular.

I genuinely believe that the Neufelds and Hersheys of the world wrote about and interacted with people from the borderlands believing they were doing the right thing. Racism, after all, can operate as common sense—as a normal way for white people, especially missionaries, to define their relationships with nonwhite people. They believed in their paternalism and they believed in their racial superiority as a sociohistorical fact. And yet it is in that process, in living with and among Mexicans in the borderlands (and in urban missionary centers

---

16 Neufeld, 41–42.

17 Harry Neufeld, "God Works in Los Ebanos," *Christian Leader* 9, no. 5 (April 1945).

18 Neufeld, "God Works in Los Ebanos."

with Latino and African American populations), that Mennonites first began to see and live into their whiteness.

I would not have been able to grasp this without spending countless hours in Mennonite archives reading primary documents such as their missionary reports. I write more about this in my book, but suffice it to say here that while much has been written about how peace activism and nonresistance shaped Mennonite identity throughout the twentieth century, we still know little about the role of evangelical missions in shaping that same identity. The two—peace work and missionary work—cannot be separated.

What really stood out for me in those documents—from conference meeting minutes to magazine articles to missionary reports—was the manner in which a people whose own journey had created beautiful and deep connections to the land and to place, people whose own migration experiences had been traumatic and difficult, began to parrot racist discourses about the borderlands and the people who lived there. In the mission field, far from their Midwestern homes, ethnic Mennonites became white Mennonites.

The South Texas region where the Mennonites first arrived remains contested land. A land with a history of violence and resistance. It is a region where Texas Rangers lynched Mexicans, killing them at random, and also where the oldest Latino civil rights organization—the League of United Latin American Citizens (LULAC)—started in 1929. Here, Mennonites arrived like every other missionary group—unaware of the region's history, the violence, the dispossession. Few of the MB leaders, for example, understood the significance for a border community of having a church building with bullet holes from battles tied to the Mexican revolution.

Relation to place has been a critical point in much of the Mennonite and Anabaptist history. That focus makes sense given that many of the Mennonite immigrants to the United States settled in defined locations across the East and Midwest, and later the West. The cities and towns in which they ended up—Hillsboro and Newton, Kansas; Reedley and Fresno, California; and Goshen and Elkhart, Indiana—historian Paul Toews called "holy places."[19] But as I think about things now, it is clear to me that studying Mennonite missions outside of these holy places can reveal as much or more, perhaps, about Mennonite identity and history. Perhaps that is the value of studying the missionary projects of Mennonites in the twentieth century: they turn us inward, to study a group of people whose ethnic and racial transitions are seen most clearly when observed from the outside in. I tried to do this in *Latino Mennonites*—to show that by studying the origins and development of Latina/os, and other nonwhite

---

19 Paul Toews, "The Quest for the Mennonite Holy Grail: Reflections on 'The Mennonite Experience in America' Project," *Direction Journal* 26, no. 1 (Spring 1997), 43.

Mennonite populations in the Mennonite Church, we can gain a deep and significant knowledge about Mennonite and Anabaptist history.

For those of us working on rewriting the Mennonite story in the United States, deterritorializing Mennonite studies—moving the story away from its current ethnic and place-based trappings—has the potential to open new avenues that take us to the various locations where Mennonite history occurred: in the West, the South, the Pacific Northwest, the US/Mexico borderlands, and beyond. Doing so can help us better understand how racism and oppression take place, how people of color have redefined the Mennonite experience, and what the range of Mennonite and Anabaptist history can teach us about religious experiences in the United States and across the globe. I know that in my corner of the world, in the *barrios* of the US/Mexico borderlands, there are many stories yet to be told.

# A Postcolonial Response to Felipe Hinojosa's *Latino Mennonites*

Hyejung Jessie Yum

## Situating Mennonites in a Postcolonial Context

Felipe Hinojosa's book *Latino Mennonites: Civil Rights, Faith, and Evangelical Culture* is a courageous emerging voice in Mennonite academia—a setting where racial difference has not been reflected much. I will begin my response to Hinojosa's book by resituating in a postcolonial context Latino and Black Mennonite struggles within white normalized society.

The normalization of white subjects and racialization of the others cannot be separated from a Eurocentric racial ideology constructed through colonial violence over hundreds of years.[1] And in the modern era, colonialism has been a major force for the birth of European capitalism through colonial settlement processes, slavery, and acquisition of raw materials.[2] Today, neoliberal capitalism, which many postcolonial thinkers identify as a neocolonial force, still functions to maintain asymmetric racial hegemony.[3] For example, free trade and international division of labor are often followed in actuality by violation of human rights and discriminatory laws, reflecting racist ideologies inscribed within harmful social norms and practices.[4]

---

*Hyejung Jessie Yum, a PhD candidate at the University of Toronto, researches postcolonial Mennonite peace theology. She has been an editor of* Korean Anabaptist Journal *since 2016 and recently collaborated on the launch of* Seeds of Peace, *a peace ministry in the multicultural context of Toronto. A version of this article was published as "21세기 메노나이트 정체성과 인식론의 전환에 대한 필요성,"* Korean Anabaptist Journal *19 (Winter 2019): 48–55.*

1 Ania Loomba, *Colonialism/Postcolonialism* (New York: Routledge, Taylor, and Francis Group, 2015), 112–39.

2 Loomba, 22.

3 Loomba, 256–57; Joerg Rieger and Kwok Pui-lan, *Occupy Religion: Theology of the Multitude* (Rowman & Littlefield, 2013), 33, 38, 42, 63, and 133; Kowk Pui-Lan, "Feminist Theology and the New Imperialism," *Political Theology* 8, no. 2 (2007): 145.

4 Raul Delgado Wise, "Migration and Labour under Neoliberal Globalization: Key Issues and Challenges" in *Migration, Precarity, and Global Governance: Challenges and Opportunities for Labour*, eds. Carl-Ulrik Schierup et al. (Oxford University Press, 2015), 25–45. Wise argues that neoliberal capitalism revolves around the global monopolization of finance and labor exploitation and that it relaunches imperialism. In particular, he

Within Mennonite communities, race relations have also been situated in a larger social context under colonial influence. When European Mennonites migrated to North America, they went from a persecuted ethno-religious minority group to a group racially and religiously normalized as white Christians.[5] In the twentieth century, for example, white evangelical and American pop culture influenced the Swiss-German and Russian Mennonites to incorporate white Christianity in their identity and theology.[6] As Hinojosa highlights, their resulting affinity for white evangelicalism significantly influenced the missions of these Mennonites to Latino and Black communities. Contemporary Mennonite racial relations are not unstained by colonial influence either, given that European Mennonites have been complicit in constructions of the white norm at the cost of displacements of Indigenous populations.[7]

A distinctive postcolonial condition[8] that calls us to rethink this Eurocentric Mennonite identity in North America is the continual migration of multiethnic Mennonites from Congo, Indonesia, Mexico, and many other countries. With contextual sensitivity, I will call for a shifting of the dominant Eurocentric view toward an ethno-culturally polycentric and hybrid view of Mennonite identity and epistemology.

## Hybrid Mennonite Identities

Colonial discourse has constructed Europe as authoritative and the source of the universal subject, while making the Other strange and provincial, thus justifying inequalities.[9] Postcolonial thinkers such as Homi Bhabha, however, have debunked the resulting Eurocentric racial ideologies. Bhabha's notion of hybridity is of an ongoing process that challenges a binary demarcation of "au-

---

points out the proletarianization of migrant workers under the international division of labor, often followed by racial, ethnic, and gender discrimination.

5 I demonstrate this claim in detail in my other article in this issue: "Unsettling the Radical Witness of Peace: A Decolonizing Investigation of Mennonite Migration from Russia to Manitoba in the 1870s."

6 Felipe Hinojosa, *Latino Mennonites: Civil Rights, Faith, and Evangelical Culture* (Baltimore, MD: Johns Hopkins University Press, 2014), 12.

7 Rita Dhamoon, *Identity/Difference Politics: How Difference Is Produced, and Why It Matters* (Vancouver: UBC, 2010), 74. In her analysis of the processes of the racialized gendering in the colonial context of the nation building, political scientist Dhamoon points out that European Mennonites were one of the favored immigrant groups by the government to expand whiteness in Canada. See my other article in this issue, "Unsettling the Radical Witness of Peace."

8 HyeRan Kim-Cragg, "A Postcolonial Portrait of Migrants as Vulnerable and Resistant," *Practical Matters* 11 (Spring 2018): 3.

9 Kim-Cragg, 29–30.

thentic" versus "impure," and "superior" versus "inferior."[10] Using this critique of binarism, Bhabha's postcolonial resistance embraces the intermixing of identities and cultures.[11]

Joining this postcolonialist conversation, Hinojosa contributes to the pluri-ethnic Mennonite voice in Mennonite academia by adding an explicit voice of *Meno-Latinos*. Rather than essentializing a Mennonite identity inherited from sixteenth-century Europe, he traces various factors—such as the struggle for racial justice, the farmworker movement, and evangelicals in twentieth-century North America—that helped shape a hybrid identity of "Meno-Latino/a."[12] This historical description of various influences opens up the possibility of understanding contemporary identities of both European and racially minoritized Mennonites in a religiously and culturally hybridized way.

In a Mennonite context, non-European Mennonites often feel confusion about their identity—not because of their religious conviction but because of their cultural differences from the normalized and centralized European Mennonite culture and identity.[13] In a recent *Vision* article, for example, Chinese Canadian Mennonite Brian Quan writes about the confusion surrounding Chinese Canadian Mennonite identity, asking the question, "What does it mean for a church made up of Chinese Canadians to identify itself as Mennonite?"[14] In order to recognize both his Chinese heritage and his Mennonite heritage, he interprets "peace" by connecting it to a Confucian concept of "harmony" in Chinese philosophy.[15]

Inspired by Quan's cultural hermeneutics of peace and Hinojosa's hybrid identity of Meno-Latinos, I claim that in North America, Mennonite identities and understandings of peace have been formed not only by European Mennonites' experiences of persecution and conscious objection to wars but also

---

10 Homi K. Bhabha, *The Location of Culture* (Brantford, NY: Routledge, 2004), 37–38, 54–55.

11 Bhabha, 54–55.

12 Hinojosa, *Latino Mennonites*, 145, 175.

13 Kelly Bates Oglesby, "Ain't I a Mennonite?," *The Mennonite*, September 27, 2016, accessed July 15, 2020, https://webcache.googleusercontent.com/search?q=cache:16v5yS-gXr18J:https://themennonite.org/opinion/aint-i-a-mennonite/+&cd=1&hl=en&ct=-clnk&gl=us. In the article, Oglesby, an African American Mennonite, shares ongoing questions about her Mennonite identity that were raised by her cultural difference from the dominant Mennonite culture, as well as her fear of creating new traditions unlike those of ethnic Mennonites.

14 Brian Quan, "The Global Church Lived Out in a Local Congregation: The Chinese Mennonite Church in Toronto" *Vision: A Journal for Church and Theology* 19, no. 2 (October 1, 2018): 11.

15 Quan, 12.

by Latino and Black Mennonites' objection to racial persecution and injustice against migrant farmers; Chinese Mennonites' longing for harmony; and Korean Mennonites' resistance to colonialism, and their longing for reconciliation in the divided peninsula.[16]

## Epistemological Shift

Despite the increasing numbers of multiethnic Mennonites, the experiences of these Mennonites have only recently begun to get attention in Mennonite discourse and practice. Recent institutional changes of Mennonite leadership, for example, such as the hiring of an African American executive director[17] and a Korean American denominational minister[18] in Mennonite Church USA, show the beginnings of a structural change of interracial relations that stands in contrast to the struggles of the Minorities Ministry Council detailed in Hinojosa's book.

However, ethnic and cultural differences have still not been much reflected in the authorship of Mennonite scholarship. *Latino Mennonites* is one of only a few books about racial relations written by a nonwhite Mennonite scholar in North America. In this sense, Hinojosa's painstaking research—collecting scattered notes and interviews of Latinx and interracial experiences as Mennonite academic sources—challenges the epistemological domination of European voices in Mennonite academia.

Producing such knowledge is an important role of scholarship, and that knowledge cannot be separated from power.[19] Power shapes whose knowledge is treated as authentic, credible, and universal and whose is considered syncretic, heretical, and subjugated. Throughout our history, Mennonites have understood this—how hegemonic religious discourse has legitimated the persecution of some, marginalizing their knowledge as heretical rather than different.

---

16 Mennonite Church USA, "Join the North and South Korea Day of Prayer on May 20," April 30, 2018, accessed July 15, 2020, http://mennoniteusa.org/news/join-the-north-and-south-korea-day-of-prayer-on-may-20/.

17 Mennonite Church USA, "Glen Guyton Called to Serve as Next Executive Director of Mennonite Church USA," February 9, 2018, accessed July 15, 2020, http://mennoniteusa.org/news/glen-guyton-called-serve-next-executive-director-mennonite-church-usa/.

18 Mennonite Church USA. "Executive Board Staff Transitions: Sue Park-Hur Begins as Denominational Minister," March 20, 2018, accessed July 15, 2020, http://mennoniteusa.org/news/executive-board-staff-transitions-sue-park-hur-begins-as-denominational-minister/.

19 Michel Foucault, *Discipline and Punish: The Birth of the Prison*, trans. Alan Sheridan (New York: Pantheon, 1977), 184.

We might ask whose knowledge and identity today have been understood to be authentic and credible Mennonite knowledge and identity and whose has not. According to Bhabha, however, "Authenticity . . . do[es] not guarantee anything, it seems."[20] Instead, a postcolonial imagination calls for an interstitial creativity between the binary poles of center and periphery. In the in-between space, antagonistic and different meanings conjoin, producing new knowledge through ongoing interactions.[21]

I hope Mennonite scholarship in the twenty-first century will pay attention to the creative potential of ongoing intercultural hybridization among multiethnic Mennonite identities and cultures in epistemological mutuality. Considering a globalizing context, the epistemological shift from a Eurocentric view toward racially and culturally polycentric and hybrid views may not seem optional. In any case, it is necessary. Given the asymmetric epistemological power balance status quo, postcolonialists endorsing epistemological mutuality need to start questioning the dominant discourse mostly occupied by European male perspectives. Power/knowledge operates intersectionally on multiple axes of factors such as gender, class, race, disability, sexuality, and so on, so the discourse—constructed through our repeated citations—together with affirming and critical comments on certain knowledges, shapes our social reality in churches and society.[22]

For this reason, I appreciate Hinojosa's painstaking work. Having grown up in South Korea, I chose to become a Mennonite ten years ago while living in Los Angeles, and I continue to be a Mennonite now that I live in Toronto. Personally, this scholarly work on Mennonite history and theology allows me to breathe in Mennonite academia and encourages me to be myself—as a Korean, a migrant, a woman, and a Mennonite.

To wrap up my response at this "Migration, Borders, and Belonging" gathering, I hope that the more we are open to crossing borders in our knowledge, the more people will find a place of belonging in our scholarship in this migration era.

---

20 David Huddart, *Homi Bhabha* (London: Routledge, 2006), 43. Huddart writes this exact phrase in order to explain a transformative implication of Bhabha's concept of mimicry.

21 Bhabha, *The Location of Culture*, 54–55.

22 Dhamoon, *Identity/Difference Politics*, 91. Intersectionality provides a theoretical tool to name and analyze how asymmetric power functions to deepen violence when various historical and social factors intersect. In this view, there is no pure racism, sexism, and ableism because the multiple factors in power relations simultaneously constitute one another. See also Nancy J. Ramsay, "Intersectionality in Theological Education," *Spotlight on Theological Education* (April 2015): 7–10.

# Book Reviews

Jen Gobby, *More Powerful Together: Conversations with Climate Activists and Indigenous Land Defenders*, Fernwood, Winnipeg, MB, 2020. 250 pp. $26.00. ISBN: 9781773632513.

The week before the Global Climate Strike in September 2019, a group of several hundred youth gathered on the steps of the Canadian Museum for Human Rights in Winnipeg, Manitoba, and staged a "die-in." I listened from the sidelines as the young organizers spoke passionately and strongly about their grief, fear, and anger over facing a world changing rapidly from climate change. They invited the adults standing to the side to participate with them as they symbolically lay down on the steps and "died." As rain fell from the sky, we lay down on the ground, but one young Indigenous activist stayed standing, fist in the air. The young activist called out, "I'm standing here because I'm not dying. I refuse to die. My ancestors fought so hard for me to be here. Indigenous people are never going to die. We're going to stay here and fight for our lands, no matter what it takes." For seven minutes, representing seven generations into the future, we lay in silence, contemplating those words, lamenting the hurting planet and the uncertain futures these young people face. When the seven minutes were over, we rose up, singing hopeful songs.

The youth die-in was a profound and powerful instance of people from many generations coming together to insist on change. It was an important reminder for me that in the fight against climate change, it isn't simply the earth and its plants and creatures that we advocate for but also the lives and livelihoods of people all over the world, especially those on the margins. With these thoughts in mind, I joined the climate strike the next week, which drew over ten thousand people in Winnipeg and millions around the world.

Jen Gobby's book *More Powerful Together* opens with a vivid description of her experience at the Global Climate Strike in Montreal. She describes her excitement, the optimism of the crowd, and the lingering feelings of hope after the event. She then describes finding out that Indigenous activists had experienced racism and violence from non-Indigenous people attending the protest. Gobby recounts being surprised but reflects that perhaps she shouldn't have been. The climate strike in Montreal ended up being a microcosm of the wider world. Racism, colonialism, and other forms of domination are playing themselves out in social movement spaces as they are in many other parts of life, rendering the work ineffective at best and incredibly damaging at worst. The antidote, Gobby writes, is to work toward creating a "movement of movements" in which diversity and collaboration have the power to create "decarbonized *and* decolonized ... systems" in Canada (6).

To construct her argument, Gobby interviews activists and Indigenous land defenders. She also provides a thorough review of the scholarly literature on climate change, inequality, social movements, and social change. Gobby presents a strong overview of the climate and inequality crises in Canada and the social movements that have surfaced to address them. The people she interviews identify settler colonialism, capitalism, and worldviews that justify domination, as the root causes of these crises. These root causes "have bred systemic disconnection from land and from each other, cutting us off from the knowledge and relations we need to get ourselves out of this mess" (54).

After envisioning alternatives to those systems of destruction, and taking stock of what is working and what isn't working in environmental movements today, Gobby discusses how to overcome the various barriers that are hindering movement efficacy and transformation. The most significant barriers are the relational tensions within and between movements, which lead to siloing and fragmentation. She writes, "damaged relationships hinder our ability to think across difference and forge powerful alliances strong enough to radically transform our world from one of destruction of people and planet to one of healing, justice and mutual flourishing" (179). The solution, she posits, is that "strong, just relations are the means and ends of building a better, climate safe world" (6). Gobby concludes that it is through working better together and through building relationships based on "justice, equality and reciprocity" with each other and with the land that we will gain a truly transformative ability to create such changes (214).

*More Powerful Together* is a timely and important book for anyone looking to learn about how change can happen. This book was an important reminder to me, as someone who works in environmental education and conservation, to consider how forms of domination may be present within the work I am doing. Gobby, and many of the people she interviews, state that it is not enough to address only ecological crises; we must also learn to see that social crises are deeply interrelated with ecological crises. Gobby argues that both ecological and social crises "are symptoms of a deeper pattern of dysfunctional relationship based on domination" (10).

As the climate movement has become more mainstream, many Christians have become interested in the environment and involved in creation care efforts. Yet, in my experience, it is rare to hear about creation care efforts that also seek to address the damages done by colonial and capitalist systems. Many in the church, myself included, benefit from these systems in the form of wealth, access to land, and/or positions of privilege. That makes it difficult to confront the ways that colonialism, racism, and other forms of oppression are present within our churches.

Gobby's book makes it clear that we cannot afford to continue to relate to each other and the earth in the ways we have been relating. She also makes it clear that everyone has a role to play. Anabaptists have a long history of resisting state-sanctioned violence and status quo relations. Might it be possible to step into those roots again and work toward a decarbonized and decolonized church and world? *More Powerful Together* offers us practical ways of moving in that direction.

Zoe Matties *is a Mennonite settler living in the Red River Watershed and Treaty One Territory. She works for A Rocha Canada as Manitoba Program Manager.*

**Bryan Stone, *Evangelism after Pluralism: The Ethics of Christian Witness*, Grand Rapids, MI, Baker Academic, 2018. 151 + vii pp. $22.00 (paper). ISBN: 080109979X.**

Evangelism makes me uncomfortable. Even when I was a teenager doing summer mission trips in Africa as part of a team intent on winning Uganda for Jesus, the prospect of going up to a stranger and telling them to accept my religion gave me a queasy feeling. I later learned that Uganda is a majority-Christian nation and the strangers who accepted my tracts and listened to my stammering pleas were probably just being polite. This did not make me any more comfortable with evangelism.

And yet, the stories of the apostles in the New Testament show a community eager to spread the good news of Jesus Christ, and I can see why. This good news is transformative and renewing, capable of bringing hope into a despairing world. To evangelize is to show someone that they are more deeply loved than they realize, that there is a community where they can be fully themselves, and that the systems that dehumanize them will not have the last word.

Is it possible to recover this kind of evangelism—an exuberant sharing of "a reason for the hope that is in you"— from beneath the imperialism and self-righteousness with which evangelism has (quite fairly) become associated?

Bryan Stone's *Evangelism after Pluralism* aims to help readers navigate the complicated waters surrounding evangelism. The book is a follow-up to Stone's *Evangelism after Christendom: The Theology and Practice of Christian Witness* (Grand Rapids, MI: Brazos, 2007), but it can be fruitfully read and appreciated without any familiarity with Stone's earlier work. Though the book is subtitled "The Ethics of Christian Witness," Stone's central aim is not to discern whether evangelism is ethical or not but to show how closely connected Christian ethics and Christian witness are. Indeed, Stone even claims that "ethics is evangelism" (9).

As Stone defines it, "Evangelism is the noncompetitive practice of bearing faithful and embodied witness in a particular context rather than an attempt to produce converts by first safeguarding the credibility or helpfulness of the good news" (13). All too often, the framework through which people approach evangelism is through a competition in a battleground of worldviews. If one wins a convert, one has enlisted them from "the other side" to "our side." At worst, this framework reinforces an "us versus them" mindset and treats members of other religious and nonreligious groups as a threat. But even at its best, this competitive framework promotes questionable sales tactics and flattening the gospel into a commodity.

Stone's discussion of the "winning converts" framework helped me understand some of my own discomfort with evangelism. If a person's religious convictions are part of their core identity, inviting them to change their convictions—no matter how compassionately—is telling them that there is something wrong with who they are, that they need to change fundamentally. If a person's religious commitments aren't part of their identity, inviting them to change their commitments is basically asking them to adopt a new "brand" (93), a set of cultural markers without any inner transformation. Evangelism, then, either involves an implicit condemnation of a person created in God's image or a superficial facsimile of the gospel. Proselytizing is either too judgmental to be good news or too hollow to be news at all.

Stone argues that these two pitfalls are two sides of the same coin. The more colonialist, sanctimonious attitude toward non-Christians and the more privatized, domesticated version of Christianity are both consequences of Christians allying their cause to what Stone calls "empire." In a fascinating chapter, Stone describes how evangelism can easily become a way of "playing chaplain to the empire" (27) as Christians become preoccupied with Christianizing their societies and neglect the work of proclaiming the radical message of the kingdom of God. This discussion will no doubt be of interest to chaplains, pastors, and missionaries working within Anabaptist traditions.

Cornel West writes, "Justice is what love looks like in public." Stone's book suggests that evangelism is what worship looks like in public. Not coincidentally, evangelism also looks a lot like work for justice. Stone makes the familiar but still important case that Christian witness is political, offering an alternative to the stories empires tell to justify their own power.

In contrast to the "winning converts" framework, Stone proposes a different model for Christian witness, centered on giving faithful witness to beauty. Rather than seeking results by selling or defending a worldview, evangelists should seek to testify to the beauty of God's work in Christ carried on by the Holy Spirit. Just as an impressionist painter tries to express the beauty of a night sky as they see it, so witnesses try through words and actions to express the beauty that has captivated their imagination. Evangelism is not so much a duty to be carried out but rather an abundant gift to be shared freely. "A faith born out of a response to beauty," Stone writes, "inclines organically, naturally, and perhaps even necessarily toward sharing" (120). If contemporary Christians want to discover the same missionary fervor as the biblical apostles, we should not grit our teeth and push through our discomfort but should rather re-awaken our imaginations to the divine beauty we can't possess but can only revel in. Not only is the culture pluralistic, but Christian witness is pluriform—evangelism is not about securing uniformity of opinion but freeing different witnesses to show others the facets of divine grace that uniquely inspire each of them.

The epilogue, titled "The Meaninglessness of Apologetics," is the least persuasive section of the book. It's unclear whether Stone is arguing that Christians should abandon apologetics as a pursuit or—as he argues with evangelism—pursue it in a different mode from what we usually imagine. Lacking a sustained engagement with how apologists understand their task, this epilogue feels more dismissive than the chapters that precede it.

Evangelism after Pluralism is an accessible, well-written treatment of an uncomfortable topic from a theological perspective. Though Stone is ordained in the Church of the Nazarene, his emphasis on nonviolence, embodied community, and dialogue resonates with Anabaptist commitments. I hope this book brings us closer to the day when people will associate evangelism not with competition but with a shared appreciation for the beauty of divine grace.

RUSSELL P. JOHNSON *is a postdoctoral fellow at the University of Chicago and a member of Chicago Community Mennonite Church.*

**John G. Flett and David W. Congdon, eds., *Converting Witness: The Future of Christian Mission in the New Millennium*, Lexington Books/ Fortress Academic, Lanham, MD, 2019. 240 pages. $110.00. ISBN: 978-1-9787-0840-2.**

*Converting Witness* is a festschrift edited by two of Darrell L. Guder's former PhD students at Princeton Theological Seminary. John Flett and David Congdon honor Guder's influential role in the development of missional theology and missional hermeneutics, giving voice to an international array of scholars who appreciate Guder's work as a catalyst for new insights in their diverse fields. The work is soundly these authors', not a summary of Guder's thought with a few reflections. Beyond the introductory first chapter, the chapters are not a close reading of Guder's published works; rather, authors in their own scholarly perspectives expound on themes that Guder engaged. The authors share Guder's commitment to scholarship for the Christian church, enabling scholars and practitioners to find something of relevance in this academic volume, even if only a single chapter.

Flett and Congdon open with a robust yet concise summary of Guder's life and work. With careful footnoting, they trace the influences, primary themes, and trajectory of Guder's theology. A reader not already familiar with Guder can become acquainted with the person behind the work and grasp the scope of his scholarship.

Eberhard Busch is one of three Swiss or German authors in the volume, appropriately so because Guder holds Swiss citizenship, spent his early career in Germany, and is an avid English translator of German theology. Busch, Karl Barth's former assistant, expounds upon Barth's gathering, upbuilding, and sending functions of the church. Busch insists on the missional task of every member of the Christian church. Christine Lienemann-Perrin, of Basel, explores the etymology and history of the term "Christendom," surveying its different uses by Christians in Europe, North America, and the Global South. Believing the concept stifling for missiological discourse, she calls for a global movement to transcend the binary split between Christendom and post-Christendom, "to avoid altogether that term [Christendom] at least for a while and replace it by describing the intended phenomena as precisely as possible" (73). Henning Wrogemann of Germany assesses current trends in the globalization of mission, observing an increase in mission efforts worldwide, diversification, and surprising directions in missiological movement. He proposes an adaptable theology of mission that is both doxological—with dimensions of "prophetic criticism, power, communal-physical experience, and [invoking] the name of Jesus Christ"—and *oikumenical*, "with aspects of solidarity, plurality, cooperation, and ecology" (206).

From a distinctively Roman Catholic perspective, Stephen Bevans explores the missional mark of catholicity as one of four Nicene marks of the church. Though he relies heavily on Vatican II, Protestants will also find much relevant material in his chapter.

From Fuller Theological Seminary (Pasadena, CA), Richard Mouw recommends conceptualizing the church as an organism rather than an institution, as distinguished by Abraham Kuyper. Interestingly, Mouw offers the only direct and sustained critique of Guder in the entire volume, judging Guder's emphasis on the parish context as "unnecessarily restrictive" (143). Also from Fuller, Wilbert Shenk emphasizes Guder's call for the church to experience ongoing renewal through "life-changing encounter with the Word" and "deep conversion to God's mission as the foundation on which new structures and practices can be developed" (217). Drawing on Ezekiel's prophetic vision of dry bones, Shenk points out that renewal begins on the margins of the church and results in mission.

Three Western Theological Seminary (Holland, MI) faculty are featured. George Hunsberger offers a theological reflection on church planting—affirming its importance, clarifying its nature and *telos*, and exploring its biblical foundations. He recommends "a church spawning imagination, recognizing our midwife relationship to what the Spirit is birthing" (161). This and Benjamin

Connor's feature on missional Christian practices are likely the most relevant chapters for ministry practitioners. Regarding Christian practices as inherently missional, Connor translates two of Guder's core concepts—incarnational witness and communal formation for walking worthily—into a practical theology of Christian practices within congregations. New Testament scholar James Brownson briefly examines two challenges emerging for missional hermeneutics since its development in the 1990s: the universality/particularity tension and missional hermeneutics as primarily an academic movement of rational discourse.

Four authors address intercultural and interreligious engagement. Congdon overlays Rudolf Bultmann's program of demythologization with the framework of intercultural hermeneutics at the intersection of the biblical text's ancient culture and that of contemporary readers. He examines Bultmann's categories of preunderstanding and self-understanding, concluding that an intercultural hermeneutic simultaneously translates the proclaimed message from one historical context to another and eschatologically "transpropriates the kerygma to ever new contexts" (114). Peruvian scholar Samuel Escobar points out that Latin American Evangelical missiology has understood the church as missional from the beginning. He highlights the complicated and problematic missiological relationship between European and American Christians and the peoples of Latin America, and recommends a new approach of Integral Mission that incorporates evangelization. Seong Sik Heo interrogates Lesslie Newbigin's reluctance to engage in interreligious dialogue. From his perspective in Korea, he reviews Newbigin's writings on religious pluralism, considers Newbigin's cultural context, and proposes steps toward engaging in interreligious dialogues in Asia as "a way of Christian pilgrimage" (179). Deanna Womack—in conversation with Guder, Newbigin, and John Mackay—explores from the American Protestant context how a commitment to mission might be reconciled with the Christian "calling to live as loving neighbors alongside people of many faiths" (184). She calls for the conversion of American mission so that Christians do not privatize their faith, reduce it to a simple truth for converting souls, or clothe it in the garb of white supremacy.

Coincidentally, *Converting Witness* was published the year Princeton Theological Seminary temporarily closed Stuart Hall for renovations—the 1876 Venetian Gothic academic building where Guder taught as Professor of Missional and Ecumenical Theology from 2002 to 2015.[1] As Guder enlarged students' imaginations for the apostolic, missional vocation of the church, it was as if

---

1 "Princeton Historic District," nomination form, National Register of Historic Places, United States Department of the Interior National Park Service, May 15, 1975, https://npgallery.nps.gov/GetAsset/8ef7085f-a375-4f72-827c-2acc409f972f, accessed January 6, 2020, 5.

the conversation occurred within a stone monument to the very Christendom Guder critiqued.

In 2019, scaffolding was erected around Stuart Hall. Guder uses the metaphor of scaffolding to describe theology and ministry's need to become "missional." "We would not need that scaffolding if our theological work were shaped by the *missio Dei*," Guder writes, "truly focused upon the formation and equipping of the church for its apostolate."[2] The term "missional" has become wildly popular among Western Protestants, yet some scholars now call it into question. The same day Guder was formally presented with this festschrift, scholars at a Gospel and Our Culture Network Forum on Missional Hermeneutics debated—with Guder in the room—dropping the term altogether.[3] Some wondered, Is the term so tied to vestiges of colonialism that it can only issue a partial diagnosis of the church's underlying problems?[4] Is it so offensive and misunderstood that different scaffolding should be erected?

Though the title might suggest that *Converting Witness* would interrogate the current and ongoing function of missional scaffolding in the new millennium, it hardly does so. With a few fleeting exceptions, most authors build upon Guder's accomplished critical work—and indeed, he has done much—and proceed with the already-defined missional task without deeply interrogating it. A tribute worthy of Guder might better critique these theoretical starting points, as Guder himself demonstrated in his own scholarship.

Rev. Sarah Ann Bixler *is an instructor in formation and practical theology at Eastern Mennonite Seminary in Harrisonburg, Virginia. She is completing her PhD in practical theology at Princeton Theological Seminary (PTS). After earning her MDiv at PTS, Sarah worked with Guder to launch and administer the Center for Church Planting and Revitalization at PTS from 2016 to 2019. She has a BA from Eastern Mennonite University and has worked as a middle school teacher, youth minister, curriculum writer, and Mennonite conference administrator. Sarah is ordained for teaching ministry by Virginia Mennonite Conference. She and her spouse, Benjamin Bixler, along with their three school-aged children, are the latest stewards of the historic Lincoln Homestead in Linville, Virginia.*

---

2 Darrell L. Guder, *Called to Witness: Doing Missional Theology*, The Gospel and Our Culture Series (Grand Rapids, MI: William B. Eerdmans, 2015), 168.

3 The festschrift presentation occurred on November 24, 2019, during Princeton Theological Seminary's reception at the American Academy of Religion and Society of Biblical Literature annual meeting in San Diego, California.

4 Drew Hart, respondent, "James Cone, Blackness, and Missional Hermeneutics," Gospel and Our Culture Network Forum on Missional Hermeneutics, American Academy of Religion annual meeting, San Diego, CA, November 24, 2019.